PROFESSIONAL
PRACTICE
DEVELOPMENT

PROFESSIONAL

PRACTICE

DEVELOPMENT

Meeting the Competitive Challenge

E.W. Brody

PRAEGER

New York
Westport, Connecticut
London

Library of Congress Cataloging-in-Publication Data

Brody, E. W.
    Professional practice development : meeting the competitive
challenge / by E. W. Brody.
      p. cm.
    Bibliography: p.
    Includes index.
    ISBN 0–275–93102–1 (alk. paper)
    1. Professions—Marketing. I. Title.
HD8038.A1B76   1989
658.8—dc19   88–28574

Library of Congress Catalog Card Number: 88-28574
ISBN: 0-275-93102-1

First published in 1989

Praeger Publishers, One Madison Avenue, New York, NY 10010
A division of Greenwood Press, Inc.

Printed in the United States of America

The paper used in this book complies with the Permanent
Paper Standard issued by the National Information Standards
Organization (Z39.48–1984).

10 9 8 7 6 5 4 3 2 1

For Nina,
my biggest fan

Contents

Preface

Professions in the United States today are caught up in an era of change of unprecedented magnitude. For several reasons, the professions are being stripped bare of the various protective devices that long have made them bastions of conservatism, privilege, and wealth. As a result, practitioners find that graduation from a preferred school into a traditionally rewarding profession is no longer sufficient to insure success. Instead they find a marketplace in which they must compete with better-established colleagues for the patronage of increasingly skeptical consumers of professional services. Few are prepared to cope with such conditions. Colleges and universities that train prospective professionals seemingly consider such subjects as practice management and practice development unworthy of their attention. Academicians instead tend to perpetuate myths of professional collegiality, literally setting up their charges for post-graduate culture shock.

Professional school graduates thus often find themselves in circumstances not unlike those that confront nonswimmers without life preservers as their boats sink. Those life preservers were supposed to be part of the economically assured futures that many of them had selected four to eight years earlier. Between the time would-be professionals embarked on professional careers and the time they find their economic ships are sinking, however, the life preservers had been removed.

Removal has been carried out by a society increasingly disenchanted with government, institutions, corporations, and those who serve or appear to serve them. A series of actions, positive and negative, originating in different areas, have quietly removed all of the protective devices that had been installed over the decades to protect the professions. Some had been specifically oriented to assist practitioners. Others were beneficial to organizations generally. All are gone. Some professional life preservers have been removed by social change. Others have been stripped away through economic and regulatory change. The reasons are of no consequence to those seeking to swim in shark-infested competitive waters.

The winds of social change grew in intensity in the United States with mounting disillusionment over the Vietnam War. Schisms caused by the war were compounded by battles over the Pentagon Papers, the Watergate scandal, and other traumas inflicted on the body politic. Resulting disillusionment with government soon spread to other institutions, formal and informal, including the professions.

The trends involved doubtless influenced what would prove to be fateful actions by the Federal Trade Commission and other agencies dealing with the ethical codes of professional societies. Over a relatively short period of time, regulators and courts struck down all competitive prohibitions and limitations among professionals. Code of ethics provisions that precluded advertising were among the first to go. Prohibitions that forbade professionals to solicit one another's clients were removed as well.

Practicing professionals in most disciplines adjusted to the changes with relative ease. At first, social pressures were sufficient to discourage significant use of mass media advertising, despite removal of legal and regulatory barriers. The circumstances were reminiscent of those that prevail when electrified fences are removed from pastures; cattle are slow to react save in the face of external stimuli.

Appropriate stimuli for the professions were not long in coming. A single compelling motivator was developing in almost every profession: overpopulation. Colleges and universities had enrolled more students in most professions than the national population could support. Shortages of practitioners that had prevailed in many professions during the 1960s were being replaced by surpluses. Before the decade of the 1970s began, for example, medical school deans were already warning of the oversupply of physicians that developed in the 1980s.

The same conditions soon emerged in almost every profession. With them came progressive erosion in professional ability to hold the line on aggressive competition through peer pressure. Newcomers to the professions perceived that they could not afford the ethical luxuries of their established senior colleagues. The result was a surge in promotional activities across the professional spectrum that shows no sign of subsiding. As the 1980s draw to a close, it appears instead that competition may continue to mount through the remainder of the century.

As competition increases, however, professionals will face other challenges. Mounting skepticism induced toward professionals by such factors as the public debate over rising health care costs will loom large among them. So will continuing decline in public confidence in channels of communication and the messages they contain.

These conditions in combination will require new professional communication strategies that embrace the term *communication* in its broadest sense, encompassing professional environments and behaviors as well as messages and media. Such strategies are not new. They have developed rapidly in recent years among organizations seeking to minimize potentially damaging conflicts with consumers and others. They are applicable with relatively little change in the professions.

This book was written to provide adaptive guidance for professionals committed to building successful practices on solid foundations of quality services that meet consumer need. Nothing less is adequate to support a successful practice development program. Given the depth of commitment necessary to provide quality services, however, practice development is a relatively easy task.

The processes described in the following pages are readily applicable in all professions and by all professionals. They are amenable to use by those with established practices and by newcomers to their professions. They require no more overt promotion than individuals consider appropriate in their individual circumstances. The key to successful practice development, in the ultimate analysis, is not promotion but substance. Creating realities deserving of consumer support, in fact, constitutes the bulk of the developmental effort. A relatively few easily learned communication techniques thereafter suffice in almost all circumstances.

Perhaps the only significant variation in practice development that occurs across professions involves breadth of practices. Most can be categorized as broad-based or narrowly based. The broad-based draw clienteles from large populations, as in medicine and dentistry. Clienteles for the narrowly based professions, such as architecture or engineering, are drawn from relatively small groups.

Within, and to a certain extent across, the two categories, practice development needs are relatively constant. Neither can afford a revolving door syndrome, where clients or patients depart as rapidly as they arrive. Recruitment and retention require that professionals consistently provide quality services and effective communication support. Neither objective is easily achieved, but few in the professions today expect to earn their livelihoods easily.

Professionalism, in fact, in recent years has come to mean more than membership in a group classified as a profession. Professionalism means dedication to high standards of performance in any endeavor. This book, like most books, is a product of many professionals in a host of disciplines. Those in health care, in architecture, and in engineering who have been served by the author's consulting firm are foremost among them. Many of their ideas are incorporated into the professional development concept advanced here.

Members of the academic community, especially Dr. Richard R. Ranta, dean of Memphis State University's College of Communication and Fine Arts, and Dr. Dan Lattimore, chairman of the college's Department of Journalism, have provided invaluable support. Colleagues in the department, in journalism education, and in the Public Relations Society of America also have made important contributions. The sure hands of Alison Bricken and her colleagues at Praeger Publishers also are to be seen in the finished book.

Most of the merit in the following pages is attributable to the combined contributions of those listed above. The inevitable flaws are mine alone.

PROFESSIONAL
PRACTICE
DEVELOPMENT

1

Professionals in Contemporary Society

The special status traditionally granted to professionals by domestic society is eroding. Storm tides of change are washing away the foundations of systems that made a privileged class of physicians, attorneys, accountants, and other professionals. The changes originate in a society that has been in a state of radical flux for more than a decade. Only now, however, have the trends become so broad and so deep as to demand professional attention and response.

Waves buffeting the professions are products of technological, social, economic, and demographic changes that no longer can be called new. The United States is in transition from the industrial age to the age of information. What long was a national economy has become international in scope. National income distribution patterns are changing, and the population is aging rapidly.

Most professionals are adapting to the new technologies with relative ease. They are experiencing difficulty, however, in coping with new values and standards embodied in personnel and clienteles. The difficulties are increasing rapidly. Once sacrosanct professional judgments are subject to second opinions—legal if not professional. In part as a result, the preferred economic and social status once all but guaranteed by professional degrees is fading.

Professional practices once were virtually immune to cyclical changes in national and international economies. Several factors contributed to these conditions. Most professions deal in problem solving. Problems occur without regard to contemporary economic conditions. Numbers of practitioners in most professions have been limited, creating relative immunity from economic law. Finally, and perhaps most importantly, clients generally have respected or tolerated systemic limitations or conditions imposed by professionals for their own convenience, for example, physicians' crowded waiting rooms and the tortuous pace of the legal system.

OLD VERSUS NEW

Client and patient tolerance levels in recent years have been declining. Fewer and fewer among them accept such conditions without protest. Most protestors object with their feet, seeking professional assistance elsewhere. Building and maintaining profitable practices necessarily become more difficult in these circumstances.

The process becomes especially difficult among those guilty of self-indulgent traditionalism. Professionals involved assume—or have been taught to assume—that client-practitioner relationships are governed by an immutable set of laws graven in granite and unquestioningly accepted by everyone. In acting on these assumptions, they create conditions predestined to discourage practice development.

Most damaging among these anachronistic laws of client-professional relationships are several in which practitioners take great comfort:

1. Professionals are the embodiment of all knowledge in their disciplines and should be approached only with great deference.

2. Within the self-established boundaries of their disciplines, practitioners are all-knowing and must not be questioned by those of lower caste.

3. These laws always have and always will govern relationships between professionals and their clients or patients.

Mythology of this sort once may have had a place in professional practice. Many professions hark back several centuries to a time when knowledge indeed was held by very few. More important, bodies of knowledge in most professions were so small that they could be absorbed in their entirety by individual practitioners.

These circumstances led to development of what might be called temple cultures in the professions. Each generation of high priests conveyed all wisdom to a chosen few successors. Transfer occurred at temples or guild halls barred to all but priests and disciples. Supplicants would be seen only at specified times, outside the gates or in the courtyards. "The great unwashed," moreover, were expected to submit unquestioningly to those who deigned to minister to them.

Many professionals' expectations of patients or clients have not changed perceptibly over the years. They expect total and unquestioning conformity to systems designed for the convenience and benefit of professionals rather than for those in need of their services. Patients and clients are expected to accept professional decisions as tantamount to the word of God and to behave accordingly. Failure to follow instructions is a cardinal sin, and questioning professional propriety is heresy.

THE TIDES OF CHANGE

New generations of clients and patients are refusing to tolerate professional arrogance of this sort. Those involved are better educated, more demanding, and, of late, increasingly sensitive to abuse by "the system." Their sensitivity is a product of a decade or more of socioeconomic and demographic as well as technological change. Many of the changes have also overtaken the professions, rendering practitioners more economically vulnerable than ever before.

In most professions, practitioner ranks are growing more rapidly than the populations they serve. Resulting surpluses create more options for consumers of professional services and encourage more aggressive competition. By far the greatest changes, however, are those that have occurred among patient and client populations.

Socioeconomic Conditions

Economic pressures would have produced many of the changes without significant increases in practitioner ranks. Change in the domestic economy in the last quarter of the twentieth century has reshaped the lives of organizations as well as of individuals. Organizations experienced the first impact, but the results soon were visited on managers and workers alike. Declining competitiveness produced market losses in many industries, from automobiles and steel to clothing and textiles. Losses were met with radical responses, from accelerated automation and introduction of robots to "downsizing," plant closings, and "outsourcing," foreign and domestic. Waves of mergers and takeovers soon added to organizational and individual economic woes.

Worsening economic conditions dislocated hundreds of thousands of workers, managers, and executives. Many ultimately found new jobs. As politicians repeatedly pointed out, more jobs have been created than have been lost. The new jobs tended to be less well paid than the old, however, and many workers remained unemployed for extended periods of time.

Deteriorating economic conditions brought women into the work force in increasing numbers. Household incomes have remained at relatively high levels, but not without price. Child care has become a major problem. Health care costs continue to rise. School systems deteriorate. Career ladders are clogged with survivors of the downsizing era. These and other problems have taken a psychological as well as an economic toll.

As is often the case, structural economic change was first recorded in Bureau of the Census data showing marked deterioration in the economic position of the nation's middle class. By 1988 the wealthy were capturing a growing share of the nation's wealth, primarily at the expense of the middle class. At the same time, popular perceptions of society were changing. For the first time in history, most U.S. workers had come to believe that future generations would be less well off than those that went before.

Educational Change

These conditions persist, unfortunately, in the face of radically changed and still changing societal conditions. At mid century, little more than 5 percent of the national population had completed a baccalaureate degree. At the dawn of the twenty-first century, almost half of the national population will have been to college. More than a quarter of them will have completed degree programs, and graduate degrees will be as common as baccalaureates once were.

Increasing exposure to higher education is changing clients and patients in two ways. First, higher education is designed to produce skepticism, to predispose the educated to challenge the status quo, to contest the old order. Second, higher education induces an appetite for knowledge that is readily satisfied in contemporary society. Advancing technological and transportation systems enable publishers to develop national newspapers such as the *Wall Street Journal*, the *New York Times*, and the *Christian Science Monitor*. Television has not been far behind. Cable News Network reports regularly on the forward march of science, business, and politics. Even network television responds to the broader interests and increased intellectual capacity of the nation with reports taken from the pages of professional publications such as the prestigious *New England Journal of Medicine*.

Access to knowledge. Virtually every development in every profession quickly becomes common knowledge in an information society. The newest in medical treatments, in construction technologies, in legal decisions, and in accounting standards is transmitted instantaneously through the media to an increasingly interested population. Clients and patients, as a result, are privy to a growing volume of information once available only to the high priests of the professions. So strong has this trend become that the *New England Journal of Medicine* forbids advance publication of its articles in the mass media. The journal's objective, according to editor Arnold Relman, is to insure that subscribers have an opportunity to read the journal before patients start asking questions about content.

Enhanced media capabilities are equally applied, however, in informing audiences that no profession is without its share of ineptitude or incompetence. Audiences may be overimpressed by such reports. It is equally possible, however, that professionals are overly perturbed by suggestions that they are less than omnipotent. Whichever the case, information concerning the burgeoning capabilities of professionals is accompanied in the media by scattered reports of incompetence and resulting litigation.

Unquestioning acceptance of professional authority has been supplanted, for these reasons, by a pervasive demand—silent or expressed—for involvement in decision making. Clients and patients no longer accept and act blindly on any direction given them. They want to know the whys, the wherefores, and the alternatives. Moreover, they expect to have a voice in deciding which alternative is most acceptable. They expect to help determine, in other words, the breadth, depth, and intensity of the services they acquire. Professionals who ignore these characteristics of the new client do so at their peril.

Militant consumers. Today's patient and client predispositions are a natural outgrowth of a consumer movement that has existed for decades but only recently has assumed militant form. The era of militancy began when General Motors Corporation ''gave birth'' to consumerist Ralph Nader. Nader and his book, *Unsafe At Any Speed,* would have gained little attention had not GM attempted to discredit the book by seeking to embarrass Nader. The GM effort, complete with detective surveillance, sparked a deepening distrust of corporations and institutions that persists to this day.

Militant consumerism now is as much a problem in the professions as in business and industry. Engineers, attorneys, architects, accountants, and other professionals are as apt to find themselves embroiled in malpractice suits as are members of the health care professions. Most of the litigation, moreover, is accompanied by mass media exposure that compounds client and patient tendencies toward suspicion and distrust. Coverage is most pervasive where juries make substantial damage awards, further complicating professional life in two ways. Malpractice insurance rates rise, and more prospective litigants are alerted to the economic potential of the process.

Professional relationships, for these several reasons, are less frequently undertaken by clients with any sense of durability of commitment. They instead tend to be viewed as casual liaisons subject to abandonment whenever ''something better''—or something that may appear better—comes into view.

THE PROFESSIONAL CHALLENGE

More and more professionals also are looking diligently for something better, and for much the same reasons that prevail within the population as a whole. The professions have become overpopulated, inducing greater competition. Resulting competitive wars most often are being waged in ways that create considerable expense but few benefits for the combatants.

Several factors contribute to these circumstances. Traditionalism is the biggest culprit. Professional schools, regardless of academic quality, perform in exemplary fashion in inculcating their students with what might be called the professional culture. They are virtually brainwashed in the ''right'' ways to do things, which almost invariably are the ways that things traditionally have been done.

Professionals consequently persist in viewing their practices from traditional and personal perspectives rather than those of their clienteles and of society. Their perspectives are not irrational. They are highly illogical, however, in a era in which professional success is a function of consumer satisfaction. Professionals today should be managing their practices to satisfy their clienteles rather than attempting to manage clienteles for their own satisfaction. While these conditions exist, professionals will continue to expend enormous amounts of time, effort, and other resources in ways that produce little if any results.

Mounting Competition

Competition developing within and across professions has been created by economic or market pressures. Supply has been outstripping demand in medicine, law, and other areas. Colleges and universities are graduating hundreds of physicians, accountants, attorneys, and other professionals who entered school under conditions different from those existing today. Most professions require at least five years of post secondary education. As many as eight years may be necessary between matriculating and practice. A great deal of change can occur in the interim, as has been the case during the 1980s.

Today's surplus of physicians, for example, was anticipated by medical school deans as early as 1980, but the impending problem seldom was recognized among matriculating students. Most had been encouraged in their academic pursuits by parents who perceived professional credentials as tickets to the good life. Their sons and daughters often graduate expecting first year incomes of fifty thousand to one hundred thousand dollars or more and anticipating two- to threefold increases in less than five years.

Economic disappointments among young professionals often produce one or both of two reactions. The first is a willingness to market professional services using promotional strategies once foreign to professionals but recently legitimized by the Federal Trade Commission. The second is a tendency to embrace innovative, nontraditional service delivery systems. Some physicians have elected to practice in health maintenance organizations, avoiding competitive environments on an individual basis but nevertheless draining patients away from private practitioners. Others have opted for more competitive tactics. The long-extinct house call has come back to life, for example, in many large cities.

Aggressively applied in competitive markets, techniques such as these often produce rapid practice growth, most of it at the expense of more established practitioners. While conditions vary from one locale to another, competition for clients and patients is intensifying from month to month. The trend appears almost certain to continue, other than in nursing and other health specialties in which professionals serve as employees rather than independent practitioners.

Many of today's professionals thus find themselves faced with what may be the greatest challenge of their careers: how to build and maintain profitable practices in the face of increasingly aggressive colleagues and fast-changing market conditions.

A Practical Alternative

Those who achieve professional success through the 1990s and beyond will almost inevitably follow a different path. Contemporary conditions require that professionals recognize and adjust to two basic facts: their clients and patients have irrevocably changed, and professional success can be achieved only by meeting their needs.

What is necessary, in other words, is accommodation. Professionals who wish to prosper must accommodate to the nature, needs, and desires of those they wish to serve. Practitioners must find ways to satisfy their own definitions of success while satisfying clients' and patients' definitions of successful professional relationships. The way can be found when professionals first accomplish two objectives. First, they must attach personal meanings to the word *success*. Second, they must come to understand the changing nature of society and the implications of social change for their practices. Only then will they be able to comprehend the expectations of clients or patients and establish the foundations of successful practices. The successful will provide service for profit rather than seeking profit through service. The distinction is small but significant.

Defining Success

Every professional wants a successful practice. No two, however, define success in precisely the same manner. Wealth, power, prestige, and professional satisfaction are the most sought-after components. Each of these elements varies in importance among individuals. Variation is created by differences in personal perspectives and circumstances. Some value tangible more than intangible rewards, although the reverse also may be true. Most also find their values changing over time. Change may be produced by success or otherwise. Power and prestige often become paramount objectives among those who have achieved wealth. Many senior practitioners, however, have abandoned all trappings of success to teach or otherwise seek self-actualization.

Those who achieve success invariably have considered these and other factors in creating their own definitions of the word. Success seldom is found by chance. It is almost always the product of a carefully developed plan created to enable the professional to reach specific goals. "More" and "bigger" may be among individuals' objectives but are almost never goals in their own right. More money is of little value without the time to spend it. Bigger practices, unless carefully developed, are prone to become more demanding than rewarding, especially for those who prefer to practice their professions rather than become managers.

PROFESSIONAL PERSPECTIVES

Professional success in contemporary society is created by several factors. One consists of ability and willingness to meet the needs and desires of patients or clients. The other is reputation. None of these terms, however, is applied in traditional fashion.

Reputation

Professional reputation involves more than many professionals realize. Practice growth is strongly influenced by reputation. The reputation involved, however, is that of the practice rather than of the professionals involved.

Professional reputation and practice reputation, in other words, are not one and the same. Professional reputations are created by practitioner knowledge and skill. A professional's reputation might best be described as the sum of colleagues' perceptions of the practitioner.

Practice reputations, in contrast, encompass every attribute of the practice, including personnel, facilities, and environment. Professional reputation thus is necessary but not sufficient to success in practice development. Knowledge and skill must be accompanied in individual professionals by other attributes.

One of them is that human characteristic referred to in the healing arts as "bedside manner." The term refers to an ability to empathize with patients, to leave them not only healed but convinced that the professional has a real interest in them as individuals.

In other professions, bedside manner involves an ability to identify with clients and their needs and interests as well as the professional challenge at hand. The practitioner's primary challenge in these circumstances is to concurrently meet client needs and standards of professional excellence. Other criteria, however, must be met as well.

Ability and Willingness

Professional success requires both ability and willingness on the part of practitioners. These characteristics are found together less frequently than many believe to be the case. Ability involves more than professional competence. The word refers equally to practitioner insight, understanding, and responsiveness in assessing the roles of the parties involved.

The word *roles* is intended to convey complexity and discourage stereotyping. It is used to suggest that professionals must look beyond "patient," "client," "nurse," "draftsman," and all of the many other labels too readily applied in contemporary society. In so doing, they are more apt to see clearly the needs, hopes, and aspirations of all involved.

Changed perceptions. Clear vision, in turn, should induce change in perceptions and a new perspective on the functions of the professional practice. It is especially important to realize that the relative prosperity of professional practices is governed by their ability to satisfy the needs, desires, and expectations of all of the parties. Ability to succeed is a function of practitioner capability to recognize and respond to these facts.

Level of recognition on the part of practitioners is readily seen in their definitions of the term *professional practice*. Some narrowly define the term *practice* to encompass only the activities of professionals. Diagnosis and prescription in medicine, design in architecture, and sales in real estate are functions that legally can be performed only by the high priests of the professions involved. Professional practice, in the eyes of narrow constructionists, is limited to such activities. They also tend to see paraprofessional and clerical personnel as necessary evils. In so doing, they encourage staff members to adopt similar attitudes toward clients or patients and may risk infecting themselves with the same virus. The results can be deadly to the practice.

Other professionals see their practices in broader terms. They define *practice* to include all personnel, all services rendered, and those to whom services are provided. Extremists among the broad constructions go so far as to include their offices, buildings in which they are housed, and neighborhoods in which buildings are situated as components of the practice.

The differences in perspectives are critical because they govern two other vital elements. The first is the nature of the practice. The second is the manner in which it is perceived by clients and patients.

Practice defined. Professional practices consist of people serving people. Most services rendered are usually provided by clerical and paraprofessional rather than professional personnel. Professionals who care only for their professions and their profits inevitably are emulated by subordinates. The result is an insensitivity to human concerns that quickly becomes obvious to all save those involved. The insensitivity too readily is interpreted as lack of caring, with predictable results. The practice, as the word is used in reference to groups of patients or clients, quickly comes to resemble a passing parade rather than a standing army.

Variation in Professions

These conditions readily can develop regardless of the nature of the profession, a term that can be applied to any number of occupational specialties. As used here, *professional* applies only to traditionally independent practitioners whose economic welfare is governed by ability to attract and retain the patronage of clients and patients. At a minimum, physicians, attorneys, accountants, dentists, optometrists, chiropractors, podiatrists, engineers, and architects fall within this category. Management consultants and counselors in a host of other areas may also practice independently rather than as employees. The content of this book is equally, although not universally, applicable to all who function in such circumstances.

Differences in practice patterns within the several professions defy any effort toward applying universal standards. Accountants, engineers, and architects, for example, seldom find it necessary to be available to clients other than during conventional business hours. Physicians and dentists, on the other hand, must be prepared to meet patient needs at almost any time. Office locations and the amenities offered also vary in importance. Client comfort and convenience are usually more important in the health professions than elsewhere.

Successful practices share one critical attribute. They are client oriented. Practitioners view their professions from the perspective of those they serve. Their long-term success is assured by the manner in which they deliver services as well as by the characteristics of services delivered.

To assure that performance standards are maintained, successful practices are staffed with personnel committed to the welfare of clients or patients as well as employers. Personnel are governed by policies, procedures, and compensation systems designed to encourage this level of commitment. Perhaps most important, they are equipped with internal and external communication systems designed to retain as well as attract patients or clients.

PRACTICE DEVELOPMENT

Practice development deals in equal parts with two primary determinants of successful professional practice. One is the ability to attract patients or clients. The other is the ability to retain them. Professionals' circumstances today are not dissimilar from those of most businesses. All of their efforts toward growth and prosperity are equally dependent on their ability to attract and retain customers.

Business and industry spend billions of dollars annually in attempting to achieve these objectives. Their expenditures, over the years, have become equally distributed between the two objectives. Public relations, advertising, and marketing programming may bring customers to the business person's door; considerably more is necessary to bring them back on a repetitive basis.

Successful practice development requires a parallel approach. Communication techniques through which patients or clients are first attracted may be far different from those applied in merchandising. They are designed to produce the same basic result, however, and should proceed on the basis of similar rules.

Merchants often are admonished never to induce demands they cannot satisfy. Unsatisfied demand produces customer dissatisfaction. Dissatisfaction drives customers into the arms of competitors. More simply stated, the rule might be "never promise what you can't (or won't) deliver." Prospective customers (in this case, clients or patients) otherwise may be only transient components of the professional practice.

Retention of customers or clients is equally complex. Development involves creating and marketing new services to attract patients or clients. Retention requires creating practice conditions that discourage existing clienteles from departing for greener pastures. Only when the back door is firmly closed, when no patients or clients are being unnecessarily lost, should developmental efforts begin. The first of them should be directed toward existing clients or patients to capitalize on a proven business principle that is equally applicable in professional practice: existing customers are the best prospects for new products or services.

Professionals, like merchants, must address a simple but important question:

what new or improved services can I offer my existing clientele on a mutually advantageous basis?

Only when retention problems and the needs of existing clienteles have been addressed should professionals examine alternative paths to practice growth. A broad range of techniques is available. Most are applicable in multiple professions, but few are useful in every profession or by every professional. While all are legally free to advertise, for example, many senior professionals adhere to standards once imposed by restrictive codes of ethics that prohibited advertising. Equally effective tools are available, however, that will produce identical results, often at lower costs.

The Attrition Problem

Attrition among clients and patients is the most damaging disease of professional practices. Patients and clients are recruited, directly or indirectly, at considerable cost. Senior practitioners usually have attracted clienteles through years of professional effort. Younger and more aggressive practitioners often win them through relatively expensive professional development programs. In either case, they are the practice's most costly assets. They have been bought and paid for, whether in time and effort or in dollars. Their loss therefore is doubly wasteful. Past investment and future earnings depart the practice together.

Other than in unusual circumstances, neglect is the primary cause of patient and client attrition. Professionals too often are inattentive to what might be called the nonprofessional components of their practices. Three often-neglected elements—office location, office environment, and office personnel—can be especially troublesome. Each varies in impact with the nature of the profession involved but all require more attention than they usually receive.

Environmental Factors

Two variables govern levels of patient or client sensitivity to the environments they experience. One is extent of exposure. Clients seldom visit the offices of their accountants and engineers, for example, but most health care services are rendered on practitioner premises. The second is the amount of stress clients or patients experience when services are rendered. Stress levels tend to be low where architects, engineers, and financial consultants are involved, but are usually relatively high in the offices of physicians, dentists, and others in the healing arts.

Client or patient age and maturity also contribute to sensitivity to professional environments. Most people suffer from anxiety in varying degrees when in unfamiliar surroundings or circumstances. Almost everyone experiences apprehension in dealing with the unknown. The new mother whose infant becomes sick and the youngster going to a dentist for the first time are therefore apt to be hypersensitive to their surroundings. Subsequent visits are less stressful, but professionals' office staffs seldom differentiate. Caught up in the demands of their jobs and working in familiar surroundings, they often are insensitive to the needs of patients or family members.

These circumstances apply, although to a lesser extent, in almost any professional practice. New clients readily recall horror stories they have heard about members of the profession. The stories may have dealt with excessive charges or professional errors or both. They add to apprehension or anxiety. They also magnify the emotional and psychological impact of first encounters, creating lasting influences on new professional relationships.

Office Locations

Impressions created by locations of professional offices can be equally troublesome. Office locations are usually selected for convenience. More often than not, however, they are chosen for the convenience of professionals and their staffs rather than that of patients or clients. Locations that meet the preferences of all involved seldom exist. The needs of all parties should be considered when choices are made, but the health of the practice should be a primary concern. Practice health is a function of client or patient patronage. Client and patient preferences for office locations tend to be governed by safety and convenience.

Safety refers to the nature of the neighborhood in which professional offices are situated. Convenience refers to ease of access. Neither the courthouses around which attorneys prefer to practice nor the hospitals near which physicians prefer to locate are necessarily attractive by these standards.

Office Environments

Office interiors are as influential as environments in a practice development sense. Offices, from client and patient standpoints, consist of three primary components: waiting rooms, working rooms, and professionals' private offices. Each, to a greater or lesser extent, can be an asset or liability to the practice. The extent of their influence is governed by amounts of time patients or clients spend in them.

These circumstances suggest that waiting rooms require special attention. Waiting room conditions are especially influential when patients or clients are apt to encounter delays in seeing professionals. The greater the potential for delay, the more important the waiting room environment.

The same principle should be applied to consultation rooms. These may be dentists' or physicians' treatment rooms or the conference rooms of attorneys or accountants. Consultation or working rooms usually are more important in the health care professions. Practitioners' office staffs often are instructed to place patients in these rooms as their predecessors depart, leaving them alone to await professional attention. Long waits, compounding any discomfort patients may experience, are not unusual.

Professionals' private offices are no less important but in different ways. Comfort remains a factor but confidence here becomes a major concern. Most professionals see to it that their private offices are comfortable. They often are less sensitive, however, to the impressions those offices convey concerning their professional capabilities.

A drafting table or partially completed building model in the office of a senior architect, for example, suggests creative rather than mere business activity. Prospective clients in such an office might logically assume that senior members of the firm take an active role in project development. A paper-laden desk, in contrast, might suggest clients' needs are secondary to management concerns.

Condition of practitioners' desks tends to be more important where personal services are involved. Patients and clients pay for professional time. They should be made to feel that all attention is focused on their needs. Distractions and interruptions—visual or otherwise—should be avoided.

Office Staff

Location and office environment may contribute to or detract from potential for practice success. Their influence is almost negligible, however, in comparison with the potential impact of clerical and paraprofessional personnel. Attributes exhibited by these individuals often contribute more to the success or failure of a professional practice than any other element.

Office personnel may exercise only marginal influence on quality of services delivered to clients or patients. Their activities are the primary molders, however, of perceptions of those services. In a sense, personnel hold telescopes to the eyes of patients and clients. Held in one way, telescopes magnify the stature of professionals. Held in another, they diminish that stature.

Clients and patients assume—rightly or wrongly—that every word and deed of office personnel is ordered or condoned by their employers. The friendliness of receptionists, the concern of staff members, and the understanding of those responsible for collections are seen as extensions of the professional's personality. Coldness, lack of concern, and brusqueness are similarly interpreted.

Few professionals adequately understand the extent to which the characteristics of their personnel influence practice success or failure. Failure might have been too strong a word a decade or more ago. Professional practices, especially in medicine, law, and accounting, could be distinguished from one another then only by size and degree of success. They might have been alternatively described as moderately successful, successful, or very successful. Increasing competition now has created potential for failure as well.

Practitioners' knowledge, skill, and "bedside manner" are primary contributors to practice success. These are the professional attributes that first attract clients and patients. The continued health of professional relationships, however, is governed primarily by the behavioral characteristics of others in the practice.

Their attitudes and actions, more than any other factors, strengthen or weaken professional bonds.

The Bottom Line

The will and ability of professionals to control the variables described above govern success or failure in practice development. Developing competition in the professions has encouraged practitioners in every discipline to become involved in organized practice development programs. Many have been highly successful. Others have been dismal failures. Differences between the two almost always can be traced to the factors discussed above.

Simply put, professionals' ability to attract new patients or clients can be more than offset by environmental negatives. The most successful practice development program produces no discernible results when losses offset gains. These conditions create what practice development consultants call the revolving door syndrome, with existing clients or patients exiting as rapidly as new ones are attracted.

Bottom-line success in practice development for these reasons requires what has been called an inside-out process. The process involves three parts. First, any internal weaknesses—any practice attributes that might encourage development of a revolving door syndrome—must be eliminated. Second, paraprofessional and clerical personnel must be reoriented where necessary to be made a part of the practice development process. Only when these steps have been accomplished can the process be extended beyond the walls of the practice with any significant potential for success.

DEVELOPING THE PRACTICE

With the professional house in order, practitioners can turn to the more traditional aspects of practice development. These encompass all activities designed to induce practice growth. They also include a number of preliminaries necessary to insure that the practice will develop in keeping with an overall plan.

Strategic planning is vital to the long-term success of every practice development program. The process is neither difficult nor mysterious. It involves (a) identifying opportunities for practice growth, (b) determining which offer greatest long-term potential, and (c) preparing to capitalize upon them.

Strategic planning begins with environmental assessment. This is a process through which professionals first evaluate and then continuously monitor three environments. First is the practice environment, involving all of the external factors that bear on the welfare of the practice. Second is the client or patient environment, consisting of social, economic, and other trends that may influence attitude, opinion, and decision making processes among these groups. Third is the internal environment, encompassing all those factors that may make the practice attractive or unattractive to existing or prospective clients or patients.

Environmental assessment produces lists of problems and opportunities. In one sense, problems and opportunities may be opposite sides of the same coin. Environmental problems produce opportunities for engineers. Health problems produce opportunities for physicians and others in the health care sector. In another sense, problems can be threats to professional practices. Decline in numbers of public works projects challenges the economic viability of civil engineering practices. Changing demographic trends can produce similar difficulties in some medical specialties.

Appropriate professional responses are necessary to guard against emerging problems potentially dangerous to the practice. Changes in practice patterns, diversification of services, or development of new specialties may be in order. Numerous options are usually available to those who successfully anticipate changing conditions. Preparedness, in other words, is the key to success.

Charting a Direction

Data generated through the environmental assessment process enable professionals to objectively examine their practices and to establish developmental goals and objectives. Goals and objectives must be expressed in demographic as well as economic terms. Economic or dollar goals are inadequate for practice development purposes. They specify no direction for the process that follows. Success in practice development requires specifying (*a*) groups to be served and (*b*) the nature of services involved.

An architect contemplating contemporary economic conditions, for example, might logically conclude that more work will be available in the health care sector than in manufacturing for the remainder of the century. Specialization in nursing homes and other extended care facilities might be among resulting practitioner strategies. Organizations active in this sector then would become a major pool of prospective clients, and communication strategies would be developed accordingly.

Health care professionals examining a growing trend in the business community toward managed care programs might similarly conclude that large numbers of prospective patients can be more readily reached through employers than otherwise. Such a decision might suggest developing on-site services for employees and a communication strategy oriented toward employers.

The same basic process is applicable in any professional practice. External conditions suggest alternative development strategies. Each strategy, in turn, requires a different set of professional services and implies dealing with a different set of decision makers. The characteristics of decision makers, in turn, suggest appropriate communication strategies.

Decisions as to practice development are most frequently made on the basis of relative advantage, real or perceived, by prospective clients or patients. Advertising agencies have gone into the public relations business, and vice versa. Architects and engineers have similarly expanded into each other's turfs and beyond. Architects especially have become more entrepreneurial in their practices, expanding into interior design on the one hand and landscape design on the other. Professionals such as these have essentially changed the nature of their services in order to create competitive advantages.

Those in the health care professions find themselves more restricted in their potential. Physicians can become qualified in several specialties, although few have done so. Dentists can become involved in subspecialties, but most abandon general dentistry in the process. Each of the health care professions nevertheless must accommodate to the demands of a changing society in order to prosper in a competitive environment.

The Role of Research

Formal research may or may not be necessary to assist in decision-making processes. Accurate data as to the interests, needs, and desires of existing and prospective clients, however, is essential to success.

A great deal of information is readily available to professionals. Professional magazines arguably are among the best sources. They tend to be especially productive for practitioners who live outside major metropolitan areas. These areas, in which competitive conditions tend to be most intense, often spawn new or innovative services or promotional strategies that can be quickly applied in other settings.

Care is necessary, however, in assuming that communities involved are comparable. Data needed to estimate comparability usually can be quickly obtained through the U.S. Commerce Department's Bureau of the Census or from professional or industry associations. Many university libraries house extensive collections of government documents, and some business colleges maintain research programs to support local or regional commercial and professional development.

Professionals also have at their disposal an extremely valuable but often overlooked source of data: their existing clienteles. Periodic surveys of these groups can be highly productive in several ways. First, data can be readily obtained as to perceived desirability of existing and proposed services, facilities, and environments. Equally important, such surveys can provide professionals with objective assessments of the strengths and weaknesses of their personnel.

In larger practices, survey techniques also can be productively applied on an internal basis. They often yield valuable ideas concerning practice development and also enable professionals to monitor the activities of managers and supervisors. Too many professionals assume total dedication on the part of all practice personnel. These conditions seldom occur other than in unusual circumstances or where rewards are made a function of practice success. Insight into conditions within the practice thus is necessary to the design of productive communication efforts.

Establishing Communication Strategies

The communication process is at once simple and complex. Prospective message recipients are easily identified given any well-designed practice development strategy. Messages can be crafted with relative ease as well. They must be designed in keeping with the needs and desires of recipient groups involved but otherwise are not unusually demanding.

Channels of communication, unfortunately, are another matter. Those that immediately come to mind often are impractical, inappropriate, or both. Traditional advertising and marketing techniques, for example, are of marginal value even where acceptable in terms of professional ethical standards. As professionals in these fields readily confess, major changes in media audiences render the mass media relatively ineffective even where ethically acceptable.

Changes in media audiences have been described in the advertising industry as "fragmentation." Television audiences in the United States, for example, once were served primarily by three network stations in each major market. Almost all of these markets now are also served by cable systems and multiple independent stations. The same circumstances have occurred in the newspaper field. Local newspaper readership totals have declined steadily with the advent of national newspapers, especially *USA Today*, the *Wall Street Journal*, and the *New York Times*. Local business, sports, and other special interest newspapers have taken a toll as well. The result has been a continuing slide in market share among all of the mass media. Each serves a smaller percentage of potential readers or viewers today than ever before.

In addition, from the professional's perspective, the mass media have always been troublesome in terms of cost and efficiency. Relatively small percentages of their audiences at any given time are prospective consumers of professional services. A large percentage of the costs associated with mass media advertising thus become money down the drain.

Program Development

Professional development programs require a different approach to communication. The primary question that arises in their design is readily expressed: what channels of communication will reach the greatest number of prospective users of service at lowest cost per prospect? Answers vary with the nature of the professional practice. Obstetricians and pediatricians are interested in relatively youthful markets. Accountants' interests are confined largely to businesses of one kind or another. Architects and engineers are interested only in those who deal in construction projects.

Within many disciplines, specialization also plays a role. Relatively few attorneys are general practitioners. Most maintain more or less specialized practices. Some practice exclusively in the business community. Others handle damage or liability cases. Advertising consultants may specialize in specific industries; public relations counselors often concentrate in financial or governmental relations. In each case, potential numbers of clients or patients decline as a percentage of mass media audiences.

These circumstances militate toward diverse but selective communication strategies. Selective communication channels can be readily used to economically convey messages to existing and prospective clienteles. They include a host of printed materials as well as audiovisual programs circulated in person, by mail, and through supplementary channels. Educationally oriented programming can be used to supplement the communication effort where appropriate.

Costs need not be excessive. A great deal of information and guidance is available through most professional associations, directly or through practice development workshops. Further assistance can often be obtained through colleges and universities and through local, regional, and national consultant organizations. Practice development programs that prove effective and productive over extended periods of time usually require professional management. Do-it-yourself approaches occasionally succeed but more often than not involve greater than necessary costs.

Managing the Process

Management is as important to the practice development process as to the practice itself. Process productivity, in fact, is a direct function of management control. Communication is an imprecise process at best. Results must be monitored and processes often must be adjusted to produce optimum benefits. Professional management is necessary, but few professionals should make the effort. Their time is better spent practicing their own professional skills.

Larger professional groups often may find it beneficial to establish internal practice development units. In small- to middle-size practice, consultant organizations usually constitute a more economical approach. Skilled consultants in the communication disciplines invariably are conversant with the strategic planning process as well as with communication. Most offer a broad range of services to professionals.

Without exception, these services should be provided under strict budgetary limitations. The professional development program should be precisely defined at the outset both as to techniques and anticipated results. Each component then should be "costed out" to create an accurate, functional budget.

Professionals should require periodic progress and status reports and use them to monitor systemic efficiency. This approach should be taken, in fact, even where alternative approaches to practice development are employed. It should be used to assess the work of internal departments or any others who assume developmental responsibility. Practice development should be viewed as a profit center. Professionals should expect to see measurable benefits and should accept nothing less.

IN SUMMARY

Contemporary professionals are practicing in a world far different from that of just a few years ago. It is an increasingly competitive world populated by clients and patients who have been traumatized by the economic, social, and technological changes of the recent past. They are individuals who harbor little loyalty and are quick to take offense. These conditions demand that professionals bent on development of successful practices depart from traditional methods in order to attract and retain clients or patients.

Innovative practice development strategies are necessary in two areas. The first involves retaining existing clients or patients. The second is directed toward attracting expanded clienteles.

The first, or client retention, phase requires professional attention to the practice's internal and external environments. The internal environment involves the conditions to which patients are subjected. They range from the location of practice offices to levels of sympathy and attentiveness rendered by clerical and paraprofessional personnel. The external environment is that within which the practice functions. It includes competitive factors and suggests strategic responses.

The second, or practice development, stage is directed toward attracting additional clients or patients. The process may employ traditional promotional techniques such as advertising, but these tend to be less productive than once was the case. Fragmentation among media audiences would suggest alternative communication strategies even where professionals have no hesitancy in employing mass media.

ADDITIONAL READING

Dizard, Wilson P., Jr. *The Coming Information Age: An Overview of Technology, Economics, and Politics*. New York: Longman, 1982.

Drucker, Peter F. *The Frontiers of Management: Where Tomorrow's Decisions Are Being Shaped Today*. New York: Dutton, 1986.

Drucker, Peter F. *Innovations and Entrepreneurship: Practices and Principles*. New York: Harper & Row, 1985.

Glueck, William F. *Organization Planning and Development*. New York: American Management Association, 1971.

Harrington, H. James. *The Improvement Process: How America's Leading Companies Improve Quality*. New York: McGraw-Hill, 1987.

Lawler, Edward E. *High-Involvement Management*. San Francisco: Jossey-Bass, 1986.

Meyer, John W., and W. Richard Scott. *Organizational Environments: Ritual and Rationality*. Beverly Hills, Calif.: Sage, 1983.

Mitchell, Arnold. *The Nine American Lifestyles: Who We Are and Where We Are Going*. New York: Macmillan, 1983.

Oxford Analytica. *America in Perspective: The Social, Economic, Political, Fiscal, and*

Psychological Trends That Will Shape American Society for the Next Ten Years and Beyond. New York: Houghton Mifflin, 1986.

Stevens, Art. *The Persuasion Explosion: Your Guide to the Power and Influence of Contemporary Public Relations.* Washington: Acropolis, 1985.

2

Charting a Course

Strategic planning is vital to the long-term success of practice development programs. The process is neither difficult nor mysterious. It involves (a) identifying opportunities for practice growth, (b) determining which offer greatest short- and long-term potential, and (c) capitalizing on them.

Strategic planning begins with environmental assessment. This is a process through which professionals first evaluate and then continuously monitor three environments. First is the practice environment, involving the external factors that bear on the welfare of the practice. Second is the client or patient environment, consisting of social, economic, and other trends that may influence attitude, opinion, and decision-making processes in these groups. Third is the internal environment, encompassing all factors that may make the practice attractive or unattractive to existing or prospective clienteles.

COMPONENTS OF ASSESSMENT

Environmental assessment produces lists of problems and opportunities. In one sense, problems and opportunities may be opposite sides of the same coin. Environmental problems produce opportunities for engineers. Health problems produce opportunities for physicians and others in the health care sector. In another sense, problems can be threats to professional practices. Decline in numbers of public works projects challenge the economic viability of civil engineering practices. Changing demographic trends can produce similar difficulties in some medical specialties.

Appropriate professional responses are necessary to guard against emerging problems potentially dangerous to the practice. Changes in practice patterns, diversification of services, or development of new specialties may be in order.

Numerous options are usually available to those who successfully anticipate changing conditions. Preparedness, in other words, is the key to continuing success.

Points of Beginning

Data generated through environmental assessment enable professionals to objectively examine their practices and to establish developmental goals and objectives. Goals and objectives must be expressed in demographic as well as economic terms. Economic or dollar goals are inadequate for practice development purposes. They specify no direction for the process that follows. Success in practice development requires specifying (*a*) groups to be served and (*b*) the nature of services involved.

An architect contemplating contemporary economic conditions, for example, might logically conclude that more work will be available in the health care sector than in manufacturing for the remainder of the century. Specialization in nursing homes and other extended care facilities might be among resulting practitioner strategies. Organizations active in this sector then would become a major pool of prospective clients, and communication strategies would be developed accordingly.

Health care professionals examining a growing trend in the business community toward managed care programs might similarly conclude that large numbers of prospective patients can be more readily reached through employers than otherwise. Such a decision might suggest developing on-site services for employees and a communication strategy oriented toward employers.

The same basic process is applicable in any professional practice. External conditions suggest alternative development strategies. Each strategy, in turn, requires a different set of professional services and implies dealing with a different set of decision makers. The characteristics of decision makers, in turn, suggest appropriate communication strategies.

Basic Alternatives

Fundamentally, professional development programs are designed to induce practice growth by assisting professionals in selling more services to more clients or patients. Every professional practice can expand by selling

1. existing services to prospective clients,
2. new services to existing clients, and
3. new services to prospective clients.

Practice development strategies necessarily involve one or more of these techniques. A number of developmental formulas can be developed by examining the three basic approaches in the context of (*a*) the four primary marketing variables—price, place, time, and promotion—and (*b*) the relative strengths and weaknesses of the practice, real and perceived.

Relative Advantage

The phrase "relative strengths and weaknesses" refers to differences in skill and ability among professionals and practices. Differences occur by chance or are developed by design in firms and individuals. In either case, the word *relative* is critical. Potential for practice development in any geographic area is governed more by differences among practitioners or firms than by any absolute measure of capability. The relative strength of the most highly skilled specialist (or firm) in a marketplace is not a function of absolute knowledge or skill level. It is a measure of differences between his or her knowledge and skill levels and those of his or her peers.

If differences in knowledge and skill levels among peers are small—if all rank between 7 and 9 on a 10-point scale—none can be considered relatively strong or weak. If, on the other hand, one ranks at 5 while the others all rank between 1 and 3, the former enjoys a significant relative advantage despite the fact that he or she may be blessed with only moderate knowledge and skills. Relative strength or weakness thus is a product of group rather than individual circumstances.

Perception versus Reality

Relative strength may be either real or perceived. Perceived strength is as productive in practice development as real strength. The perceptions of clients or patients—existing or prospective—are their realities. If professional A is perceived as superior to professional B, it makes no difference that they may be equal in skill or that B may be superior to A. While long considered of little or no importance by professionals, perceptions govern the destiny of practice development efforts.

Professionals rightfully have been disdainful of popular opinion because it seldom accurately reflects reality. Peer opinion is appropriately considered a superior indicator of proficiency. With rare exceptions, however, peer opinion exerts little influence on success, while popular opinion is vital to practitioner welfare.

Simply put, consumers' decisions concerning professional services are based—rightly or wrongly—on perceptions of firms or individuals involved—accurate or inaccurate. Consumers behave in keeping with their perceptions. Only rarely are consumers influenced by opinion, favorable or unfavorable, among peers of those whose services they are considering. Architects may influence clients in selecting engineers. Surgeons may govern selection of anesthesiologists. Other than in these circumstances, however, opinion among professionals usually carries little weight among lay people.

Marketing Variables

Consumers, marketers tell us, are influenced primarily by four major variables in making purchase decisions with regard to services, professional or otherwise. The variables are price, time, place, and promotion.

Practice development deals only infrequently with price and promotion—or communication, as the function is better named in professional settings. Time and place, however, require careful practitioner consideration. Although varying to some extent across professions, time and place—or convenience, if you prefer—exert a strong influence over purchase decisions.

Consumer preferences as to time and place are at the heart of the fast food industry's success. In addition, however, these factors have brought us minor emergency clinics, opticians and optometrists in shopping malls, dentists in department stores, and store-front accounting practices.

Proximity or access readily may be perceived as factors influencing speed and quality of service as well as convenience. Their influence on changing patterns of consumer behavior cannot be understated. They therefore deserve careful consideration on the part of every professional.

Other than by adding to the range of professional services offered or by attempting to cover a broader geographic area, most changes in professional practices deal with one of the marketing variables. A great deal of carefully conducted research often is necessary to evaluate practice potential associated with anticipated change in any variable.

Alternative Perspective

Practice development alternatively can be viewed as an effort to deal with change. The process is designed to conform realities to the perceptions and expectations of existing or prospective clients or patients. Change can be induced in either area.

Where professionals are not accurately perceived by prospective users of their services, professional development tasks are relatively simple. Practitioners need only correct false perceptions among those who have been misled while engendering or reinforcing accurate perceptions among others.

The problem is more complex where existing or prospective clients accurately perceive professionals or their organizations but find the realities involved unacceptable. Practice managers then must select from among alternative courses of action:

1. Change reality to appeal more strongly to existing and/or prospective client groups.
2. Change reality to appeal to a broader range of prospective clients.

3. Appeal to prospective clients in a larger geographic context.

4. Accept circumstances in which practice growth will occur only with change in the size or makeup of the geographic area being served.

All of these possible courses of action must be carefully considered as professionals approach the development process.

THE DEVELOPMENT PROCESS

Practice development is a complex but logical process easily mastered by professionals. The process involves multiple phases. First among them is an examination of the practice environment as described above. Demographic and competitive conditions in the community require special attention. They are valid indicators of potential problems and prospective opportunities in practice development.

The second phase involves examining the practice in the context of community data. It requires a careful analysis of client or patient groups in light of competitive conditions as well as demographic trends.

The third phase consists of two parts. One involves compiling and analyzing practice development alternatives. In the second, the most attractive alternatives are brought together to form a cohesive development plan.

The first two phases are diagnostic. They describe the practice as it exists. The third produces a design for the practice as the professional would like it to be. Only when these phases have been completed can developmental processes begin.

The initial phases are much akin to those employed in strategic planning, marketing, and public relations. Professionals in those and other fields often create auras of mystery around their specialties. Mystery discourages the uninitiated from entering the temple without a priest. No shaman is needed, however, to apply logical processes in reaching practical objectives.

Overall, the development process is designed to produce controlled but continuous growth in preselected practice areas. The objective is optimum economic reward with minimal risk. Achievement requires several preliminaries. First, professionals must define precisely the groups and geographic areas they want to serve. Second, attrition in contemporary client or patient groups must be halted. Third, practice growth must be induced in areas previously selected.

None of the preliminaries are readily completed. Professionals often find in defining constituencies and geographic scope of practice that their office locations are inappropriate to contemporary demographic patterns. Halting attrition in existing clienteles requires analysis of factors that most influence patient and client behavior. They include practice environments as well as professional knowledge and skill. Major renovations in office facilities and extensive behavioral change among personnel often is necessary to meet changing patient or client standards. Those who would succeed in increasingly competitive practice environments have no choice but to conform to these standards.

THE ASSESSMENT PROCESS

No professional practice functions in a vacuum. All are influenced by conditions and trends in communities they serve. Communities may be local, regional, national, or international in scope. All consist of individuals and organizations whose demographic and socioeconomic characteristics control the developmental potential of professional practices. They limit opportunities in some areas while creating them in others.

Environmental assessment, as the process is called in strategic planning, thus involves examining communities to assess developmental potential for (*a*) existing products or services and (*b*) alternative products or services. Demographic and socioeconomic conditions must be examined in light of two questions:

1. What is the growth potential for existing practice services?
2. What other services might the practice profitably provide?

The questions are more complex than they appear. Responses require analysis of community characteristics. Is the population aging or growing younger? Are migration trends positive or negative? What are the prospects for commercial and industrial growth? Most important, what do these characteristics imply for the professional practice?

In a practice development sense, community demographic characteristics encompass trends in the professional discipline as well as the community. The assessment process, in other words, deals with both supply and demand. Demand for professional services—existing and potential—can be calculated by examining population growth patterns. Supply, a more complex variable, can be estimated by examining existing and prospective conditions within professional disciplines.

Community Demographics

Demographic and socioeconomic data concerning every community in the United States are available from a host of sources. They include the U.S. Commerce Department's Bureau of the Census; state, county, and local Chambers of Commerce; industrial development organizations; and colleges and universities. Data from such sources provide clear insights into existing community conditions and prospective developments.

A broad range of data can be used by professionals in examining communities in which they work or are considering establishing practices. Significance of the data varies across professions, but all are worthy of examination.

Summary data compiled by the Bureau of the Census often are most helpful.

They describe populations by age, marital status, family size, educational level, occupational category, and income level. Data are available for states, counties, metropolitan areas, cities, and U.S. Postal Service ZIP code zones. Data are most meaningful where comparable figures for several decades are compared to reflect developmental trends.

Complementary Data

Complementary commercial and industrial development data also are available from state, county, and municipal agencies. Taxing agencies maintain records of assessed valuations and tax revenues. Planning organizations monitor amounts of land zoned for specific purposes. Agencies responsible for road, sewer, and utility development maintain long-range development plans. Reviewed historically, data these organizations provide are accurate predictors of geographic development in the community.

The nature of individual practices determines the relative value of available data. Those in the healing arts, for example, usually find demographic data more enlightening. Age is a highly sensitive indicator of need for specific health care services. Household income levels are indicators of economic potential. In contrast, population growth rates, community income levels, and data from planning organizations are strong indicators of practice potential for architects and engineers. To a lesser extent, these data also are predictors of practice potential for attorneys, accountants, and other professionals.

Competitive Factors

Accurate analyses of need for professional services require more than an assessment of factors indicative of demand. The supply side of the equation also must be analyzed. Supply analyses in professional practice must extend beyond mere head counts. Numbers of practitioners in any discipline are but one indicator of supply. Their subspecialties, ages, and reputations must also be weighed in estimating existing and prospective levels of competition.

Data necessary to supply analyses in individual professions are less readily available than demographic information. Yellow Page listings in telephone directories, for example, may list practitioners only in broad categories. Those involved in financial analysis and reporting, for example, may be categorized as bookkeepers, accountants, and certified public accountants. Numbers in each category may be significant. The data would be far more helpful, however, were practitioners listed by age, years in practice, and practice specialty. Aging professional populations imply greater potential for newcomers than otherwise might be the case. By the same token, high percentages of generalists suggest practice potential for specialists, and vice versa.

Information about the latter factors often can be obtained through professional grapevines. More accurate data usually are available from licensing agencies and professional associations and, occasionally, from professional directories. Some law directories, for example, list practice specialties. Medical directories do likewise. Engineers are licensed within relatively narrow specialties.

Qualitative data concerning colleagues' services are least available but most valuable in competitive analyses. Professional grapevines may be enlightening as to colleague perceptions but seldom can be considered valid indicators of client or patient opinion. Consumer directories occasionally provide information as to the perceptions of prospective patients or clients. More often, formal research is necessary. Market research firms usually are open to such assignments, but costs are relatively high. Investments involved may be worthwhile, however, in highly competitive environments.

PRACTICES AND COMMUNITIES

With demographic and competitive data in hand, professionals are prepared for the next step in the process: analyses of their own clienteles. Is the practice clientele representative of the sum of existing and prospective clients in the community? Why might specific subgroups be under- or overrepresented? How has the clientele changed in recent years?

Few clienteles are representative of the populations professionals serve. Most tend to evolve over time to reflect practitioners' personal preferences. Many develop more by chance than design. In neither case are they apt to produce the best possible economic results.

Evolutionary Development

Practices develop in evolutionary fashion in response to practitioner predisposition. Most newcomers to a profession accept any and every client coming to their doors. Ultimately, however, professionals tend to attract and gravitate toward those who require services they prefer to provide.

Two factors appear to influence these developments. First, most individuals prefer to do that which they do well. Second, they are inclined to neglect less appealing tasks. Recipients of preferred services therefore obtain the best the professional has to offer and quickly spread the word in their communities. Others drift away, and the practice evolves accordingly.

Development by Chance

Occasionally, however, professionals stumble into specialties or subspecialties and subsequently exploit their experiences for economic gain. Many of the nation's leading subspecialists in law and accounting have seen practices develop in this manner. A relatively few trust and estate clients encountered early in general law practice, for example, frequently have led professionals to specialize in that sector. The same has been true in labor law and other specialty areas.

Many an accountant in like fashion has become progressively more involved in one industry to the exclusion of others. More often than not, this has been the extent of professionals' practice development activities.

The relatively few senior professionals in any discipline or subdiscipline may find these circumstances satisfactory. Many may be approaching retirement. Others will have achieved such prestige in their specialties as to attract ample numbers of clients or patients in the most competitive of environments. Other than in these circumstances, practice development programs are all but essential to professional and economic security.

PRACTICE ANALYSIS

Considerable information is required in the decision-making phase of practice development. Although obtained from a variety of sources, all of the data involved are designed to assist in developing responses to two sets of questions. The first set deals with professional practices as they exist:

1. What firms or individuals make up the current clientele?
2. To what extent do they differ from those of past years?
3. Why have client profiles changed?
4. To what extent does the existing clientele represent a cross-section of the clienteles of all professionals in the community?
5. Why do any significant variations from the average practice clientele exist?

Responses to the second set of questions logically lead to development of a set of practice objectives.

1. What is the economic potential of identifiable groups within the existing and prospective clienteles in the community?
2. What steps might be taken to reduce attrition and/or enhance practice development among the most economically attractive groups?
3. In what order should those steps be taken?

The First Questions

Analyses of existing clienteles are readily accomplished in some practices but are complex in others. The variation arises out of numbers of clients or patients involved. Few engineering or architectural firms, for example, have more than a few dozen active clients at any time. Practices in the healing arts, in contrast, may number patients in the hundreds or thousands.

Differences in numbers should not be permitted to impede analytical processes. Results increase in significance with the difficulty encountered in obtaining them. Professionals in smaller practices usually are constantly aware of changes in their practices. Similar changes in large practices are difficult to discern.

Existing clienteles. Criteria by which change in clienteles can be measured vary with practices involved. Indicators used in the healing arts differ from those in law or accounting. In most instances, however, necessary data are similar. They deal with more or less comparable practice characteristics.

Durability of relationships always is significant, as indicated by numbers of years during which professionals have served their average clients or patients. Depth of relationship, measured in the extent to which clients or patients use available services, is equally important. In the healing arts, depth of relationship in some instances can be measured in terms of numbers of family members served. In accounting and law, diversity of assignments is a similar indicator.

Analyses over time. Analyses always should be conducted repetitively. Year-to-year change in practice patterns always is more significant than any single year's data. In and of itself, however, change is neither necessarily good nor necessarily bad. Numbers of new clients or patients ideally should increase with each passing year. Attrition rates among older clients or patients should be no worse than stable.

Client or patient use of newer services usually increases more rapidly immediately after services are introduced than later. In the absence of an intervening factor such as technological change, use of older services also should increase, but at a slower rate. Overall change in types of clients or patients served is not necessarily suggestive of practice deterioration. Changing demographic and socioeconomic patterns often are responsible.

Reasons for change. Changes in client or patient profiles that do not reflect demographic or socioeconomic change require further research. Patients and clients do not merely drift in and out of professional practices. Their behaviors are influenced by internal or external factors that must be identified.

Only to a limited extent is change inevitable. Patients relocate or pass away. Companies disappear through acquisition, merger, or liquidation. Other than in such circumstances, clients or patients are either drawn away or driven away. Reasons must be identified before they can be remedied.

Community norms. Research of one sort or another usually is necessary to identify causes of attrition among patients or clients. Research costs can be high, however, and scope of anticipated research therefore should be limited to areas of importance.

Limitations are most readily established by examining community norms. Special attention should be paid to the demographic and sociographic patterns. Declines in birth rates, for example, necessarily limit growth in pediatric practices. They also tend to reduce numbers of architectural and engineering assignments involving new schools, playgrounds, and similar facilities.

Practitioners active in professional associations usually gain insight into prevailing community trends through contact with colleagues. Others can obtain pertinent data from national practitioner organizations. Professional journals such as *Medical Economics* and commercial reporting services are equally helpful.

Further research usually can be economically justified only where individual practice trends run counter to data obtained from such sources.

Further Analyses

Information professionals acquire in comparing profiles of their practice's community data is also valuable in identifying practice development alternatives. Where initial efforts are oriented toward identifying trends within practices, further analyses are designed to focus on community trends.

Differences between community and practice patterns often suggest productive developmental strategies. Needs for services and facilities change in keeping with changing demographic patterns. Those who identify pertinent trends early can modify or add services attractive to growing or emerging groups.

Economic potential. Developing new or modified professional services can be justified economically only where sufficient numbers of prospective users exist or will exist. Professionals often must acquire additional knowledge, skill, or technology in order to meet group needs. Revenue potential must be adequate to justify investments involved.

No investment should be seriously considered until sufficient numbers of prospective users for new services have been identified. Accomplishing this objective requires analyzing community growth trends on the one hand and competitive factors on the other.

In most cases, professionals look first to existing clients or patients and only afterward toward those of competitors. Architects whose practices are concentrated in office buildings, for example, more readily might expand into interior design than into another area of architecture. Those anticipating such a move, however, are best advised to make economic projections based on existing clienteles. Economic gain at the expense of others may develop over time but seldom should be considered in short-term economic analyses.

Curbing attrition. Attrition control efforts usually are focused on two broad areas. One involves conditions that may cause otherwise satisfied clients or patients to seek professional counsel elsewhere. The other consists of those attributes of competitive practices that also may encourage such behavior. In the latter situation, professionals seek to establish relative as opposed to absolute competitive advantages from the perspective of clients or patients. Of the two techniques, the former is the more important.

Habit and inertia are strong governors of human behavior. Unusually strong stimuli are necessary to induce change. Retailers' sales and promotions essentially are designed to provide such stimuli to shoppers. Advertising and discounts are expensive. Investments involved are recovered only to the extent that they attract new shoppers who subsequently change their shopping patterns.

Resistance to change is even greater where professional services are involved. Client loyalty is usually stronger than that surrounding commercial transactions.

Professionals usually need maintain no better than average standards in order to retain loyalty.

Quality of professional service, in fact, only infrequently is involved in client or patient attrition. Departures are almost universally triggered by unthinking or insensitive behaviors on the part of paraprofessional or clerical personnel. Such behaviors usually arise out of professionals' failures to establish and enforce social performance standards among their personnel. Professionals' concerns too often are limited to quality of technical service in an era in which personal factors are increasingly important. Human relationships can be enhanced, however, with relatively little effort.

Developing new services within professional practices is advisable only after attrition among existing client or patient groups has been reduced to minimal levels. Attrition usually can be reduced more rapidly and, in the short term, more productively. Accomplishing this objective requires more information, however, than can readily be obtained through analyses of patient or client records. Seldom will professionals' files give any indication of why former clients sought professional assistance elsewhere.

Practice attrition may result from controllable or uncontrollable causes. Little can be done to limit most forms of uncontrollable attrition. Business sales and mergers, relocation of corporate headquarters, and turnover in executive personnel lead to unavoidable practice changes, for example, among attorneys and accountants. Job changes, change in marital status, and death can result in practice losses for dentists and physicians.

Controllable losses are another matter. Clients or patients are easily offended by practitioners' paraprofessional or clerical personnel. They may find waiting rooms too crowded or otherwise uncomfortable. They may be inconvenienced by lack of timely response to requests for service. Any of a number of factors can turn a client into an ex-client or a patient into an ex-patient in a matter of moments. Quality of professional services only rarely is involved. Reasons for attrition must be known, however, if losses are to be stemmed.

Research alternatives. Causes of attrition are more readily identified where numbers of clients or patients are small. Architects, engineers, and others whose clienteles usually involve smaller groups are more apt to be aware of problems that lead clients to seek professional assistance elsewhere. In large medical, dental, and accounting practices, patients or clients can more readily drift away unnoticed.

Where the latter circumstances prevail, only two practical options exist. Practitioners can make direct contact with departed clients or patients, or professional researchers can be engaged to obtain necessary information. Direct approaches may or may not produce accurate data. Individuals often are less than candid in dealing with those they perceive as having been involved in earlier problems. Research can be relatively costly but nevertheless is worthwhile. Attrition of uncertain origin over time can economically cripple a professional practice. More important, continuing attrition can negate the potential benefits of the most productive professional development effort.

Where research costs appear prohibitive, professionals may find one other option worthy of consideration. Periodic surveys of existing clients can be highly effective early warning systems. They also can be used in identifying potentially productive services and otherwise cement patient or client relationships.

CREATING DEVELOPMENT PLANS

In taking necessary steps to curb attrition among patients or clients, professionals complete the first portion of any comprehensive practice development program. The analyses involved lead to three other strategies that usually become part of the process:

1. Expanding services to existing clienteles
2. Enlarging clienteles for existing services
3. Developing new services to attract larger clienteles

Development plans that achieve the greatest success involve all of these strategies. Seldom, however, are they applied concurrently. Most professionals instead use them in the order listed above. The sequence is dictated primarily by economic factors.

Considerable time, effort, and expense go into practice development, whether the process is organized or conducted on an ad hoc basis. Professionals, as a result, have significant investments in each and every client or patient. It is economically foolhardy to aggressively seek to expand a professional practice while attrition goes uncontrolled.

Controlling Personnel

Change in personnel behavior often requires change in fundamental employee-employer relationships. For more than a decade, business and industry in the United States have been responding to an essential conflict that remains largely unattended in professional practices. While crying out for performance, most were paying only for attendance. They were getting what they were paying for, no more and no less. As has been demonstrated in ever-increasing numbers of organizations, however, performance readily is forthcoming where four conditions exist:

1. Employer expectations are completely and accurately spelled out to all personnel.
2. Qualitative and quantitative performance standards are established for every employee.

3. Rewards are based primarily on performance and granted in temporary form, for example, as bonuses rather than wage increases.
4. The system applies to every individual in the organization.

Reward need not be entirely monetary, but systems must engage the self-interest of individuals involved. As one highly successful manager described the underlying philosophy, "When you've got them by the pocketbooks, their hearts and minds will follow." Unfortunately, the converse is equally true, as illustrated in the experience of a consultant called upon to assist a physician in bringing order out of office chaos. The physician complained, "No matter how hard I try to get a break in the middle of the day, I always seem to wind up working through my lunch hour." Careful examination of his practice procedures revealed the following facts. Office policy called for patients without appointments but requiring attention to be seen at the end of the day. Personnel all were salaried and expected to work as long as patients remained to be seen. To avoid having to work late, personnel were asking "emergency cases" to come to the office in late morning rather than at the end of the day, effectively eliminating the doctor's lunch hour but preserving their own preferred departure times.

The moral is a simple one. All other factors equal, people will serve their own needs first; those of others later. Where practitioners' paraprofessional and clerical personnel see no linkage between behaviors and paychecks, they are far less likely to be considerate in handling professionals' most valuable assets: their clients and patients. Personnel management systems thus must create linkages necessary to assure appropriate worker responses.

External factors. Uncontrolled or inadequately motivated personnel arguably account for 80 to 90 percent of professionals' problems in client or patient attrition. Most of the remainder usually are due to the sort of uncontrollable circumstances described earlier. Mergers and acquisitions necessarily induce changes in consultant relationships, as do relocation and death in individual circumstances.

Most controllable attrition beyond that originating with practice personnel arises out of competitive factors that can be successfully anticipated and minimized in many if not most cases. Strong motivators are necessary to consistently lure away patients or clients. Most such incentives in recent years have been convenience oriented.

The accelerating pace of domestic society, compounded by economic conditions that have led more and more women into the work force, have created circumstances in which time is the typical individual's most valuable resource. Products or services offered more conveniently than competitive products or services therefore are highly attractive to prospective consumers.

Considerable controllable attrition in professional practices in recent years has been attributable directly to the strong appeal of convenience factors. At first physicians referred sarcastically to emerging minor emergency clinics as "doc-in-a-box" operations (alluding to a similarly named chain of drive-in hamburger stands). Many of the most sarcastic ultimately were forced to respond to convenience medicine by moving offices to more convenient locations, by opening satellite offices, or by creating their own minor emergency clinics.

Minor emergency clinics might never have come into vogue had physicians earlier been more accessible to patients. Restricted office hours and the nearly interminable waiting that patients experienced created the "drive-in doctor." More recently, as a physician surplus developed, entrepreneurial doctors in some markets started offering house calls at all hours.

Other professions. The same pattern is developing in other professions as numbers of practitioners grow in relation to the populations they serve. Dentists now practice nights and weekends in department stores. Opticians have opened large laboratories in shopping malls and rented adjacent space to optometrists. Accounting practices are being eroded by tax preparation services on the one hand and by people rental services on the other. In each case, the trend was predictable and might have been negated by timely professional response.

Two simple steps can enable professionals to avoid most difficulties of this sort in the future. First, they must stay abreast of developments in their fields through professional journals and mass media. Second, they must adjust their service delivery systems to make them attractive enough to retain patients and clients.

Expanding Services

Three basic elements other than price are involved in consumer purchase decisions. The three elements are time, place, and usefulness. Put another way, people acquire products and services because they are offered at a more appropriate time, in a more convenient place, or with greater utility than competing products or services. In relative terms, price usually is a secondary consideration.

One or more of the three basic elements have been made more attractive to consumers of professional services in each of the innovative approaches discussed earlier. Store front legal clinics capitalize on place, on ease of consumer access. Minor emergency clinics' services are enhanced because they are available during periods when most physicians' offices are closed. Those who prepare income tax returns offer a small fraction of the services provided by bookkeepers and accountants at consequently lower cost.

These concepts are vital to professionals in examining alternative approaches to expanded services. Expansion of services need not be carried out on a large scale. Smaller often can be better. Chain stores, for example, have increased patronage in recent years by steadily adding products or services in the form of small specialty departments. Grocery stores have added delicatessens and bakeries. Clothing stores have added optometry and dental offices.

Two perspectives. These changes must be viewed from two perspectives. Large retailers involved have added services to expand sales volumes at the expense of traditional professional practices. Concurrently, however, professionals involved have limited their practices to cater to specific audiences. Dentists who practice in chain stores, for example, usually are generalists. They leave more complex procedures to other specialists. Income tax preparers function in like manner.

At the other end of the spectrum, physicians in minor emergency centers have become more specialized. They have narrowed the breadth of their practices and appeal to clients primarily in terms of time and place rather than of form of service.

Expansion alternatives. Preparation for expansion of professional services requires examining primary services in two contexts, vertical and horizontal. Those who employ professionals in one discipline often employ others as well. Horizontal expansion involves enlarging professional practices to encompass multiple disciplines. Many who employ professionals also necessarily proceed to acquire other products or services. Vertical expansion involves offering one or more of those products or services.

Professionals must examine not only the specific services they provide but the results that consumers anticipate through use of the services. Consultation with professionals in most cases is among the first in a series of steps that clients or patients undertake to achieve predetermined objectives. Achieving objectives in some cases requires the services of other professionals as well. Achievement almost invariably requires procedures or products beyond those traditionally available from professionals first consulted.

Consider, for example, prospective owners of high-rise buildings who engage architects. Before the buildings are complete, these individuals will require additional professional services. Engineering services will be essential. Interior designers probably will become involved as well. So will general contractors, small armies of subcontractors, and legions of material vendors.

Health care delivery patterns are not significantly different. Those who call on general practitioners often require the services of specialists. They also may need hospitals, therapists, pharmacists, and providers of a broad range of health-related hardware or supplies for home or hospital.

Vertical expansion. The process through which professionals offer nonprofessional services or products that necessarily will be required by their clients or patients is vertical expansion. Were physicians to offer home health services such as visiting nurses or therapists, they would be expanding their practices vertically. The same would be true of architects who offer color renderings of buildings they design or who provide direct construction supervision. Accountants, in like manner, might offer computer programming services.

Provision of such services can and should be beneficial to clients as well as vendors. Vendors usually benefit in that their profits increase through marginal expansion of staff or facilities. Clients benefit in two ways. They save time that otherwise would be necessary in acquiring services involved and they acquire ''single source responsibility.''

The latter concept permits clients to avoid the sort of difficulties that can arise where, for example, an auto manufacturer and a dealer each hold the other responsible for correcting a mechanical defect. The buyer is caught in the middle between two organizations each disclaiming responsibility and pointing to the other.

Horizontal expansion. Where vertical expansion involves offering services or products beyond the scope of traditional practices, horizontal expansion is more a supermarket approach. The concept involves providing multiple professional services through a single organization. Architectural firms might pursue horizontal expansion, for example, by establishing engineering and interior design divisions. Accounting firms might establish management consulting units.

Several alternative forms of what might be called horizontal expansion have been employed in the health care professions. Perhaps most popular among them has been the multidisciplinary clinic, often a partnership but occasionally nothing more than a gathering of physicians in synergistic specialties in a single building or location.

The latter concept also has been successfully employed where legal or ethical barriers have prevented expansion through a single legal entity. Opthalmologists, opticians, and optical laboratories, for example, often are found operating independently within the same walls for mutual benefit. Pharmacies and firms offering medical appliances often are established in close proximity to one another for the same reasons.

Horizontal and vertical expansion both deserve consideration on the part of all professionals. So do the expansion alternatives discussed earlier. Many physicians today doubtless regret that they failed to offer minor emergency facilities and house call services within their preexisting practices. Their failure to do so may or may not have resulted in attrition in their practices but inevitably produced a decline in prospective patient populations.

Expanding Clienteles

Professional clienteles are most readily enlarged through vertical or horizontal expansion of services. They also can be expanded through more traditional means, but with greater difficulty. Professional schools are graduating practitioners in most disciplines at unprecedented rates at a time when the nation is suffering what has been called a "birth dearth."

The increases in professional populations, combined with the decline or stabilizing in numbers of prospective clients are producing inevitable results. Newcomers to the professions are finding it increasingly difficult to establish traditional practices. As a result, they are turning to nontraditional techniques and eroding potential for expansion among traditional clienteles in the process.

Alternative approaches. Professionals can expand traditional practices in these circumstances only by achieving unusual distinction and recognition in one or both of two areas. The areas are professional expertise and practice environments.

Both distinction and recognition are necessary. Both can be achieved, but only with considerable innovative effort.

In general, distinction and recognition are more readily achieved in non-professional than professional contexts. Lack of knowledge and emotional barriers long have induced clients and patients to value "bedside manner" and other people-oriented practice characteristics more than professional expertise. Achieving distinction and recognition in nonprofessional practice areas, however, often involves departure from traditional practice management techniques.

Two primary nonprofessional areas are involved: office environments and office personnel. Each can be a facilitator of or a barrier to practice development. Neither traditionally has been granted adequate attention by professionals. Their primary concerns have been efficiency rather than humanity.

Physical environments. Efficiency in office environments traditionally has been evidenced in easy-to-clean but aesthetically barren waiting and consultation rooms. Chrome and plastic furnishings and vinyl tile floors have been indigenous to the healing arts and prevalent in other disciplines.

These characteristics may be appropriate in clinic settings or where practitioners are dealing with client and patient groups who expect nothing more. Even among these groups, however, austerity may be viewed as evidence of a lack of caring that reflects ill on the professional aspects of the practice.

Office personnel. The circumstances are little better and often worse where paraprofessional and clerical personnel are exposed to clients or patients. Individuals involved almost invariably have been employed for their technical expertise. Any ability on the part of those involved to relate to or sympathize with those on whom the practice depends has been coincidental.

In the best of competitive conditions, these circumstances are barriers to development of client or patient loyalty. In today's environment, they can be deadly. They create conditions that encourage patients or clients to depart for anything that even vaguely resembles more people-friendly environments.

Problem or opportunity? Physical and human environments alternatively can be viewed as problems or opportunities. Pragmatically, the worst of existing conditions constitute the greatest opportunities for salutary change. Professionals who long have neglected patient or client reactions to office environments can readily reverse this pattern.

Two steps are necessary. Each can be accomplished by the professional or delegated to a qualified consultant. The first involves redecorating and reequipping the office to meet the needs and desires of patients or clients. The second involves changing management systems to ensure that office personnel are responsive to patient or client needs.

The latter component usually requires change in reward and accountability systems. Performance-based compensation mechanisms almost invariably are necessary. So are audit systems to keep the professional abreast of the extent to which personnel are meeting contemporary practice requirements. Fortunately, both are readily installed in a manner in which they are welcomed by all involved.

Developing New Services

Only when practice environments have been recast as practice attributes should practitioners turn to developing new services. The processes involved are complex, time-consuming, and often expensive. Potential for error and economic loss can be minimized but not eliminated. Effective practice development programs, however, ultimately proceed to a point at which development of new services is necessary and appropriate.

The term *new services* is somewhat misleading. It encompasses services that are truly new, but it more often refers to services otherwise available that logically can be offered as part of the professional practice. The extent to which this is the case is most evident in medical practice. Very few physicians today "go outside" for routine laboratory tests, X rays, and other services that can readily be offered internally.

Whether new in the real sense or merely new to the practice, professionals should approach development of additional services with caution. Several factors require especially close attention. They include the cost of providing the service, the extent to which it potentially will be used by existing clients or patients, and the extent to which it will enhance the attractiveness of associated professional services.

Developmental costs. Development of new services invariably involves a broad range of costs, fixed and variable. Both varieties of cost require careful examination and analysis in assessing the economic potential of individual services. Economic potential also should be viewed in negative as well as positive terms. Assessment should deal with potential for loss as well as potential for profit.

Three or four factors generate most costs. They are personnel, equipment, space, and, in some circumstances, inventory. Each is a variable that may or may not make any service a good match for a specific professional practice at any given moment. The best match occurs where contemporary practice circumstances enable professionals to accommodate additional services within existing resources.

Availability of unused space, for example, may make a space-intensive service more practical than an equipment-intensive service. Existence of adequate personnel resources within the organization also can reduce start-up costs as opposed to circumstances in which additional workers must be hired.

In general, loss potential increases with the extent to which long-term financial commitments are necessary. Space-intensive services may require expanding offices, which in turn may necessitate renegotiating leases. Services requiring extensive equipment can be equally burdensome and loss potential may be equally great. While equipment often can be leased rather than purchased, most contemporary leases are the equivalent of time-purchase agreements.

Analytical processes. Professionals should begin preparations for expanding services by compiling exhaustive lists of services that might be offered. Lists usually are most readily compiled by reviewing contemporary literature in the profession and associated fields. The latter should be included because the process should include analysis of horizontal as well as vertical expansion potential.

Information necessary in compiling lists of services usually is readily obtained through professional journals, especially those that deal with practice management. *Practice management* here refers to the business aspects of the profession rather than to the management of professional services. Potential information sources also include professional meetings and associated exhibits and the staffs and libraries of professional associations.

With lists of potential expansion areas completed, professionals next should examine the extent to which the several services are available in the community they seek to serve. This process also should encompass horizontal as well as vertical perspectives. Professionals should assume that innovative services developing in more competitive markets ultimately will arrive in their communities. Sound business principles demand that they consider carefully whether preemptive action might be appropriate or necessary. Many a professional has regretted knowingly ignoring the development of an innovative service beyond the boundaries of his or her own practice area.

The result of the analytical process should be a relatively short list encompassing opportunities of two types. First are those involving relatively low costs and minimal risk of loss. Second, but of equal if not greater significance, are those which might be damaging to the practice if introduced by competitors. Finally, those services on the list should be ranked in order of relative desirability for practitioner action.

At this point, preliminary analytical processes are complete, and the professional should have four lists at hand. They should provide, in order of importance, steps to be taken in

1. reducing attrition in existing practices,
2. expanding services for existing clienteles,
3. expanding clienteles for existing services, and
4. developing new services to expand clienteles.

IN SUMMARY

Practice development is a logical, three-phase process. The first phase involves examining the practice environment. The second requires examining the existing practice in the context of the environment. The third consists of defining and analyzing alternative approaches to the developmental process. The pattern involved is much akin to the processes used in marketing and public relations.

Environments are important in that external conditions largely determine the growth potential of the practice. The nature of populations that professionals serve limits the potential of existing and prospective professional services. En-

vironmental potential is most readily analyzed by examining community demographic data and competitive conditions. Demographic data are indicators of
community development trends that in turn point toward areas of practice potential. Competitive circumstances permit professionals to evaluate the relative
potential for practice development in those areas.

Analyses of existing clienteles provide additional guidance as to developmental
potential. They focus primarily on the extent to which the practice is serving
specific population subgroups and are designed to show why each might be
overrepresented or underrepresented. Most practices evolve by chance or in
keeping with professional preferences. The absence of well-designed plans in
these circumstances may lead professionals away from areas of significant developmental potential.

Practice analyses require careful examination of existing clienteles to accomplish multiple objectives. They serve to define patterns of change in professional
practices and lead practitioners to examine underlying causes. They also involve
comparing individual practices with others in the community as to relative
strengths and weaknesses. Most important, they induce professionals to examine
the economic potential of practice subgroups and assess alternative approaches
to better serving those groups.

When developmental alternatives have been identified, economic analyses are
in order. New or expanded services can be justified only where substantial user
potential exists and initial costs are reasonable. Preliminary estimates of user
potential are best confined to existing rather than prospective clienteles.

Practice development plans incorporate one or more of four strategies designed
to reduce attrition among existing clienteles, expand services, attract additional
clients, and develop new clienteles by providing additional services. The developmental process usually is most productive where these strategies are applied
sequentially rather than concurrently.

Reducing attrition should always be the first step in practice development.
The process involves two components. The first consists of eliminating sources
of internal friction that may induce patients or clients to seek assistance elsewhere.
Practice personnel are a primary source of friction, and attrition control usually
requires installing performance reward systems designed to induce improved
staff behaviors. The second component of the process involves addressing those
attributes of competitive practices that may be attractive to clients or patients.
Most are convenience oriented and can be successfully countered through competitive strategies.

The same sort of problem-solving approach is applied in expanding services.
The objective of the process is to make the practice more attractive to existing
and prospective clients or patients. Relative attractiveness from a consumer
standpoint relates to one of three attributes other than price. They are time, place,
and usefulness. Professional development requires making the practice competitively attractive in one or more of these contexts. The same attributes are
involved in expanding clienteles and developing new services.

ADDITIONAL READING

Duck, Steve. *Human Relationships: An Introduction to Social Psychology.* Beverly Hills, Calif.: Sage, 1986.

Falcione, Raymond L., et al. *Organizational Communication.* Vol. 5. Beverly Hills, Calif.: Sage, 1980.

Hamilton, Seymour. *A Communication Audit Handbook: Helping Organizations Communicate.* New York: Longman, 1987.

Kreps, Gary L. *Organizational Communication.* New York: Longman, 1986.

Pope, Jeffrey. *Practical Marketing Research.* New York: amacom, 1981.

Rothman, Jack. *Using Research in Organizations: A Guide to Successful Application.* Beverly Hills, CA: Sage, 1980.

Ruben, Brent D., ed. *Information and Behavior.* Vol. 1. New Brunswick, N.J.: Transaction, 1985.

Wimmer, Richard D., and Joseph R. Dominick. *Mass Media Research: An Introduction.* 2nd ed. Belmont, Calif.: Wadsworth, 1987.

3

Formulas for Success

Organizations and their clienteles share a common element: people. Organizations consist of people. The individuals who consume the products and services that organizations offer also are people. People—consumers and producers—thus are the primary concern of successful organizations.

The word *organization* is all-inclusive. It applies equally to manufacturers, distributors, and retailers; to providers of services; and to not-for-profit entities of all kinds. Each is composed of people. Each is dependent upon people.

Dependency increases where organizations deal in services rather than products. Quantity and quality of products are readily measured using generally accepted standards. Quality of service is another matter. Essentially, the quality of a service is what buyers say it is. It is what they perceive it to be.

The mechanism through which perceptions are formed is more complex than many suspect. Perceptions, especially where services are involved, are more than a set of visual impressions. They are shaped as consumers compare what they expected with what they experienced.

A special organizational vulnerability to misperception arises in many professional practices. Practitioners are sought out by clients or patients to apply professional knowledge and skill toward solution of problems. Clients and patients may spend hours in the temple of medicine, law, or accounting, but only minutes with the high priest in the sanctuary. The remainder of their time is spent with novices, acolytes, and other retainers in anterooms and other chambers. Perceptions are shaped accordingly.

Since clients and patients lack the knowledge and skill to measure professional competency, other factors influence their evaluations of the quality of the services they purchase. Quality of service, from their perspective, encompasses the environment in which it is rendered and the behaviors of every individual involved.

Professional success thus is governed by the total experience of the client or patient. Practitioner expertise is necessary but not sufficient.

Successful practitioners thus must master more than the knowledge and skill on which their professions are based. They also must deal with the two human components of their practices: personnel on the one hand, clients or patients on the other.

CRITERIA FOR SUCCESS

A great deal of research in recent years has produced consensus among experts concerning the characteristics of successful organizations. The bulk of the research has dealt with larger, nonprofessional organizations. The results, however, are no less applicable in professional practice.

Successful organizations are consumer oriented. They succeed by inducing customer satisfaction. They share six characteristics that produce that result:

1. demanding performance standards,
2. insight into consumer desires,
3. managed consumer expectations,
4. designs for consumer satisfaction,
5. investment in performance, and
6. investment in people.

Demanding performance standards require real effort on the part of organizational personnel. Meeting those standards, however, also instills in them a sense of pride in accomplishment. Knowledge of consumer desires enables organizations to work effectively toward meeting them. Organizational effort can be directed toward meeting consumer standards, modifying consumer expectations, or both. Investment in performance and people insures continued organizational success. Investment means recruiting the best and the brightest and rewarding them for superior performance. The process thus comes full circle. Demanding performance standards are accompanied by rewards for those who meet them.

All of these characteristics are essential in inducing development of the single element that produces success in professional practices: consumer satisfaction. Unfortunately, these elements are not readily acquired. They can be developed, but only with the support of practice personnel at every level and in recognition of the vital role of the consumer.

Most important from the standpoint of the professional, quality of service is what the client or patient says it is—no more and no less. More technically prone scholars contend that quality is conformity to specifications. They miss a vital element: the consumer. The consumer's definition of quality is the only definition that counts. Looking at it another way, professionals provide high quality service by doing well the things that clients and patients consider important.

Clients and patients evaluate services by comparing their expectations with their perceptions of services they receive. Expectations and perceptions extend far beyond what a professional would encompass with the term *professional service*. Every characteristic and component of the service and the environment in which it is rendered enter into consumer judgments.

Professional reputations thus are a product of the extent to which practitioners meet or exceed patient and client needs and expectations. Knowledge and skill play a role in creating reputations, but the extent of their influence is almost inevitably smaller than professionals would prefer. Success in competitive environments therefore requires attention to those factors of greatest importance to consumers. Each must be managed with the same diligence extended to the professional aspects of the practice. Successful professionals, in essence, manage practices as businesses committed to serving customers and clients.

Management here refers not to money but to people and the manner in which they respond to their environments. Professional practices are usually oriented in one of two directions, toward generating profit through delivery of services or toward producing services to generate profit. The two concepts are very different despite their apparent similarity. The former is dollar oriented while the latter is quality oriented.

COMPONENTS OF QUALITY

Defining quality in the context of professional services is no easy task. Services are intangible and, at least to some extent, invisible as well. They can be neither weighed nor measured, but they can and must be evaluated by professionals from the point of view of their clients and patients.

Delivery of a service involves a performance in an environment. The process consists of an act or series of acts undertaken by one or more persons in one or more settings. Unlike services, settings or environments can be measured. So, too, can the behaviors of individuals involved in delivering services. Quality of services therefore can be indirectly measured by examining these elements.

Environments

In the context of professional services the word *environment* refers to neighborhoods in which professional practices are located, to buildings in which they are situated, and to the offices within those buildings in which practices are housed. Environment might better be described as the "seeable" part of the professional service. The word also encompasses practice furnishings, equipment, and the appearance and demeanor of individuals involved. It includes everything that can be seen by the patient or client.

Performance

Every individual inhabiting a professional environment is involved in performance or delivery of services. Some may be involved only indirectly, as in the case of a draftsman in an engineering or architectural office or a laboratory aide in a physician's office. Others, such as design or nursing personnel, are in direct contact with clients. Each of them, however, directly or indirectly influences the way in which professional services are perceived.

Researchers suggest that four characteristics of practice members are most impressive—positively or negatively—from the perspective of patients or clients. These characteristics are responsiveness, empathy, reliability, and assurance. Each is an individual attribute that inevitably attaches itself to the practice as well as members of its personnel complement.

Reliability. Consistent, dependable and accurate delivery of a service is termed reliability. It involves doing what an individual or organization promises to do.

Unfortunately, reliability is a variable within and across types of organizations. It is considered a vital part of truly professional deportment in advertising and public relations but is treated with cavalier abandon in many of the health care disciplines. Advertising and public relations practitioners consider it a cardinal sin to miss media deadlines but physicians are notoriously poor in keeping appointments.

Responsiveness. Reliability and responsiveness are closely related to one another. Responsiveness refers to willingness and readiness to provide professional services in keeping with patient or client needs.

As in the case of reliability, responsiveness can mean different things in different professions. Among advertising agencies, it may involve working late to change the price in an advertisement. For a dentist, it may mean going to the office to help a patient on a holiday or during a weekend.

Assurance. Knowledge and courtesy come together to create assurance, to assure the client that his or her needs are being met. Assurance is a sense that all is well. It occurs in visitors to the practice environment when they are met by individuals who are at once competent and nice, knowledgeable and friendly.

Assurance creates confidence and trust. It produces a feeling that all is well. It induces clients to confidently place their physical, legal, or economic welfare in the hands of professionals without hesitation. And it predisposes those involved to resist the siren song of professionals' competitors.

Empathy. The ability to feel and respond to the needs of clients and patients is called empathy. The word refers to the commitment that successful professionals make to those who come to them for help. Empathy is a commitment to identifying and satisfying client needs. It involves individual interest and attention on the part of every member of the practice in every client.

Each of these elements—reliability, responsiveness, assurance, and empathy—is characteristic of quality in professional practices. Each of them is necessary in meeting client definitions of quality. Quality in professional service means much more, however, from the practitioner perspective.

COMMITMENT AND QUALITY

Professional commitment to quality in the sense in which the word is understood by clients is but the first step on a long path. Commitment to quality requires that practitioners create environments and organizations equally committed to excellence. Such commitment requires acceptance of several basic principles beyond those which delegate definition of quality to users of professional services:

1. Quality requires ongoing effort.
2. Quality is everyone's responsibility.
3. Quality requires leadership and communication.
4. Quality begins with integrity.
5. Quality is built in, not added on.
6. Quality requires keeping promises.
7. Quality produces profit for all.

Continuity

Perhaps the most difficult attribute of quality service for many to accept is the continuing demand it makes on committed organizations. Quality is not among those goals that can be labeled "achieved." It is not a mountain to be climbed or a river to be crossed.

Quality is an attitude, a mind set, a commitment. It requires continuing effort, day to day, month to month, year to year. What has been done acceptably can be done well; what has been done well can be done better. The path has no end, and the effort can not be confined to one or a few individuals in any organization.

Responsibility

Professional commitment to quality seldom is adequate to assure practice success. This is the case even where practitioners are prepared to substitute client or patient definitions of quality for their own. Except in the (rare) case of a professional practicing without paraprofessional or clerical support, practitioners alone cannot maintain quality standards.

Where others are involved, their support is essential, and this principle applies whether or not they come into direct contact with patients or clients. No one works in a professional practice without clients. Everyone performs a service for someone else.

Some members of professional practices perform external services. Others perform internal services. The draftsman and laboratory worker, as discussed above, are no less important to overall quality of service than the designer or nurse.

In no case can service quality be delegated. Quality of service is the sum of the performances of all involved. In the same manner, client or patient perceptions of quality are the sum of hundreds of moments of interaction between them and members of the practice team.

Leadership and Communication

Professionals committed to providing quality services quickly find themselves involved in much more than mere professional practice. Consistent quality service requires leadership and communication. Leadership is essential to quality and communication is essential to leadership.

Quality requires getting the job done for the client day in and day out, under any and all conditions. It is hard work that requires real commitment, commitment that can be induced only through genuine leadership at every organizational level.

Management and administration are inadequate to sustain committed service by organizational members over an extended period. Leadership, even inspirational leadership, is invariably necessary, and even leadership may not always be sufficient.

Integrity

Quality service and organizational integrity are inseparable in successful professional practices. Consistent service quality develops only where fairness governs organizational value systems.

Service-minded organizations are incompatible with "win/lose" attitudes, with systems in which client interests are sacrificed on the altar of profit. Levels of worker pride necessary to sustain successful professional practices by providing quality services are impossible to achieve in these circumstances.

Only integrity on the part of professionals and their organizations—nothing more and nothing less—will induce the consistency of quality performance necessary to long-term success.

Quality by Design

The same principle applies in developing quality within organizations. Where quality is to prevail, it must be a primary rather than a secondary concern.

Quality of service is pragmatically more a matter of philosophy than of any other element. Quality develops where it is part of everyday life rather than something to be added later. The circumstances are much akin to those that apply in manufacturing or construction. Each and every component of the finished product must be selected and installed with care if quality is to result. Anything less predestines the product to less than adequate quality.

Quality for Profit

The latter concept is especially important where professionals consider organizational productivity. Productivity and profit, to a far greater extent than many realize, are governed by quality. Quality literally is a profit strategy. Quality is the best route to economic success.

Profit in any organization originates in one of two areas: Differentiation from competition and cost efficiency. Differentiation, or buyer perception of superiority, enables organizations to grow more rapidly, to develop more customer loyalty. Cost efficiency involves greater profit margins.

Excellence contributes to both of these objectives. Quality of service differentiates one organization from another. Service organizations may look alike to prospective clients or patients, but they don't "feel" alike. Excellence is a strategy that is both important to clients and hard to imitate. It is something that cannot be bought but that must be created from within.

Quality also lowers costs. Professional practices can grow in only three ways. They can attract new clients or patients. They can provide more services to existing clients or patients. And they can reduce losses in clients or patients. Poor quality of service detracts from organizations' ability to perform in all of these areas, and the reverse is equally true.

Poor reputations make for negative word-of-mouth publicity. They discourage existing clients, and research shows that each of them is likely to tell nine or ten others of his or her problems. These circumstances are dangerous where products are involved and deadly in service organizations. Because services cannot be seen, people tend to ask acquaintances for advice. Word of mouth is a major governor of success in service organizations; negative word of mouth is a killer.

Poor quality is no less destructive inside the organization. Poor internal support systems frustrate personnel and encourage them to quit. The more committed the worker to quality, the higher the frustration level and the more likely the resignation. These conditions produce higher personnel turnover rates and higher recruiting costs. Higher turnover leads to poorer quality of service and undermines patient or client loyalty.

Fortunately, the reverse also is true. People find it more fun to work for organizations that deliver superior service. They prefer to work in achievement cultures where everyone is trying to do his or her best. They sell their friends on coming to work for their employers rather than telling them to stay away.

The same sort of differences in results occur in other areas. Poor service produces errors that must be corrected, leading to higher costs. Poor service also produces higher marketing costs and tends to induce lower prices, both of these elements leading to reduced profitability. A reputation for poor service requires more marketing effort with consequently greater expense, and prices may have to be adjusted downward to compensate for perceived organizational deficiencies on the part of prospective clients or patients. In other words, lower prices tend to be an outcome of poor service, while high quality can command high prices.

SERVICE BARRIERS

While quality service inevitably is more beneficial to organizations and their clients or customers, many continue to fail through failure to provide quality. In most cases, one of five primary problems is involved:

1. Management misinterprets consumer desires.
2. Management fails to translate consumer desires into functional policies.
3. Workers fail to conform to management specifications.
4. The organization fails to communicate adequately with clients or patients.
5. The organization fails to deliver the service that consumers expect.

Each of these areas of potential failure is more complex than it appears. In addition, each relates to the primary concept established earlier: quality is defined by the consumer.

Misinterpretation

No organization can succeed while delivering a service no one wants. Legions of organizations, however, have managed to deliver unsatisfactory products or services and have paid the price.

One of the most striking examples of recent decades involved changes in automotive buying patterns that occurred in the United States during the 1970s and 1980s. This was a period during which fully 25 percent of what had been an almost exclusively domestic market was lost to overseas manufacturers. The reason was U.S. manufacturers' failure to understand and react to basic changes in the preferences of automotive buyers.

Domestic manufacturers offered chrome instead of quality, size rather than economy, and conversation instead of service. They forgot that the primary need of their customers was reliable transportation, that they literally were selling transportation systems rather than automobiles.

The Germans, Japanese, Swiss, and others capitalized on the tunnel vision of the U.S. auto industry. They introduced quality products at lower prices and supported those products with quality service. The result was inevitable.

Performance

The same results could as easily have developed in other circumstances. Accurate management perceptions of consumer needs are inadequate to success unless (*a*) perceptions are translated into quality service specifications, and (*b*) workers perform as specified.

Performance is especially important. The concept is far broader than first appears to be the case. Performance begins before services are rendered and continues after the fact. It encompasses the warmth and sincerity of the welcome extended to patients or clients as well as after-the-fact support.

Those who answer professionals' telephones, for example, can be highly productive or wholly counterproductive in terms of practice development. Callers readily discern whether or not their calls are welcome, whether professionals' receptionists are really interested in seeing that needs are met.

The same range of response usually is induced, by design or otherwise, after clients or patients are served. Affirmative responses occur where, for example, a dentist calls surgical patients when his work day is over to make certain that they are comfortable.

The reverse tends to be true where professionals "take the money and run." Potential for negative response has been compounded in recent years by marketers' efforts toward more personalized services. Consider, for example, the potential reaction of an individual used to getting after-service calls from his auto dealer when he is ignored by his physician after discharge subsequent to out-patient surgery.

Several steps are necessary to insure that follow-up procedures are followed. First, the procedures involved must be clearly specified to all involved. Second, individuals responsible for handling follow-ups should be held responsible for seeing that they are made as specified. Finally, performance should be monitored to assure that follow-ups are made.

Communication

Communication between professional organizations and those they serve is a complex process. Handled well, it can strengthen relationships between the groups. The reverse, however, is equally true.

Complexity arises out of the fact that communication begins before organizations come into direct contact with patients or clients. Information received early concerning professional services more often than not is conveyed by word of mouth or by inference.

Inferences are apt to be drawn from a diversity of information available to prospective prospects or clients. How "good" is the practitioner's office address? With what community causes or organizations is he or she publicly identified? How is he or she depicted in the mass media?

Factors such as these often are more significant in individuals' decisions concerning acquisition of professional services than otherwise is the case. The intangible nature of services makes "prepurchase" examination difficult. Prospective users thus are predisposed to seek out other sources of information in reaching buying decisions.

Service Delivery

Success and failure in the delivery of professional services are equally complex concepts. They involve the extent of professionals' promises (expressed or implied), the manner in which those promises are perceived by clients, and, most important, the extent to which the two concepts match one another.

As indicated earlier, quality of service is defined by recipients. Their definitions are created as they compare preconceived expectations with experiences. The best of services may be perceived as inadequate where expectations are unrealistically high. The worst of services, in like manner, may be acceptable where expectations are unrealistically low.

Delivery of quality in professional services thus involves a great deal more than meeting standards of excellence as established by professional peers. Clients and patients are seldom aware of them. If aware, they usually lack adequate knowledge to judge professional performance.

"Nonprofessional" aspects of professional practice are another matter. Clients are very much aware of delays in waiting rooms, courtesy or discourtesy among paraprofessional or clerical personnel, and other such "little things."

THE PERFORMANCE GAP

Professional and other perceived shortfalls in organizational performance come together in professional practices to create performance gaps. These are chasms between what patients or clients want and receive, or between what they believe they have been promised and what they receive. Whatever the origins of these problems, they can be deadly to the professional practice.

Problem potential expands when services are labor intensive, when they require interaction between providers and receivers, and when they are decentralized. Numbers of individuals involved usually increase with labor intensity, multiplying potential problem sources. Potential for misunderstanding increases in proportion to the volume of communication required in delivering services. When services are provided at multiple sites, overall potential for difficulty further increases. Managerial or supervisory oversight deteriorates as a result.

Magnitude of performance gaps is governed by two variables, one readily controlled and the other relatively difficult to manage. The variables are the ability and the willingness of personnel to perform as organizations require. Ability of those involved can be controlled to some extent in most organizations; willingness to perform is another matter.

Level of willingness determines the extent to which workers expend discretionary effort. Discretionary effort is effort greater than that required to keep from getting fired or to do the job properly. The nature of services, as opposed to products, creates greater than average gaps between these points. Product quality is more readily measured than quality of services. In the automotive industry, for example, evident differences between "fit and finish" quality were

Figure 3.1
Willingness/Ability to Serve Clients and Patients

```
Willingness                 Ability

                    Able              Unable

Willing              A                  B


Unwilling            C                  D
```

major contributors to domestic manufacturers' loss of market share. Differences in the quality of their service operations as compared with those of competitors was more difficult to measure.

Simplistically, workers can readily be categorized as to their ability and willingness to perform (see figure 3.1). They may be able or unable, willing or unwilling. High performance workers (A) are willing and able. The willing but unable (B) readily can achieve high performance levels. Managers' primary challenge is inducing behavioral change in those who are (C) able and unwilling and (D) unable and unwilling.

Willing and able workers expend 100 percent of discretionary effort to achieve organizational objectives. They are reliable, responsive, reassuring, and empathetic. They best serve patients or clients as well as the organization and themselves. Practitioners' primary challenge is in changing the behavioral patterns of remaining personnel or in separating them from the organization.

CLOSING THE GAPS

Concerted effort on the part of professionals is necessary to close the gaps in service quality. A number of steps are necessary to accomplish that objective. Direct efforts toward improving quality by inducing workers to invest 100 percent of discretionary effort is most important. Other factors, however, contribute to professional success in gaining worker commitment. The latter include the following:

1. A productive research program dealing with perceptions of service quality from the standpoint of workers as well as of clients

2. Recruiting and retention strategies in keeping with contemporary labor market conditions

3. Employee knowledge and skill development programs

4. Performance-based reward systems designed to encourage behaviors that will contribute to the economic health of the practice

5. Open communication systems within the practice

Collectively, these steps assist professionals in creating understanding of practice and client needs among workers. They are designed to generate information and, most important, to convey to employees the interdependent nature of their jobs.

Research Programs

The value of market research in professional practices has increased with growing practitioner need to induce total commitment on the part of clerical and paraprofessional personnel. Professionals traditionally have been concerned with research only as necessary in maintaining contemporary professional knowledge. Benefits inherent in the use of research in practice development have largely been ignored.

Two circumstances have led more and more professionals to reconsider the value of market research. One is the increasingly competitive environment in which most professionals practice. The other is an increasingly competitive personnel marketplace. Successful practice development in these conditions requires insight and understanding on the part of workers as well as professionals.

Insight and understanding are produced by credible information. While information may be obtained by means other than research, credibility is another matter. Employee-employer relationships in the United States have traditionally been so adversarial as to render any employer statement open to question. Availability of valid research data provides valuable reinforcement for professionals attempting to induce employees to work toward enhanced organizational performance. Data also can be used (see chapter 8) to measure worker performance and to enable managers to allocate rewards accordingly.

Research can be externally or internally oriented. Externally oriented research is usually designed to discover perceptions of the practice among prospective clients. Internally oriented research may be directed at existing clients or at practice personnel. Both varieties of research are designed to identify the practice's relative strengths and weaknesses—perceived and real—in the eyes of the groups involved. Practice development demands that professionals capitalize on their own strengths and on competitors' weaknesses while correcting weaknesses in their own organizations. Correcting may involve altering misperceptions or changing realities, as circumstances require.

Recruiting and Retention

Perceptions of the practice also are important in recruiting and retaining qualified personnel. Perceptions in the community and especially among existing personnel exert considerable influence on practitioner ability to recruit and retain superior personnel in competitive markets.

The basic principle involved functions in two ways. First, organizational reputations govern the extent to which they attract applicants. Organizations perceived to be superior thus have larger talent pools from which to draw when vacancies occur. Second, worker ability to move from one job to another is a function of individual ability.

Organizations perceived as desirable by workers thus inevitably are in a position to strengthen their personnel complements at the expense of those seen as less desirable. The good get better, in other words, while the poor get poorer. Organizations that find themselves in the latter category soon may find their survival threatened as a result.

Worker Development

Organizations that offer their personnel opportunities for personal growth enjoy a distinct advantage in competitive labor markets. Personal growth involves more than wages. The concept involved is based on providing workers with opportunities to improve knowledge and skill levels to a point at which they can improve their earnings through enhanced productivity.

Improvement can be qualitative, quantitative, or both. Workers can be trained or educated to do more of what they have been doing or to handle a broader range of tasks or both. Their potential productivity will increase in either case. The organization then need only provide mechanisms through which productivity potential can be realized and rewarded.

Individual productivity can improve only where organizational systems enable workers to expand the scope of their activities. Systems and supervisors must be sufficiently flexible to enable workers to grow. Such flexibility occurs only where growth opportunities are also available to supervisors and managers, encouraging them to work with personnel rather than to become obstacles to enhanced productivity.

Reward Systems

Organizations provide productivity-based rewards in one of three forms: recognition, career advancement, and cash or equivalents. Reward system managers usually obtain best results when organizations provide considerable latitude in use of the three types of rewards. Differences among individuals at any given time may render one variety of reward superior to another.

The latter principle applies within and across reward categories. Immediate rather than deferred compensation almost universally is more attractive among younger workers, for example, while deferred compensation often is preferred by their senior counterparts. Recognition, in like fashion, often is as attractive as economic reward among those in midcareer and beyond.

In essence, incentives or rewards of one sort or another are necessary to induce workers to invest discretionary effort on behalf of their employers. Professionals who would successfully compete for workers must insure that appropriate inducements are available. Systemic flexibility enables managers and supervisors to keep a carrot—in one form or another—directly in front of every nose at all times.

Communication Systems

Organizational communication systems must be designed to insure that all members are (*a*) aware of the carrots and (*b*) made to feel a part of the organization. The latter of the two elements often is the more important. Individuals who identify with organizations, who consider themselves part of teams rather than mere employees, almost universally are more loyal and more productive. While not disinterested in rewards, they are less prone toward an approach to employers that seems to say, "What have you done for me lately?" Communication systems should discourage the latter perspective and foster the former.

The complexity of communication systems varies with organizational size and complexity. To a significant extent, formal communication techniques are employed in large organizations to replace the personal networking that prevails among their smaller counterparts.

Communication systems in most professional practices tend toward the informal. With the exception of organizations such as national and international accounting, advertising, and public relations firms, professional organizations usually are relatively small and operate in relatively few locations. Little formal communication activity is necessary where managing professionals are in daily contact with subordinates. Sophisticated systems ranging from newsletters to computer-based information systems may become necessary as organizations grow.

IN SUMMARY

Professional practices and their clienteles are interdependent entities that engage in one or, more commonly, a series of transactions. Transactions continue to occur, however, only when two conditions are fulfilled. First, there must be a continuing need for the services involved. Second, and far more important, both parties must continue to be satisfied with completed transactions.

These conditions are apt to persist only where practitioners consistently fulfill a set of rather demanding criteria, beginning with high standards of professional performance. Successful professionals also

1. maintain insight into the desires of their clienteles,
2. manage the expectations of those who consume their services,

3. design their practices to induce consumer satisfaction, and

4. invest in people and in their performance.

Only when these standards have been met can professionals produce consumer satisfaction, and only where there is consumer satisfaction will further transactions take place.

Consumer satisfaction arises out of quality of service. Quality is what clients or patients say it is. Quality, from their perspective, represents the extent to which professionals meet their preconceived expectations. Most client and patient expectations center around two variables: environments and performance.

Environment refers to professional offices, to the buildings in which those offices are located, and to the neighborhoods in which the buildings are situated. Performance refers to the reliability, responsiveness, assurance, and empathy with which practice personnel treat clients or patients.

These factors exist in any given practice only to the extent that professionals recognize that quality

1. requires ongoing effort,

2. must be made the responsibility of every staff member,

3. requires leadership and communication,

4. begins with integrity,

5. requires keeping promises to all involved, and

6. produces profit for all involved.

Quality deteriorates or fails to develop adequately, on the other hand, where one or more of a series of barriers develops or is permitted to develop. First among them are professionals' inability to interpret consumer desires and transform those desires into policies to govern the practice.

The policies must be designed to insure that personnel conform to professional standards and that adequate channels of communication are maintained with clienteles as well as employees.

Finally, and most importantly, the practice must deliver the service that clients or patients expect.

Where one or more of these obligations go unmet, a performance gap develops. In essence, a performance gap is created when personnel are either unwilling or unable to perform as required. Every worker falls into one of four categories of what might be called a willingness/ability matrix. The willing and able obviously create no problems for professionals. The willing and unable must be trained or equipped to perform as required. The unwilling can be given only one opportunity to change their minds. Neither professionals nor other members of the organization can afford more.

A no-nonsense approach to performance standards and four other performance-related efforts are necessary to insure client or patient satisfaction. First is an ongoing research or monitoring program to monitor perceptions of service quality from the perspectives of patients and clients on the one hand and of personnel on the other. After a monitoring mechanism is in place, professionals should develop personnel recruiting and retention strategies in keeping with labor market conditions. Personnel knowledge and skill development programs also are necessary, together with performance-based reward systems to inextricably link the economic welfare of personnel and professionals.

ADDITIONAL READING

Bramson, Robert M. *Coping with Difficult People*. New York: Anchor, 1981.

Dowling, William, ed. *Effective Management and the Behavioral Sciences*. 8th ed. New York: amacom, 1978.

Hickman, Craig R., and Michael A. Silva. *Creating Excellence: Managing Corporate Culture, Strategy, and Change in the New Age*. New York: New American Library, 1984.

Jamieson, Kathleen H., and Karlyn K. Campbell. *The Interplay of Influence: Mass Media and Their Publics in News, Advertising, Politics*. Belmont, Calif: Wadsworth, 1983.

Larson, Charles U. *Persuasion: Reception and Responsibility*. 3rd ed. Belmont, Calif. Wadsworth, 1983.

Peters, Tom, and Nancy Austin. *A Passion for Excellence: The Leadership Difference*. New York: Random House, 1985.

Robinson, Edward J. *Communication and Public Relations*. Columbus, Ohio: Merrill, 1966.

4

The Role of Information

Practice development is a process that consists in large part of gathering and analyzing information. The success of professional practices is governed by prevailing and developing conditions in specific communities, among practitioners in those communities, and among their existing and prospective clients or patients. Knowledge of communities, professions, and their clienteles thus is essential to practice development.

Information gathering necessary to practice development can be viewed alternatively as environmental assessment, as monitoring conditions in three environments: community, professional, and patient/client. Practice welfare is inextricably bound up in events and trends that occur or develop in these areas. Trends usually prove more significant than events. Community growth patterns are especially significant. So are demographic trends and technological developments. These elements influence numbers and economic status of patients or clients, present and future.

Information gathering can also be examined as a set of processes that equip professionals with information necessary to practice development decisions. Information can be obtained using different techniques and sources, any or all of which may be necessary or appropriate at any given time. Considerable information can be obtained from local news media. More detailed and more precise data generally is available from information sources such as libraries and research-oriented public agencies. Still more focused data may require formal research undertaken or funded by professionals.

A TACTICAL APPROACH

All the perspectives indicated above require continuing professional attention. The alternative is too many opportunities lost through inattentiveness. Most individuals have experienced such circumstances, often with regard to successful small businesses. Their usual comment is "I wish I'd thought of that."

Successful small businesses are started by entrepreneurs who have done their homework in precisely the manner under discussion here. They look at communities, businesses serving them, and prospective customer groups. Only after carefully studying all available data do they make decisions leading to successful businesses. Businesses only appear to have been successful by chance.

The same approach applies in the professions. It applies, in fact, whether professionals are starting new practices or seeking to expand existing practices. It begins at the informal information-gathering level at which most individuals simply follow their habits.

Informal Information Gathering

Information gathering processes vary only in the extent to which they are undertaken by design. Informal processes, such as reading newspapers and watching television newscasts, are driven by habit. They develop in most individuals without conscious plan.

A great deal of information is available through informal information gathering. Informational potential expands with choice of media. While most professionals read daily newspapers, for example, choice of newspapers is another matter. Few individual newspapers can be expected to keep readers abreast of national and international as well as local news. Many professionals therefore regularly read or scan multiple newspapers.

The term *newspapers* today includes national dailies such as the *New York Times*, the *Wall Street Journal*, the *Christian Science Monitor*, and *USA Today*; metropolitan daily newspapers that exist in most large cities; business newspapers that also have sprung up in recent years; legal newspapers; and a host of more specialized publications. The latter, such as *Women's Wear Daily*, and some of the ethnically oriented publications arguably are more magazines than newspapers.

Most professionals find it advisable to read more than one newspaper. Their selections are dictated by the nature of their practices. Those whose practices are sensitive to social trends are attracted to the *New York Times*, which provides intensive coverage in this area. Practitioners whose worlds are influenced by international developments, as in design and engineering, are better served by the *Christian Science Monitor*, a newspaper known for its international coverage. Where economic information is highly significant, as in real estate or financial consulting, the *Wall Street Journal* is usually considered essential reading.

Most professionals find it necessary to handle broadcast media, especially television, in much the same manner. Local and national newscasts followed by specialized news programs from the Public Broadcasting System often are on the regular viewing lists of professionals.

The logic involved is simple and flawless. Almost anything that happens in today's world can influence the welfare of professional practices. Political events influence supplies of raw materials of all kinds and in turn govern the selling prices of finished materials. Demand often fluctuates accordingly and can make significant differences in production and employment rates in specific industries and in the communities in which their plants are situated.

Professional Knowledge

The same sort of pattern is logically applied in obtaining professional information. Professional journals are a primary source of contemporary information for most practitioners. The more progressive—and often more prosperous—usually go far beyond professional boundaries in information gathering.

Architects, for example, read their own journals and then turn to those of structural engineers. Going a step further, many among them read the academic journals in their own and associated fields. Academic publications usually are more turgid in style and harder to read but often contain the latest research data from the nation's college and university laboratories.

Information obtained from professional journals often is supplemented by knowledge gained through participation in one or more professional organizations. Most larger cities, to extend the example used above, have chapters of the American Institute of Architects. The institute also operates at state and national levels. One of the primary purposes of organizational meetings at all levels is exchange of information. More aggressive information gatherers often are active members of state and national as well as local groups and, in the case, of architects, also may become associated with organizations of engineers and others whose professional interests overlap their own.

Secondary Research

Where specific subject areas temporarily become highly important, research may be used to supplement information gathered through less formal methods. Research generally is categorized as formal or informal. Informal or secondary research involves obtaining and applying information compiled by others. Formal research is designed to create new knowledge. Since secondary research necessarily is less costly, it also is more popular and usually begins at local libraries or with other information sources.

Consider, for example, the case of a physician attempting to decide where to open a second office. Physicians presumably are conversant with growth in numbers of practitioners in their specialties through reports in their professional journals. Where newcomers are rare, pressure to open second offices is slight. Little likelihood exists in these circumstances that a newcomer will upset existing patient distribution patterns. Patients will have no choice but to travel to existing physician offices wherever they may be.

The issue is more complex in more competitive circumstances. The best location for a physician's second office must meet several criteria. First, the location should be preemptive in nature. It should deny potential competitors the best location they might otherwise select. In addition, however, it should be located conveniently.

Convenience in this context applies to prospective patients rather than physicians or their staffs. Prospective patients most important in the selection process are the more affluent and, especially, those that do not yet exist. Wise physicians seek office locations in the path of growth on the part of the most affluent component of the population.

Informational requirements. Office location problems imply strong needs for several types of information. Among the more important questions that must be addressed are the following:

1. In what direction is the community growing? Where will the geographic center of gravity for the types of patients in which the practitioner is interested be found five or ten years hence?
2. How many patients of this type are apt to be living within a reasonable distance of specific potential office locations?
3. If potential patronage is too low to logically support an office, how soon is it likely to reach economically viable proportions?

The latter question is critical where professionals are concerned over potential competition. Preemptive action may be logical and rational, although expensive, where (*a*) competitive potential is high and (*b*) growth rates are equally high.

Information sources. While seemingly complex, answers to the questions posed above are not necessarily hard to obtain. Multiple organizations in most communities record and maintain data highly useful to those attempting to make office or commercial site decisions. Three types of public agencies are especially likely to maintain records helpful to the professional.

Community growth patterns usually are monitored, although for different reasons, by planning and zoning organizations and utility companies. Staff members at these agencies are often consulted by developers and are usually highly knowledgeable as to short-term developmental plans for communities their agencies serve.

Types and numbers of patients apt to be residing in specific areas at later dates is another matter. Information of this type usually can be obtained only indirectly. Planners, zoners, and utilities usually maintain development maps that show when specific parts of a community were developed. Maps showing when other sections are expected to be developed also may be available.

The maps seldom provide information as to the socioeconomic or demographic characteristics of populations but can be enlightening as to time elements. Relatively few contain accurate growth projections, although some may indicate anticipated needs for roads, utility lines, and the like. Most do show, however, when existing areas were subdivided and when infrastructure components were built. Close examination of these data can be helpful in estimating direction of growth and, by projection, the anticipated time by which any area will have developed.

More detailed demographic and sociographic data is available on request from the Bureau of the Census of the U.S. Commerce Department in Washington. Bureau of the Census documents often are maintained by chambers of commerce, industrial development agencies, and college or university libraries for the areas they serve.

Census records provide statistical information concerning the age, sex, race, marital status, educational level, and incomes of those residing in relatively small census tracts. Bureau data from current and prior census reports often can be compared to determine the extent of change taking place in any of the criteria in question. Rate and volume, examined together, are accurate indicators of change.

Census data are often sufficient to permit physicians to make judgments as to where to locate new offices. Where nearby populations are largely affluent, affirmative decisions are indicated. This especially is the case where age factors are favorable as well. Relatively young neighborhoods, for example, are preferable for obstetricians and pediatricians. Specialists in cancer and other diseases more common in aging populations might find such areas less desirable.

Where necessary, information obtained from the Bureau of the Census and local agencies can be supplemented with reports from commercial services. Formed by entrepreneurial statisticians and demographers, these services merge demographic and socioeconomic data to provide more complete and current information for economic decision making. Major research firms active in the field advertise regularly in *American Demographics*, a magazine available at most libraries.

Primary Research

Published data usually fulfill the bulk of professionals' needs for accurate information concerning events and trends that may influence the success of their practices. Available information often falls short of meeting professional needs, however, in two more specialized areas. The first consists of attitude and opinion among patients or clients, existing and prospective. The second is attitude and opinion among practice personnel.

Knowledge of client/patient attitude and opinion is vital to professionals who want to make their practices as appealing as possible in a competitive world. Data concerning practice personnel are equally important for two reasons. First, demographic trends in the United States demonstrate that availability of younger workers will decline steadily through the remainder of the century. Professionals will be competing for fewer numbers of paraprofessional and clerical personnel to fill positions in their practices. Second, worker satisfaction inevitably is reflected in the quality of services they provide to clients or patients. Professionals who expect members of their staffs to respond to the needs of their practices must be equally responsive to the needs of personnel.

Alternative approaches. Primary research can be undertaken in different ways that vary in efficiency and practicality with the nature of professional practices. In very small practices, what otherwise might require formal research can be accomplished with remarkable informality. Practitioners need only make it a matter of policy to maintain regular personal contact and open communication with clients and personnel. In very large practices, there is no practical alternative to formal survey research techniques.

Neither of these approaches is as simple or as complex as it first appears. The informality that can prevail in small practices can be productive only where (*a*) practitioners are committed to fairness and equity in their dealings and (*b*) these commitments are reciprocated by others involved. These circumstances can be made to exist, but only through continuing effort over extended periods of time. Mutual confidence is a rare commodity in an increasingly contentious society.

Informal formality. Where mutual confidence exists, professionals find openness and candor on the part of clients or patients. Practice strengths and weaknesses are discussed openly, and prompt responses insure still stronger and more productive relationships.

Circumstances of this sort require, however, that communication channels be open at all times. Responsiveness is critical. Relatively strong relationships can erode quickly when interpersonal contacts deteriorate or when responses are slow in coming.

Deterioration occurs especially easily as practices grow. Informal approaches become impractical as professionals are called upon to maintain regular, personal contact with increasing numbers of clients and patients, prospective and existing. Alternative approaches to information gathering then must be installed in time to prevent deterioration in human relationships.

Formal informality. Relatively impersonal techniques must be used to replace the more personal as practices grow and as professionals become busier. Perhaps most easily applied among them are informal questionnaires that can be used in verbal as well as written form.

The questionnaire can be a simple, single-sheet unit that can be enclosed with invoices or statements and will fold for return mailing. In the alternative, it can be administered by telephone. Many business organizations in recent years have started to use such research to evaluate their products, services, and personnel.

The after-delivery approach was first used by "big ticket" merchants, such as those who sell Mercedes-Benz automobiles. More recently, customers who use General Electric Company's in-home appliance services will find the service calls followed by (*a*) a telephone call and (*b*) a printed survey. In each case, two primary questions are addressed in detail: "Were you satisfied with the service? Were you satisfied with our personnel?"

Where responses to questions such as these are accurately recorded, tabulated, and analyzed, professionals obtain considerable information about the health and growth potential of their practices. Remedial action is advisable in the wake of negative responses, of course, to "mend fences" and to reestablish salutary relationships.

Relative practice health is indicated by the nature and number of complaints received over extended time periods—months and years. If complaints decline or, at worst, remain more or less constant in relation to numbers of clients or patients, relationships are improving or holding their own. Where complaints increase, relationships are deteriorating.

Complaints occasionally are also indicators of potential for practice expansion. The opthalmologist who encounters numerous complaints over the optician next door, for example, might consider investing in an optical dispensary. The orthopedic surgeon who receives complaints about physical therapists might productively entertain offering therapeutic services within his or her practice. Similar complaints can lead architects to expand into engineering or interior design, public relations counselors to expand into advertising, and so on.

Formal research. More sophisticated formal research techniques usually come into play in professional settings only where practitioners are seeking to identify areas of relative advantage or voids in professional services that might be exploited in professional development programs. Relative advantages exist more often than many suspect is the case. Simply put, they involve areas of client or patient concern in which a practitioner readily can outstrip his or her colleagues to achieve an economic advantage.

The concept of relative advantage is more complex than appears to be the case. In professional development, relative advantage involves client or patient interests as well as differences in professional services. Consider, for example, the scars left in the wake of major surgery. Scars may be considerably smaller where one surgeon is involved as compared with another. Differences, in other words, may exist. Other than where cosmetically significant, however, sizes of scars seldom are a major determinant in selecting surgeons. Only where cosmetic aspects are a source of concern, then, can one surgeon's ability to work with smaller incisions create a relative advantage.

Relative advantage thus involves significant differences, real or perceived, among professional services in areas that bear on the decision-making process. Reality and perception are equally important, because they are equally persuasive to those involved. Services are unsatisfactory to those who perceive them to be unsatisfactory even when they meet every rational objective quality standard. Practice development programs must address any weakness, perceived or real, identified by clients, existing or prospective. Strategies must be designed to correct weaknesses or perceptions in developers' practices and to capitalize on those afflicting competitors' practices.

Professional development strategies must be based on accurate information to assure success. Most information is obtained through formal survey techniques of one type or another. In almost every case, surveys are handled by professional researchers or by practitioners who manage the process carefully to insure that they are not identified by respondents. Information is likely to be objectively given and reflective of reality only when research sponsors are unknown to respondents.

OBTAINING QUALITY INFORMATION

Information quality often determines the success or failure of professional development efforts. Misleading data concerning community growth trends, for example, might induce a health care practitioner to invest hundreds of thousands of dollars in new facilities far from the path of community development.

Inaccurate demographic data could be similarly disastrous to almost any professional, inducing him or her to act on the basis of false assumptions concerning practice potential. Valid data readily can be obtained, however, through survey research. Knowledge of potential pitfalls in survey research, in addition, equips professionals to identify suspect data provided by others.

Accuracy in survey results is affected by the nature of the group to which questions are addressed, the content of questions asked, and the manner in which questions are presented. Each of these variables requires careful management in developing survey research projects.

Survey Respondents

Information can be gathered in survey research from a population or from a sample. A population consists of all individuals within a predetermined category. For example, the clients of all mechanical engineers in a given community would be a population. A sample, in comparison, is a smaller group selected from the population. Survey research usually deals with samples for economic reasons.

Where samples are used, one factor is critical. Samples must be representative of populations. To make samples representative, every member of the population must have an equal chance of being selected as a member of the sample. This objective is achieved through random selection, usually accomplished by applying random number tables, computer programs, or other devices.

Most professionals and professional firms deal with so few clients or identifiable prospects that population rather than sample studies are used. Identifiable prospective clients or patients can be so few, in fact, that demographically similar groups are often selected for research purposes. A general accounting firm, for example, might use the membership of the Chamber of Commerce or the Rotary Club as a research population on grounds that virtually all are business executives or professionals who may employ or influence the employment of accountants.

Population surveys can serve a dual purpose when existing clienteles are involved. They can elicit valuable information while concurrently enhancing relationships if survey sponsors are made known to respondents. If this approach is used, however, care must be taken to assure respondents that their anonymity will be preserved. Only when this is accomplished can professionals expect wholly candid responses.

Patient or client surveys conducted openly communicate professionals' concerns and their commitments to development and maintenance of superior services. They let patients or clients know that they are considered important and that their opinions are valued. This message then is convincingly enhanced when professionals respond quickly to remedy seemingly minor weaknesses that nevertheless are important to clients, such as access to telephones while waiting to see the professional.

Designing Questionnaires

Questionnaire design often is a major problem for professionals. Their perceptions of the more important or significant elements in professional practice may differ from those of existing or potential clients. This problem becomes especially troublesome for research projects designed to identify relative strengths and weaknesses from a client perspective. It often can be easily solved, however, by introducing a preliminary step in the form of focus group research.

Focus groups consist of small but representative groups of clients or prospective clients. They should be as representative as possible of populations proposed to be surveyed. Focus group members also should be selected for openness and candor, especially if chosen as representatives of organizations. When these conditions prevail, group members should be sufficiently high in the hierarchies of their organizations to have no concerns over whether excessive candor might undermine their own positions. Completely candid responses are necessary, and participants in focus groups must feel free to express themselves without reservation.

General questions. Focus group participants should be asked for comments in the following basic areas:

1. The nature of the professional services they use
2. Any other services they would like the professional to provide
3. The quality of services they use
4. The quality of the personnel they encounter

A moderator, often an outsider employed by the professional involved, usually is present to see that responses are given in sufficient detail to meet professional needs. The basic question concerning additional services, for example, is inadequate to trigger desired responses. The moderator should provide as complete a list of services as might be provided by the professional organization involved. Accounting firms, for example, are becoming engaged in a broad range of consultant services. Clients and prospective clients may be unaware of many of these services and must be made familiar with their existence in order to respond accurately to the question.

Focus group sessions usually continue for several hours to insure that all questions are thoroughly explored. Sessions are taped with prior participant consent in order that information generated by the discussion can be captured for subsequent analysis. Each area of participant interest or concern then is considered for possible inclusion in the survey questionnaire.

Types of questionnaires. There are usually two types of survey questionnaires. The more common are created for use in telephone or in-person surveys. They contain detailed instructions to interviewers as well as questions to be asked. The second type, as shown in figure 4.1, is used in mail surveys and is usually more common in research associated with professional development programs.

Mail surveys are used more often than telephone interviews for several reasons. First, telephone interviews are costly. In-person interviews are even more expensive in interviewer time. Skill is required to insure that interviewers do not inadvertently influence responses. Interviewers must be paid while being trained, as well as during the survey itself.

Mail surveys require no interviewers and, in addition, serve as communication devices for sponsoring professionals when existing clients or patients are involved. Existing clienteles are virtually always included in research surveys so that the data produced will enable professionals to compare their practices with those of competitors.

Posing the Questions

Decisions as to the type of survey to be conducted determine which type of questionnaire will be necessary. Designers develop specific questions in one or more of several formats. Those most often used are fill-in-the blank, yes/no, multiple choice, and open-ended. Each has an appropriate place in most questionnaires. Most designers attempt to limit the number of question types, however, to make respondents' tasks easier and to minimize potential for confusion.

Most of the questions should be prepared in a manner that permits multiple choice answers. Most are used with numerical response scales, usually five-point or ten-point scales ranging from "high" to "low" or from "very good" to "very bad." Scales with odd numbers of points permit respondents to hedge with middle-ground responses such as "about average." Some designers therefore use four- or eight-point scales that force respondents to come down on one side of the middle ground or the other.

Bipolar scales. Professionals' needs for knowledge of relative advantage, as defined earlier, are making so-called bipolar scales increasingly popular. Bipolar scales, as seen in figure 4.1, are designed to indicate the extent of any shortfall or gap between services as they exist and as respondents would like them to be.

Data generated through use of bipolar scales thus is far more enlightening than data obtained by questions that simply ask respondents to indicate how good or bad they consider each aspect of the professional's service. Enlightenment increases when data gathered from existing clienteles are compared with

Figure 4.1
Sample Bipolar Scale

Your responses to the questions that follow will assist us in
determining the extent to which clients of professional
organizations believe their needs are being adequately met.

Two response scales are provided for each factor you are asked to
evaluate. Please use the scale to the left of the factor to
indicate the extent to which the factor in question is important
to you. Then use the scale to the right of the factor to
indicate the extent to which your needs were met.

Values are the same for both scales, ranging from 1 (low level or
service needed or received) to 5 (high level of service needed or
received).

Level of Service Needed						Level of Service Received				
Low			High			Low			High	
1 2 3 4 5					Promptness in meeting agreed upon delivery dates/deadlines.	1 2 3 4 5				
1 2 3 4 5					Initiative in suggesting new strategies to cope with changing market conditions	1 2 3 4 5				
1 2 3 4 5					Promptness in meeting requests for information	1 2 3 4 5				
1 2 3 4 5					Initiative in providing information concerning new/pending legislation and prospective impact	1 2 3 4 5				
1 2 3 4 5					Overall level of attention to your needs	1 2 3 4 5				
1 2 3 4 5					Initiative in suggesting new strategies to cope with changing laws/regulations	1 2 3 4 5				
1 2 3 4 5					Responsiveness to your requests for information	1 2 3 4 5				
1 2 3 4 5					Initiative in suggesting new ideas for your business	1 2 3 4 5				
1 2 3 4 5					Ability to respond to sudden and unforeseen needs for service	1 2 3 4 5				

Figure 4.1 (continued)

Level of Service Needed						Level of Service Received				
Low				High		Low				High
1	2	3	4	5	Knowledge of economic trends and potential impact on your business sector	1	2	3	4	5
1	2	3	4	5	Level of overall expertise in your business sector	1	2	3	4	5
1	2	3	4	5	Initiative in suggesting new strategies to cope with emerging economic trends	1	2	3	4	5
1	2	3	4	5	Promptness in returning calls	1	2	3	4	5
1	2	3	4	5	Diligence in meeting needs of your business	1	2	3	4	5
1	2	3	4	5	Creativity in planning in context with your assignments	1	2	3	4	5
1	2	3	4	5	Skillfulness in developing interpersonal relationships	1	2	3	4	5
1	2	3	4	5	Appropriateness of publications provided to your business	1	2	3	4	5
1	2	3	4	5	Quality of work performed for your organization	1	2	3	4	5
1	2	3	4	5	Level of service provided to your organization	1	2	3	4	5
1	2	3	4	5	Frequency of contact initiated by the firm	1	2	3	4	5
1	2	3	4	5	Frequency of contact with senior members of the firm	1	2	3	4	5
1	2	3	4	5	Availability of personnel when needed	1	2	3	4	5
1	2	3	4	5	Attentiveness to long range as well as short-range needs	1	2	3	4	5
1	2	3	4	5	Quality of tax research and opinions provided	1	2	3	4	5
1	2	3	4	5	Timeliness of management letters	1	2	3	4	5
1	2	3	4	5	Ability to provide innovative responses to new problems	1	2	3	4	5

Figure 4.1 (continued)

Level of Service Needed						Level of Service Received				
Low			High			Low			High	

1	2	3	4	5	Sensitivity to cost of services provided	1	2	3	4	5
1	2	3	4	5	Initiative in suggesting additional services	1	2	3	4	5
1	2	3	4	5	Responsiveness to requests for information	1	2	3	4	5
1	2	3	4	5	Sensitivity and responsiveness to need for confidentiality	1	2	3	4	5
1	2	3	4	5	Responsiveness to requests for information	1	2	3	4	5
1	2	3	4	5	Consistency in quality of services provided	1	2	3	4	5
1	2	3	4	5	Technical competence of personnel who has served you	1	2	3	4	5
1	2	3	4	5	Interpersonal competence of personnel who have served you	1	2	3	4	5
1	2	3	4	5	Communication skills of those who have served you	1	2	3	4	5
1	2	3	4	5	Understanding of your organization on the part of those who have served you	1	2	3	4	5
1	2	3	4	5	Fairness in charges for services provided	1	2	3	4	5
1	2	3	4	5	Availability and quality of personal (as opposed to business) advice	1	2	3	4	5
1	2	3	4	5	Quality and quantity of advice provided concerning data processing	1	2	3	4	5
1	2	3	4	5	Clarity and conciseness of reports.	1	2	3	4	5

---

those obtained from prospective clients or patients (others in the community who are not part of the existing client population).

Other responses. Less sensitive response devices are used for other types of questions. Yes/no categories suffice, for example, where questions deal with such items as marital status or whether the respondent already retains a professional. Fill-in-the-blank responses are appropriate where questionnaires ask for the ZIP zones of respondents' offices or homes.

A word of caution is necessary, however, for novices in questionnaire design. Where questions are to be posed on personal matters such as household income, questions involved should be among the last on the questionnaire. Individuals who have completed several pages of questions then are more apt to respond or to mail questionnaires even if they skip questions. Where sensitive questions are asked early, on the other hand, larger numbers of prospective respondents decide not to participate and discard their questionnaires.

NEGLECTED DATA

One other source of information that can be most important in the design of professional development programs is readily accessible but often neglected by professionals: their own records. The value of information contained in these records varies by profession but nevertheless can be important.

Internal data are more apt to be of marginal value where small numbers of clients are served, as often is the case in such disciplines as advertising and public relations or in younger practices. Where the reverse is true, much information can be gained by careful analysis to determine the history of the practice. Of special interest to analysts should be changes in

1. types of clients served,
2. types of services rendered to clients,
3. geographic scope of the practice and distribution of clientele in areas served,
4. periods of time during which clients have continued with the professional, and
5. reasons why relationships were discontinued.

Two primary reasons should be asked in each case: what changes have occurred and why have they occurred? Changes in clientele may be a natural outgrowth of change in a community. They also may result from weaknesses in the professional's practice or from strong competition. The reverse may be equally true. Reasons should be identified wherever possible, and, where weaknesses in professional practices are at fault, they should be corrected.

Former clients or patients also should be added to the group to be surveyed, especially when they are sufficient in number to generate statistically valid data. Even when this is not the case, however, their responses may provide some insights into reasons for their departures from the client or patient group.

IN SUMMARY

Knowledge is as important in practice development today as it is in any profession. The communities in which professionals function and the people who populate them are in a state of change. Their attitudes and opinions ebb and flow on a near daily basis. Their needs, desires, and expectations of professionals are in flux as well. Efforts toward professional development without adequate information in environments of this sort are risky at best, futile at worst.

Practice development activities should be based on the sum of multiple information-gathering activities. These activities fall into three basic categories. One is informal information gathering, consisting largely of reading, ranging from mass media to professional journals. Another is secondary research, which deals with gathering and analyzing published information concerning demographic, psychographic, and other trends and events that influence the welfare of professional practices. The third is formal research to generate objective data concerning the attitudes and opinions of practice personnel and clienteles, existing and prospective.

Quality of information produced by these efforts, especially in formal research, is a primary determinant of success in professional development. The formal research process requires special care in several areas. They include definition of populations and selection and samples as well as design and administration of questionnaires.

Questionnaire design is of special significance. Professionally prepared and administered questionnaires can produce highly accurate data concerning relative strengths and weaknesses across as well as within professional practices. They can specify the extent to which practices and their competitors are meeting the needs and desires of existing clienteles. In this manner, they support professionals in creating and implementing highly productive practice development strategies.

ADDITIONAL READING

Breen, George, and A. B. Blankenship. *Do-It-Yourself Marketing Research*. 2nd ed. New York: McGraw-Hill, 1982.

Derber, Charles. *The Pursuit of Attention: Power and Individualism in Everyday Life*. New York: Oxford, 1979.

Fink, Arlene, and Jacqueline Kosecoff. *How to Conduct Surveys: A Step-by-Step Guide*. Beverly Hills, Calif.: Sage. 1985.

Hennessy, Bernard. *Public Opinion*. 5th ed. Monterey, Calif.: Brooks/Cole, 1985.

Robinson, Edward J. *Public Relations and Survey Research*. New York: Appleton-Century-Crofts, 1969.

Winett, Richard A. *Information and Behavior: Systems of Influence*. Hillsdale, N.J.: Lawrence Erlbaum, 1986.

5

Decision Making

Information-gathering processes in professional development prepare practitioners to successfully pursue three further tasks: short-term action, long-term planning, and, in many cases, further research.

Need for short-term action can arise from two types of data generated by the information-gathering process. One variety is statistical information indicating that clients have complaints that can be quickly and beneficially remedied. The other consists of client or patient responses suggesting that information gathering should be made a routine part of practice management. Such responses usually take the form of favorable comments or volunteered information of value to practitioners.

Other data obtained through information gathering inevitably trigger long-term planning efforts leading to major strategy decisions. Information may suggest, for example, that practitioners should either specialize or broaden the range of services they offer. Need for changes in office locations and other components of the organization also may become apparent.

Perhaps most important, further research often is found necessary in developing personnel policies and procedures to make the organization responsive to patient or client needs. Professional practices are service organizations dependent on personnel for client or patient satisfaction. Practitioners too often assume employees' commitments to practice clienteles to be as strong as their own and suffer unnecessary losses as a result.

POINTS OF DEPARTURE

Systematic information-gathering efforts inevitably yield large amounts of data. This especially is the case where survey research is involved. Unwary practitioners therefore risk becoming so involved in detail that they fail to use information to produce the best possible results. This pitfall can be avoided through a simple information management process. Information first is sorted into three basic categories. One involves real or perceived problems amenable to quick and inexpensive remedies. Another consists of real problems that can only be cured through substantial investment of time, effort, or economic resources. A third includes perceived problems that can be corrected only through extensive communication effort.

The welfare of the practice demands that professionals be and appear to be continuously responsive to patient or client need. A posture of this sort is essential in achieving the first objective of professional development: stemming unnecessary client or patient losses. This goal can be largely accomplished through appropriate handling of the first category of information.

Before proceeding, however, professionals are well advised to compile one additional body of data that can be helpful in decision-making processes. It consists of information in existing client or patient files.

Practice Profiles

Professionals should have clear composite "pictures" of their clienteles before them at all times. In some cases, such as architecture and engineering, numbers of active clients at any given time may be so few as to enable practitioners to precisely characterize their practices without reference to statistical data. Numbers and types of clients and prospective clients, longevity factors, and similar data necessary to planning can be mentally cataloged in smaller practices. Health care and accounting practices are another matter. They usually involve more patients or clients, and professionals can seldom accurately characterize their clienteles at a moment's notice.

Where the latter conditions prevail, computer analyses are advisable. Computer analyses should show length of client relationships, types of services rendered, geographic distribution of clients, and other factors useful in developing and maintaining successful professional development strategies.

Profile Analyses

Serial practice profiles are more significant than individual sets of data for planning purposes. Change in professional practices often occurs slowly and over extended periods of time, often going unnoticed by practitioners involved. It is especially easy, for example, for professionals to fail to notice that their practices are aging. Practitioners are less likely to be sensitive to demographic than other types of change because they, too, are aging.

Healthy professional practices should reflect the populations they serve rather than those that existed during earlier years. Other than as influenced by practitioner specialization, clienteles should be cross-sectional in nature. This principle is especially important in protecting against economic fluctuations. Diversity in clientele or types of assignments usually adds stability in otherwise potentially volatile conditions. Civil engineering practices preferably should involve sewer and water as well as road and bridge projects. Architects should be handling manufacturing and distribution as well as office and institutional buildings. Accounting practices should be serving recently established as well as old-line businesses. Medical and dental practices should be representative of the geographic areas in which they are situated.

Imbalances in areas such as these can be indicative of practice weaknesses that deserve early attention. Practice diversity usually works to the benefit rather than the detriment of professionals involved. Today's international economy has created so complex a set of business variables as to make it almost impossible for professionals to anticipate change in time to make practice adjustments. In a day when political instability in the Persian Gulf can produce overnight collapse in Texas and Oklahoma financial and construction markets, diversity can spell the difference between prosperity and failure in a professional practice.

The same level of attention is necessary in dealing with the results of information-gathering efforts and with the problems and opportunities they present. Practice development, in essence, must become a day-to-day component of practice management. Those who fail to deal effectively with the needs and desires, large and small, of patients and clients put themselves at increasing economic risk.

READILY SOLUBLE PROBLEMS

Survey research almost inevitably yields a host of patient or client complaints concerning matters symbolically more than substantially significant. An overabundance of such minor complaints may be indicative of deeper problems. They deserve careful examination in this context. In every instance, however, the many small irritants identified in surveys create opportunities for practitioners. Prompt practitioner response to minor problems can demonstrate responsiveness to clients or patients.

Responsiveness is valuable in and of itself in practice development. The principles involved are much akin to those applied in political campaigns. Candidates seek to engender voter loyalty through involvement, no matter how seemingly insignificant. As any candidate will attest, one thousand one-dollar contributions are far more valuable than a single thousand-dollar donation. The one-dollar contributions psychologically engage the donors and ultimately will be supported by equal numbers of votes. The thousand-dollar contribution probably was matched by an equal amount given to the opposition and represents no political commitment. Each and every contributor therefore receives a written thank-you note that also serves as a reminder to vote on election day.

Cementing Relationships

Client or patient support is as important to professionals as voter support is to politicians. While candidates' supporters express themselves at the ballot box, professionals' clients express themselves with continued patronage that ultimately can be counted in dollars. Patient and client suggestions in response to surveys thus arm professionals to demonstrate commitment through prompt response.

Practitioners can quickly install systems to see that telephone calls and correspondence are handled more promptly, to insure fresh coffee is available to clients as well as personnel, to install a telephone in the waiting room for those occasions when they may be unavoidably delayed. Actions of this sort do more than express commitment. They also communicate in much the same manner as did the survey itself. They express real concern for the needs of patients or clients.

Commitment is the key to enduring relationships. Involvement creates commitment. Direct professional response to expressed client needs creates involvement.

Tactical Approaches

Timing of responses to expressed client or patient needs is more complex than may appear to be the case. Professional responses to surveys must be undertaken on a timely basis. Timeliness, however, involves more than promptness from the standpoint of the practitioner. Initial responses should be instituted with relative speed, but others should be implemented over a period of several months.

Extended time spans are necessary to enable professionals to address more substantive problems with due deliberation. Decisions concerning the scope of the practice, the location of offices, and items of similar magnitude seldom can be taken in haste without creating undue risk. Ideally, however, the survey should mark the start of an ongoing series of practice improvements orchestrated to convince patients or clients that real and durable change has occurred.

LONG-TERM PLANNING

Long-term planning assures that change will persist. The long-term planning process, however, is the most demanding and time-consuming of the three tasks that follow completion of initial information-gathering processes. Long-term planning is governed in part by practitioner knowledge, in part by information gathered informally within the community, and in part by results of survey research. Each element has a bearing on most practitioner decisions.

Other factors may impose limitations on decision-making processes, however, and while generally beyond the boundaries of this book, they nevertheless are noteworthy here. Most limitations are imposed by prior legal or physical commitments. The legal usually are in the form of building or equipment leases that are not readily broken. They also may involve partnership or similar agreements that limit individuals' latitude of action.

Still other constraints may be imposed by limits on practice resources. Expansion of services, geographically or otherwise, almost inevitably involves investment in space, equipment, personnel, or a combination of these factors. Their availability is always limited to a greater or lesser extent, and practitioners often find it necessary to establish practice development priorities within specific resource limitations.

Establishing Priorities

One of two basic strategies usually dominates in establishing developmental priorities. One is based on purely economic concerns, while the other focuses primarily on competitive factors. The economically oriented approach suggests that the practice development process should be designed to become self-sustaining and to yield profits as early as possible.

The competitive approach, in contrast, makes short-term profit a secondary consideration and focuses instead on expanding market share. The assumption here, as in most commercial endeavors, is that market share is more important than volume in determining long-term success. Given greater market share, advocates declare, volume will take care of itself.

Neither the economic nor the competitive approach can be considered right or wrong in an abstract sense. Since professionals usually experience relatively little difficulty in obtaining necessary financing, the more aggressive of the two ultimately may prove preferable due to long-term benefits involved.

Economic strategy. The economic approach is not necessarily dollar driven. Expansion of services can require resources beyond those that can be quickly acquired through lease or purchase. Office expansion, for example, at a minimum is time-consuming and costly and in some circumstances may be impossible. Personnel in some disciplines may be difficult to recruit and train as well. Sophisticated equipment may require months in production.

Economic and common sense concerns together suggest that practitioners are well advised to establish priorities in keeping with existing and available resources as well as indicators contained in research data. Relatively low-priority opportunities that enable professionals to capitalize on existing underutilized resources, in other words, may prove least risky as well as most productive in the short term.

Capitalizing first on opportunities that merit productive use of underutilized resources also serves practice developers in another way. Where these resources can early be made productive, net investment is reduced and return is increased. Where practice volume, for example, is substantially below the capacity of existing space, personnel, and equipment, expansion adds disproportionately to profits because overhead remains relatively unchanged. This approach is especially desirable where practitioners elect to capitalize on professional development opportunities sequentially.

Sequential development techniques are often used where one or both of two conditions exist. The first is a lack of adequate resources to permit concurrent development. The second is a decision to make the professional development program self-sustaining as rapidly as possible. *Self-sustaining* here refers to a process by which developmental efforts are undertaken in order of potential return on investment. The underlying assumption, in the case of professional organizations, is that added profits from the first increment of expansion will help fund the second, and so forth.

Competitive strategy. Economic strategies of the sort described above suffice save in one set of circumstances: where competitors quickly perceive and understand colleagues' strategies and set out to frustrate them. Professionals who find themselves in highly competitive markets thus find economically oriented development strategies somewhat risky. Alert competitors may respond to initial expansionist steps with a broad range of countervailing activities.

These circumstances can be avoided, but only by accepting greater risk. Greater risk occurs where phased expansion strategies are replaced by those calling for concurrent development of multiple new services or delivery facilities or both. An architectural firm, for example, might concurrently establish interior design and engineering subsidiaries. A law firm might open Washington and New York offices and establish lobbying and governmental affairs units. A surgeon might open one or more branch offices and concurrently add physical therapy services.

Planning becomes more complex where competitive approaches are found necessary. Planners then must focus on long-term rather than short-term economic potential. Were economic resources to prevent the surgeon from concurrently opening branch offices and physical therapy units, for example, the branches probably would take precedence. A physical therapy unit at the surgeon's existing offices might be more profitable in the short term but failure to establish a presence in the community's developing areas could be costly over time.

Evaluating Alternatives

Practitioner decisions to embark on economic or competitively oriented strategies are always more a function of conditions in individual markets and practices than of any general guidelines. Numerous variables may require evaluation in determining how best to proceed. Many of them, however, should be amenable to relatively precise measurement in light of information gathered earlier.

General economic conditions and their influence on professions, conditions within professions and communities, and specific competitive circumstances all should contribute to decision-making processes. Collectively, these factors tell practitioners what level of aggressiveness may be necessary to assure success.

Economic conditions. General economic conditions usually are a valid indicator of potential competitor activity. Relatively few in any profession are apt to become developmentally aggressive where general conditions signal caution. Economic decline compounds risk and generally discourages expansion.

The impact of economic conditions, however, is a variable across professions. Relatively few new architectural and interior design practices are established, for example, when the national economy is slipping. Neither are new plastic surgery practices likely to appear during such periods. Both types of professions deal primarily in elective services. Prospective clients, in other words, are free to delay purchases and often do so in unsettled economic times.

Accounting and law practices, on the other hand, usually are little influenced by general economic conditions. The problems they are called upon to handle require attention in any circumstances. General surgeons, obstetricians, and pediatricians also find their practices relatively immune to changing economic circumstances.

Professional conditions. The influence of economic conditions in designing practice development strategies is always tempered by conditions within professions involved. At least two sets of conditions require attention. One involves supply and demand factors at national and regional as well as local levels. The other consists of conditions within the profession in the local community.

National supply and demand factors influence potential for increased local competition through the arrival of additional practitioners. Conditions in the profession within the community include the nature of existing competitive practices and the predispositions of professionals within them.

Well-established professional practices directed by senior professionals in the latter portions of their careers usually are little disposed toward aggressive professional development activities. Individuals in these circumstances more often are content to maintain the status quo. They often fail to recognize that change is inevitable and that those who are not gaining ground almost inevitably are losing.

Younger professionals in relatively new practices almost universally are more aggressive. In addition, they tend to be more sensitive to their environments and more responsive to change. They often react strongly to colleagues' professional development efforts.

Individual competitors. The competitive histories of colleagues must be considered in addition to general professional conditions and economic circumstances. In most cases, and especially where practitioners have made it a point to become knowledgeable concerning others in their professions, past performance can be a major influence on the professional development planning process.

The oft-repeated axiom concerning tigers' stripes is applicable here. They don't change. Neither do the competitive habits of professionals. Those who have been conservative and resistant to promotional strategies in the past are apt to perform in the same manner in the future. Those who have been aggressive and always at the cutting edge of change will be likely to persist in that behavior as well.

From a planning perspective, colleagues' demonstrated habits are most indicative of future performance. Habits can be modified, however, by changing circumstances in the profession or by general economic conditons. Planners must weigh the influence of habit against the strength of external forces of change in predicting potential behavior. Anticipated behavior, calculated as precisely as possible, then must be weighed in making practice development decisions.

Case in point. Consider, for example, an optometrist attempting to decide whether to first develop a training service for the visually impaired or to open a satellite office in a fast-developing, high-income neighborhood into which many of his existing patients are moving. All of the factors discussed earlier should enter into his decision.

Will any of his competitors be prone to preempt the neighborhood by opening an office before he is finished developing the training service?

Is there a substantive likelihood that a newcomer to the professional community—a new player in the game—might identify the opportunity for an optometric office?

Are economic conditons likely to encourage, on a short-term basis, the opening or expansion of optometric practices?

Calculated risk. Every business decision is based on calculated risk. Practice development decisions, although involving professionals rather than business persons, are no different from any business decision. All involve calculated risks, and no precise formulas can be applied to eliminate them. The best that can be done, as illustrated above, is to isolate and examine as many as possible of the major variables that should be considered in the decision-making process.

Business risk inevitably will remain. Professionals who want to avoid all business risk have only one option: to accept employment by colleagues in corporate settings or large practices. Academic ideals to the contrary notwithstanding, professionals who practice independently are business persons and must be prepared to make sound business decisions.

FURTHER RESEARCH NEEDS

While highly informative, research projects always create hidden risks. They can readily lull researchers and their clients into a dangerous sense of security. Organizational problems often are readily identified through data analysis. Analysts must recognize, however, that the apparent problems they identify existed on the day the data are analyzed. The breadth and depth of problems can change with considerable speed, especially where people are involved.

Two factors also can create potential for researcher bias. The first is a tendency to overly rely on data at hand. Numbers on paper tend to become highly persuasive, especially to those who work with them regularly. Research data, however, deteriorate with age. They depict conditions that existed on the date that they were gathered. Data under analysis at any given time may be weeks or months old.

Aging Data

The aging data problem can be alleviated but not eliminated. Repetitive surveys can be used to create comparable sets of data that can produce greater insights. Data sets that reflect differences in conditions over time are valid indictors of change. They show whether conditions are improving, deteriorating, or remaining relatively constant.

One of the classic demonstrations of the potential impact of aging data occurred during the Truman-Dewey race for the presidency. Pollsters showed Dewey well in the lead through the dawn of election day. So certain were the pundits of the election results, in fact, that newspapers were printed proclaiming Dewey's victory. Truman won the election. The polls were misleading because they were based on old data. The Dewey campaign had peaked before the election while Truman's momentum continued to climb.

Today's pollsters, armed with computers and sophisticated methodologies that permit them to complete nationwide surveys in hours, would not have been misled. There remains, however, a strong tendency to rely on numbers on paper despite their age and resulting problem potential.

Reliability of Data

The second factor that can distort results also involves reliability. Survey research data reflect respondents' perceptions. Perceptions may or may not be accurate reflections of reality. Ability to undertake remedial action is determined by managerial skill in differentiating between the two. Independent examination of reality therefore can be important in evaluating research data.

These conditions collectively suggest that several steps be taken. First, researchers must develop techniques to validate survey data results. Only in this manner can they successfully differentiate between perception and reality before attempting remedial action. Second, the initial survey should be made the first in a series, enabling professionals to monitor the health of their practices on a continuing basis. Finally, data available from professionals' records should be used to create a set of diagnostic indicators through which the health of the practice can be continuously monitored.

CORROBORATING RESEARCH

Problem: Clients or patients claim they're kept waiting too long in your lobby or waiting room and that your personnel are slow and discourteous in responding to telephoned requests for assistance. These are the greatest weaknesses they see in your practice. In addition, your survey data show that comparable problems apparently do not exist among your competitors. How should you respond?

First, recognize that you're dealing with two problems rather than one. Timeliness and courtesy are different factors although they may complement one another in producing negative survey responses. Each problem, in addition, in large part may be real or perceived. Variation in human responses is such that neither is apt to be wholly real or entirely perceived. In addition, intervening variables can compound perceived problems.

Second, be prepared to use any and all devices that may be available to generate information and suggest solutions to the problems, real or perceived. At all times remember that you're attacking *problems* rather than *individuals* who may have inadvertently produced them. In an era of labor shortages, professionals can no more afford to risk unnecessarily alienating personnel than they can to lose patients.

The Timeliness Problem

Most organizational problems—real or perceived—are readily addressed in terms of a series of questions. Is the problem real or perceived? Is it "freestanding" or does it relate to one or more contributing factors? If real, how can it be alleviated? If perceptual, how can perceptions be changed?

Answers to all of these questions are necessary in developing solutions. Steps toward problem resolution can be taken only with substantial risk in the absence of complete information.

Reality versus perception. Client and patient views of timeliness, to a greater extent than with most qualitative variables, usually are more a matter of perception than reality. These circumstances are most prevalent in context with the health care professions but are equally applicable elsewhere.

The discomfort that accompanies illness tends to compound impatience and reduce tolerance for delay. What to the professional may appear minor delays then produce evidence of disproportionately strong responses in survey data.

Scope of problem. Other factors equal, timeliness is no more strongly related to one than another of the several qualitative factors that concern patients or clients. Research suggests, however, that criticism has a strong tendency to spread from one area to another. Where clients or patients consider themselves aggrieved over delays, they tend to become more critical of the attitudes of personnel and other factors that contribute to satisfaction.

Considerable evidence indicates that problems involving factors such as timeliness, permitted to become chronic and extreme, can poison relationships between professionals and their clienteles. Access to data generated by well-designed surveys should permit early identification and resolution of such difficulties.

Developing remedies. Most professionals are aware of the manner in which appointments are scheduled in their offices and the extent to which they are kept. Where this is not the case, receptionists should be able to quickly generate data that will provide insight into the problem. Ideally they should log (*a*) appointment times, (*b*) client or patient arrival times, and (*c*) times at which clients or patients are seen.

A remedial strategy then should be developed that will eliminate as much valid cause for complaint as possible. Perfection is beyond virtually every individual and every organization, but near perfection can be accomplished in two ways.

First, appointment schedules can be adjusted to make them more in tune with the possible than the ideal. Professionals who always complete their days an hour behind schedule should adjust accordingly, perhaps by adding ten to twelve minutes to the time normally allocated to each patient or client.

Second, where schedules are occasionally unpredictable, patients or clients should be notified *in advance* of these circumstances. Few will be unduly critical of delays when they are aware that they occasionally occur. Advance notification works to professionals' benefit by altering patient or client expectations to adjust to practice conditions. Pragmatically, most gaps between expectations and realities can be adjusted in this manner.

The Courtesy Problem

Courtesy problems differ from scheduling difficulties in several respects. Time factors are readily measured. Courtesy is not. While time can be examined objectively, effort to evaluate courtesy is necessarily highly subjective.

Even without this difference, however, courtesy problems would be highly complex. In many professional settings, and especially where health care is involved, clients and patients are under physical or emotional stress or both. These circumstances make them hypersensitive to external stimuli. Overreaction is not unusual, and professionals never can be certain whether perceived offenses ever took place.

Potential for problems arising out of the sensitivity factor is compounded by failure on the part of most professionals to adequately control the behavior of their personnel. Paraprofessional and clerical staff members are responsible primarily for making things run smoothly. In many situations, that is equivalent to handling patients on an assembly-line basis with little regard for their feelings.

Practical solutions to difficulties of this sort, from the standpoint of professionals, require two components. The first is a policy requiring that staff members, to the best of their abilities, behave courteously. The second is a system that effectively monitors staff performance.

Policies can be written with relative ease. Compliance is another matter. Compliance can be induced in personnel only where performance is measured and rewards are granted or withheld accordingly. Where professionals are regularly surveying clients or patients, staff courtesy can be addressed in the questionnaire. Survey-to-survey change then will be a valid indicator of performance. Alternatively, professionals need only let patients or clients know of their policies and provide them with appropriate feedback devices. A simple leaflet distributed from a rack beside an office suggestion box will suffice. Periodic tabulation of responses then will provide insight into improvement or deterioration in worker behavior.

Other Difficulties

Many other difficulties and symptoms of difficulties can and should be addressed in similar fashion. Professionals' records can be analyzed to provide information on patient or client turnover or dropout rates, demographic variation, and economic trends.

Practitioners who fail to take advantage of contemporary computer technology to maintain client or patient data bases do themselves a disservice. Information necessary to track clienteles more closely than traditionally has been the case usually must be recorded in any event. The nature of services performed, the nature of the client, and similar information is regularly recorded. It can as readily and almost as economically be keyed into a small computer.

Professionals then can have at their disposal regular analyses of types of services their practices are providing, types of clients or patients using those services, and their geographic origins. Successful professional practices must adjust to changing patterns in these areas as rapidly as to economic change.

SERIAL STUDIES

Changes in practice patterns are most readily identified and monitored through serial or repetitive surveys. They best serve in professional development programming for a simple reason. Information generated through analysis of practice data often is inadequate to support estimates for future developments. Survey data usually are far more reliable.

The difference between the two types of information is simple. Analysis of practice patterns provides a picture of the past. Evaluation of attitude and opinion among patients or clients, existing and prospective, creates a window on the future.

Continuing changes in patient or client addresses, for example, may suggest a need for a branch office or for relocation when a lease expires. Mounting dissatisfaction over any aspect of professional services among prospective clients, in contrast, can signal a major competitive opportunity. Ability on the part of professionals to gain early access to information of this type can create major advantages in an increasingly competitive market for professional services.

Meeting the Need

Initial survey research produces insights into relationships between professional practices and their clients or patients, existing and prospective. The value of data increases, however, when surveys are used in serial fashion.

Change and direction of change in survey data are far more significant than any set of abstract data. This especially is the case where organizations are dealing in services rather than products. "Zero defects" may be a realizable if costly goal in a manufacturing setting. Zero dissatisfaction, however, is an impossible standard where services are involved.

Conditions that create satisfaction and dissatisfaction cannot be accurately defined. Degree of satisfaction varies with the extent to which organizational performance meets individuals' preconceived notions of quality. Any measure of satisfaction therefore is meaningless in an abstract sense. Measures become meaningful only in terms of change over time or across groups.

Where client or patient satisfaction levels consistently improve, practices become increasingly attractive to prospective clients or patients. Where satisfaction levels are stable or deteriorating, the reverse must be assumed to be the case. Change can be measured only through comparative data generated at regular intervals. Professionals who would enhance the attractiveness of their practices thus must periodically repeat surveys to determine amount and direction of change.

Research Design

While apparently more complex, repetitive surveys that show amount and direction of change are individually less costly than isolated research projects. Two factors are involved. One is reuse of designs required for initial surveys. The other is created by economy analytical processes created by contemporary computer systems.

Every research design should be developed on the assumption that it will be used repetitively to generate sequential data. Those employed in practice development surveys are no different. Where these processes are followed, survey forms, computer programs, and other materials prepared for the initial survey can be reused in whole or in part for those that follow.

Change in questions or analytical techniques is not impossible in repetitive studies. Modifications due to environmental change often are highly advisable. In general, however, research techniques, questionnaires, and materials used in initial studies can be adapted economically for subsequent use.

IN SUMMARY

Information gathering equips professionals to begin practice development in one or more of three areas. The three, usually undertaken concurrently, include short-term activities to eliminate minor irritants to patients or clients, long-term activities to strengthen the practice, and, in some cases, further research.

Short-term activities, focusing on easily remedied problems, serve multiple purposes for the professional. First, they demonstrate to patients or clients that previous research was undertaken seriously and that expressed concerns are being addressed. Second, they constitute the first of several steps necessary in reshaping the practice to meet contemporary conditions.

Survey responses almost always point to multiple minor irritants associated with the practice that can be readily corrected. Although seemingly minor, they always are meaningful to respondents and therefore worthy of attention. Removing these irritants also is a first step toward creating a new reality—the first component of communication in practice development.

Long-term activities to create a more attractive reality can be time-consuming for several reasons. Offices are not readily relocated or renovated. New personnel policies and procedures are not developed and implemented overnight.

Equally if not more time-consuming are decision making and action directed toward expansion of practice activities to better serve existing clienteles or to attract new patients or clients. These almost always require more space, staff, and equipment, which may or may not be within the physical or economic means of the professionals involved. Survey data must be analyzed in the context of resources required and available to establish developmental priorities.

Developmental priorities may be governed by economic or competitive factors. The economic factors deal with rates of return on investment that attach to any prospective service. Many practitioners establish priorities based on these rates so that new services may become self-sufficient as rapidly as possible. Where these conditions prevail, revenues from one new service can fund development of the next. Economically oriented approaches to practice development thus usually involve establishing new services on sequential rather than concurrent bases. Competitive strategies, in contrast, are more preemptive in nature. They are designed to capture market share and operate on the assumption that, given greater market share, revenues necessarily will increase.

Either strategy may be appropriate for a given practice in specific circumstances. Professional review of general economic as well as community and professional conditions usually provides ample data on which to make decisions. Conservative approaches usually are wisest where (a) economies are not in boom conditions, (b) colleges and universities are not graduating competitors at excessive rates, and (c) existing competitors are not apt to become aggressive. Otherwise, preemptive strategies are advisable.

Not infrequently, practitioners also will elect to seek more information through ongoing research. Continuing monitoring of practice environments and those groups critical to practice success is highly advisable, especially during the early years of a practice development effort. The underlying reason is simple but significant: survey data can be misleading. Survey results are akin to photographs. At best, they are accurate portrayals of conditions that prevailed at the time the data involved were collected. Information as to trends within surveyed populations can be accurately established only where surveys are repeated. Comparisons drawn across data sets then provide additional insight for professionals.

Further information also is helpful in monitoring results of short- and long-term developmental activities. Data gathered earlier concerning such subjective matters as comfort of facilities and deportment of personnel also can be misleading. Practitioners who want to monitor changing attitudes and opinion in these areas must have data from repetitive surveys.

ADDITIONAL READING

Frey, James H. *Survey Research by Telephone*. Beverly Hills, Calif.: Sage, 1983.

Henderson, Marlene K., Lynn L. Morris, and Carol T. Fitz-Gibbon. *How to Measure Attitudes*. Beverly Hills, Calif.: Sage, 1978.

Morris, Lynn L., and Carol T. Fitz-Gibbon. *How to Measure Achievement*. Beverly Hills, Calif.: Sage, 1978.

Patton, Michael Q. *Creative Evaluation*. 2nd ed. Beverly Hills, Calif.: Sage, 1987.

Shavelson, Richard J. *Statistical Reasoning for the Behavioral Sciences*. Boston: Allyn and Bacon, 1981.

Smith, Judson, and Janice Orr. *Designing and Developing Business Communications Programs That Work*. Glenview, Ill.: Scott, Foresman, 1985.

Soderberg, Norman R. *Public Relations for the Entrepreneur and the Growing Business: How to Use Public Relations to Increase Invisibility and Create Opportunities for You and Your Company*. Chicago: Probus, 1986.

6

The Nature of Communication

Success in communication requires an understanding of several critical components of the process. Some involve little more than common sense in their application. Others are more complex and demanding.

It is most important to understand that communication encompasses more than disseminating and receiving information in the traditional sense of those words. Communication does indeed occur where information is exchanged. Information is exchanged more often, in more ways, and more pervasively, however, than many believe to be the case.

Communication in professional practice development thus begins with reality and behavior. The words *reality* and *behavior* refer to what the practice is and does. The nature and environment of the practice and the behavior of professionals and their staffs communicate more efficiently and convincingly—for better or worse—than any substitute.

All other forms of communication do nothing more than substitute for or supplement the process initiated by the reality and behavior of the practice. Most are used to overcome natural barriers to the flow of information. They are employed to convey information to those who otherwise might not have access to it due to limited exposure to the practice.

Interpersonal, electronic, and printed communication can be applied to amplify, elaborate, or substitute for reality and behavior. Neither can be replaced or changed, however, by spoken, recorded, or printed words. Reality and behavior have been and will remain professionals' primary communication vehicles.

COPING WITH REALITY

In professional practice development, everything communicates. Every aspect of every detail of the practice contributes to the public's knowledge of the practice and the professionals involved. Convenience of offices and access to parking can readily be taken as evidence of professionals' concern for clients or patients. The condition of waiting rooms also says a great deal about professionals' concern for their clienteles. So do the dress and deportment of office staff and the vocal tone and inflection of those who answer when telephones ring.

In some situations, factors such as those specified above can be extraordinarily important. In locations where architects or interior designers practice, for example, the appearance of buildings and waiting rooms may reflect on their professional abilities. The efficiency of heating and air conditioning systems can similarly reflect on the capabilities of engineering firms.

These factors are important for a simple reason: neither services nor products are purchased for their intrinsic value. They are acquired for the benefits they create. Refrigerators are acquired to keep food cold. Washing machines are intended to produce clean clothes. Failure to meet buyers' expectations can quickly drive products and producers from the marketplace. The same circumstances rapidly are developing in the professions. Architects whose buildings fail to perform as promised, plastic surgeons who fail to meet patients' aesthetic standards, and advertising consultants whose creations fail to induce sales will share the same fate.

Public relations once was simplistically defined as "doing a good job and getting credit for it." The definition continues to apply, and the prescribed sequence is vital in every communication situation.

Problems Defined

Research conducted in the course of creating a practice development program is intended primarily to define (a) what clients or patients, existing and prospective, consider to be a good job and (b) the extent to which they perceive professionals as meeting that standard. Data collected in the research process tells professionals

1. the extent to which their practices meet the standards of existing and prospective clients,
2. the extent to which competitors' practices meet those standards, and
3. how to proceed toward enhancing perceptions of their practices in contrast with those of competitors.

The data invariably reveal problems and opportunities in two forms: real and as perceived by respondents. Real problems usually are found in one of two forms. Many are elements within the practice that serve as relatively minor irritants to patients or clients. Others are significant competitive disadvantages. They may include limitations on range of available services, inadequate facilities, or inept personnel.

Uncomfortable waiting room furniture and professionals' chronic tardiness in keeping appointments would classify as irritants. Relative inconvenience of offices or limits on services offered in relation to those of other professionals, on the other hand, can be classified as competitive disadvantages.

Perceived irritants or problems are another matter. Clients or patients may be unaware of facilities and services available to them. Such perceptions can be especially damaging because they enhance the relative attractiveness of competitors' practices.

Information-gathering processes serve as a first step toward correcting perceptual problems. While providing data concerning their practices, for example, survey research also initiates a communication process. The manner in which professionals handle responses can serve to enhance relationships with clients or patients. Survey questionnaires elicit information. Respondents contribute their time in response. They then await professional reaction. Perceptions of the practice and professionals involved are enhanced when substantive response occurs on a timely basis. Otherwise, the reverse usually is true.

Response Strategies

The enhancement process involves a series of steps taken in logical order within limitations imposed by professionals' resources. Parallel sets of activities usually are involved. One is designed to produce short-term improvement. Another deals with long-term efforts. A third addresses practice environments.

The short-term category consists of two subgroups. One involves a set of real but minor irritants amenable to quick and inexpensive remedies. The other consists of all perceived problems, regardless of their apparent magnitude.

The long-term category consists of real and substantive problems and opportunities that often require significant resources in their resolution. Each requires careful cost-benefit analysis in light of total resources available. Long-term activities are usually undertaken under priorities assigned on the basis of return on investment.

The environmental category deals with the physical and human environments in which professions are practiced. They can be assets or liabilities. Environments are amenable to change, but change can be accomplished only with substantial effort and usually requires considerable time.

The overall result can best be conceived of as a "parallel track" strategy: short- and long-term efforts toward modifying reality to gain competitive advantages operating in parallel with communication programs to make existing and prospective clients aware of the changes involved. The strategy should be viewed, however, as a cohesive whole. Short-term efforts can readily produce significant results and thereby lull professionals into a false sense of security. Only where long-term objectives have also been achieved can practices be competitively positioned to best advantage.

Short-Term Improvement

Achieving short-term improvements in the wake of survey research in a sense is reminiscent of a carnival shooting gallery. Respondents to research invariably point out a multitude of minor irritants that are readily remedied. Their removal always makes the practice more attractive, although the results are not likely to be durable where deeper problems exist. The situation in some ways is much akin to that which can occur after an auto accident. Victims are glad to see the bleeding stopped but remain much concerned over broken bones that still must be set.

Short-term improvements nevertheless are important to professionals in that they alter unsatisfactory realities. They enable practitioners to respond tangibly to the expressed wishes of clients or patients. The process, in a sense, establishes two-way communication and at least temporarily strengthens professional relationships.

What to do. What sorts of short-term improvements can be made? They vary from one survey to another, but many appear rather frequently on research reports. Popular among them are the following:

1. Quicker responses to telephone calls
2. Greater punctuality
3. A telephone in the waiting room
4. Access to coffee or soft drinks
5. More courteous behavior by clerical and paraprofessional personnel
6. More open communication

Need to know. The latter element can be especially significant. It appears on survey reports in several forms, but the essence of the problem is consistent. Clients and patients want to know the whys and wherefores of their situations. "That's the way it needs to be" is an inadequate answer, whether "it" is a building site or a surgical procedure. Today's clients and patients are better educated and more knowledgeable than those of a few years ago. They demand and deserve to be treated accordingly.

Overall results of short-term efforts are invariably enhanced when they are viewed as such, when they are considered by practitioners as stop gap measures to control client or patient attrition until comprehensive programs can be put in place to deal with more substantive problems.

Long-Term Improvement

While short-term programs deal with "the little things," ranging from waiting room thermostats to cold stethoscopes, professionals' long-term developmental efforts are more strategic than remedial, more tactical than environmental. They do not neglect patient or client concerns, but they are strongly oriented to developing and maintaining competitive advantages in fast-changing professional environments.

Long-term effects focus on primary determinants of patient and client behavior rather than on minor irritants—on the broken legs rather than on the bruised egos, as it were. Long- and short-term efforts must continue in parallel. The short-term variety are never sufficient to sustain a productive practice development program.

Long-term improvements are designed to induce practice growth through one of several tactics. One involves introducing new services. This is a logical practice development step where services to be implemented are not available and where real demand exists. Another tactic involves enhancing existing services. This approach can be productively applied where existing services are—or are perceived to be—inadequate.

The second approach involves a number of alternatives based on the nature of perceived inadequacies. Services can be made more convenient to users in any of several ways. They can be made more geographically convenient, as with the bookkeeping or accounting assistance available through income tax preparation services. Professionals can be made more readily accessible, as with medical services in minor emergency clinics and dental offices in department stores. They can be offered on a more timely basis, as with optical laboratories in shopping malls.

Environmental Improvement

The range of developmental possibilities is almost endless. None of them ultimately will be any more or less productive, however, than the practice environment permits. Environments consist of the physical and human factors that govern the comfort of patients or clients.

Professional practices achieve their economic potential only where the environments in which they function make those they serve feel comfortable and welcome.

Comfortable takes on added meaning in terms of professional practice. Neighborhoods and buildings must be comfortable for clients and patients, at least to the extent that they do not feel unnecessarily apprehensive. Office surroundings should be comfortable but need not be palatial.

Welcome also is a more complex word in the context of practice development than otherwise might be the case. Human surroundings should be caring as well as warm. Paraprofessional and clerical personnel must understand that they are employed to serve the needs of the practice, including clients or patients as well as professionals. They must be required to respond accordingly to the needs of all involved.

These circumstances require that professionals take a real interest in what goes on around them. They must be concerned about the manner in which the environments they create speak to their clients or patients. From the perspective of the individuals involved, environments literally speak for professionals. Discomfort and discourtesy almost always are perceived—and often accurately so—as evidence of insensitivity on the part of professionals.

Survey-generated indicators of client or patient dissatisfaction with professional offices or personnel thus require special attention. Both discomfort and discourtesy may be real or perceived. Those who are ill especially tend to be hypersensitive to their environments. Their hypersensitivity, however, in no way detracts from their ability to damage the practice. Practice personnel must be educated and trained and physical surroundings must be adjusted to any extent necessary to prevent negative reactions under any conditions.

COMMUNICATION STRATEGIES

A great deal of what professionals want clients and patients to know about their practices, and everything that practitioners do not want known, is conveyed without benefit of formal communication programs. Former and existing clients, for better or worse, constitute professionals' primary channels of communication. Present and former practice personnel are almost equally effective in communicating but usually are far fewer in number.

The disproportionate influence of clienteles and personnel—past and present—is produced by the fact that people are seldom wholly rational and logical in dealing with sources of information. As auto manufacturers and others have learned to their sorrow, buying decisions are more apt to be governed by the opinions of friends and acquaintances who have used the product than by any other factor. Those involved seldom would qualify as experts in the subject at hand but nevertheless are most influential in the decision-making process.

These circumstances should underscore the point made earlier: in practice development, reality and perceptions of reality communicate. Environmental reality compounds or diminishes the impact of the communication component of practice developmental programs by controlling client perception and reality. Perception of reality, where professional practices are involved, is disproportionately influenced by existing and former clients and by past and current personnel. Many presumably departed for greener pastures. Professionals logically can hope for no better than noncommital treatment at their hands.

These conditions logically suggest that communication in professional development programs begins internally rather than externally; that practitioners communicate first with their personnel, second with their clients, and only afterward with prospective clients. To do otherwise is to risk confusion on the part of prospective clients as a result of conflicting messages originating with others involved.

Inside-Out Strategy

The most logical communication strategy, in other words, is an inside-out strategy, a strategy designed to produce a sound foundation in reality and in the perceptions of existing clienteles before using communication to refute erroneous perceptions or attract support for a worthy reality. The inside-out strategy is designed first to enlist practice personnel and then to involve clienteles in the communication effort. As such, it implies a logical approach to communication techniques. The first step always consists of creating salutary realities or environments for groups involved. The second involves providing them with any information that may not be evident in the nature of the environments. The latter element consists of activities (as opposed to realities) that most would more traditionally categorize as communication.

Understanding of any subject or issue is more readily accomplished by two individuals in face-to-face conversation. Potential for misunderstanding becomes progressively greater with increase in distance or decline in contact between message senders and receivers.

Alternative Techniques

In general terms, communication techniques might be sorted into three categories and several subcategories in declining order of efficiency:

I. Interpersonal communication
   A. One-on-one
   B. Small Group
   C. Large Group
II. Mediated communication
   A. Electronic
      1. Interactive televideo
      2. One-way televideo
   B. Printed

Multiple options exist within each of the interpersonal and mediated communication categories. Each has advantages and disadvantages relating to group size, time requirements, and cost limitations. In general, however, efficiency in communication increases in keeping with the "closeness" of the method selected.

Within the interpersonal group, one-on-one communication is more efficient than the small group variety, which in turn is more efficient than large group communication. Interactive televideo is more efficient than the one-way variety.

Two variables govern the relative efficiency of the process. First is potential for audience response. Second is communicator ability to "read" and adjust to audiences. Both of these elements diminish steadily as groups grow larger, and they disappear at the one-way televideo level.

Efficiency in communication can refer to more than the extent to which messages are received and understood. The term also can be applied to the relative cost of alternative processes. In general, costs increase with group size and with their geographic and temporal diversity. Principals in small professional organizations usually experience little difficulty in maintaining regular face-to-face contact with all of their personnel. The process grows progressively more difficult and more time-consuming as organizations grow. Regular and frequent face-to-face communication becomes almost impossible as practices expand to encompass multiple offices or as they increase the range of their service hours to require multiple work shifts. In essence, then, every communication method beyond face-to-face contact is essentially a progressively less efficient substitute for one-on-one communication.

Interpersonal Communication

Efficiency in interpersonal communication deteriorates primarily with the size of groups involved. Deterioration is a function of communicator ability to maintain visual contact with all involved; to "read" and respond to facial expressions and other forms of body language. At a given point that appears to vary to some extent with communicator skill and experience, conversations with multiple individuals become group communication. Speakers pass the point at which they are able to assess and respond to individual reactions. They continue to read and sense collective audience response, but collective responses are inefficient in indicating the extent to which messages are received and understood.

One-on-one. These conditions encourage managers and supervisors in growing companies to maintain one-on-one contact with personnel for as long as organizational size permits. Ability to do so can be enhanced where managers remain the immediate supervisors of workers involved. As such, they can use the performance evaluation process to effectively maintain contact.

Senior managers also strengthen interpersonal relationships in larger organizations through a process called "management by walking around." The process involves getting out of the executive suite and maintaining informal contact with personnel at all levels with leisurely walking tours of the organization.

Two direct benefits occur. First, personnel take the periodic visits of senior managers as evidence of (*a*) their importance to the organization and (*b*) managers' concerns for them. Second, managers are able to hear and see the concerns of subordinates directly rather than through impersonal communication channels.

In professional practices, practitioners are faced with the same problems in dealing with clients or patients. Volume and extent of contact differ from one profession to another but the basic problem remains the same: maintaining relationships satisfactory to clients or patients.

Physicians experience difficulty in this area as practices grow and as they spend less and less time with individual patients. These circumstances require that they use every second efficiently, making real efforts during time spent with each patient to convey interest and human feeling as well as professional competence.

Principals in large accounting, architectural, and law practices have a much different problem. They usually are directly involved with clients in establishing relationships. During the ritual dances that precede the "mating" of professional and client, principals are very much in evidence. Afterward, second and third tier professionals assume responsibility for the "care and feeding" of new clients. Principals, preoccupied with managerial tasks and other prospective clients, are limited to a progressively declining volume of "hand holding."

Unless surrogates do their work with exceptional skill, new clients may come to feel they had been misled into believing that principals would be directly involved in meeting their day-to-day needs. These conditions put two burdens on the shoulders of the surrogates. First, their work must be of the quality that the client expected to obtain from the principal. Second, and more important, they must create interpersonal relationships of a quality acceptable to clients as substitutes for those earlier expected of the principal.

Most larger professional organizations attempt to build client and patient relationships using what euphemistically has been called a team approach. The plan involved calls for other members of the organization to share and, over time, largely assume responsibilities early undertaken by principals on behalf of the practice. Pragmatically, the team approach is a substitutional tactic. In addition it usually represents conscious efforts to induce patients or clients to place their confidence in a group—the practice as a whole—rather than in one individual.

The team approach is a sort of reversal of the small group approach to communication. In small group communication, communicators find it necessary to exchange information with small groups rather than one-on-one to meet time constraints. Professionals, for the same reasons, attempt to induce clients or patients to accept assistance from multiple individuals within an organization rather than from the professionals to whom they had come for help.

Small group. Traditional forms of small group communication are used in professional practices primarily in dealing with organizational matters rather than those involving patients or clients. Managers and supervisors use small group techniques in dealing with subordinates to reduce time demands imposed by interpersonal communication.

Personal involvement and contact on the part of managers or communicators is largely maintained in small group communication. This is especially the case where group members are familiar with one another and are at the same organizational level. Other than in such cases, many may be reluctant to express themselves for fear of retribution or out of timidity.

The principal challenge managers must meet in using small group techniques thus involves the makeup of the group. Efficiency and "neatness," for example, often may suggest that senior managers meet with all members of a department or other operating unit. The process can become considerably more complex where rank-and-file personnel, supervisors, and managers are separated. Separation also can reduce the efficiency of the communication process and may lead to intergroup misunderstandings.

Large group. The elements specified above are also at work in large group settings. Communication in large groups is necessarily still less efficient; a greater number of audience members fail to receive, understand, or act upon communicators' messages.

These circumstances logically lead most communicators to consider their objectives in deciding whether to use a specific form of verbal communication. Large group communication remains relatively efficient where communicators' objectives are inspirational. Efficiency levels decline, however, where the objective is informational or educational.

Differences in objectives and in individuals within given audiences account for the decline in efficiency. Communicators must exercise care in selecting techniques that best serve their purposes in given circumstances. In training personnel in new procedures, for example, one-on-one methods may be overly costly. Large group methods may be equally inefficient because of variation in the technical backgrounds or learning abilities of those involved. Small group or electronically mediated communication or both then may prove most efficient.

Electronic Communication

The term *electronic communication* in recent years has grown to include an increasing number of media or communication channels. Some are amenable to productive application in small and large group settings, thus blurring traditional boundaries between interpersonal and mediated communication.

Electronic channels are used in conjunction with interpersonal methods to enhance efficiency and economy. More and more health care professionals, for example, have patients view videotapes to learn more about specific health problems and alternative courses of treatment. So prevalent have such devices become that they prompted a *Wall Street Journal* cartoonist in 1988 to picture a physician's receptionist talking with a patient. The caption: "For $15 you see a videotape; for $30 you talk with the doctor."

The ability of videotape to deliver messages accurately and repetitively can be of considerable value in these and other circumstances. Traditional training films and slide presentations today are largely confined to videotape because of the greater flexibility and efficiency of the medium.

International organizations use "real time" satellite-based communication to keep far-flung components "up to speed" on internal information and to maintain morale. Federal Express Corporation, for example, maintains a staff of more than fifty and budgets millions of dollars annually for internal communication programs committed precisely to these objectives. The company transmits daily informational bulletins via satellite to operational units around the world. Federal's objective is to build morale and esprit de corps by letting personnel know how they're doing in meeting delivery guarantees. Federal also stages an interactive annual meeting with workers around the world using the same technology. Cost is high but results make the effort and investment worthwhile.

Printed Communication

While less apparently so, printed communication has expanded almost as rapidly as electronic methods in recent years. The factors involved in the change are the same that govern the use of virtually all forms of communication: time and cost. *Time* usually refers to elapsed time necessary to prepare a message for transmision. *Cost* refers to dollars involved, but on a per-recipient basis rather than in abstract numbers.

Decline in per-recipient or unit cost and in production time requirements in recent years has induced greater use of printed communication. The declines were created with the advent of the computer and what has come to be called desktop publishing. The term is ambiguous because the finished product rarely is produced on a desktop, but the implied increase in speed and decline in cost are real. Desktop publishing essentially enables small organizations—professional firms as well as companies—to set type and compose pages of newsletters, reports, and other documents in house rather than send typescripts to printers. Pages produced by computers and laser printers can be duplicated on office copiers or sent to printers, together with photos, as ''shooting copy'' for leaflets, brochures, and newsletters.

Reduced cost and time requirements have enhanced the efficiency of most printed messages. The changes have done nothing, however, to alter the basic attributes of print media. They remain superior communication vehicles where information conveyed must be retained and applied by recipients, as in the case of text books or instruction manuals. They remain inferior where communicators' objectives are inspirational or motivational.

Controlled versus Uncontrolled

Media mentioned within each of the categories specified above are controlled media. Content in each case is controlled by message senders. It cannot be changed by third parties or ''gatekeepers,'' as they're sometimes called.

While organizations are concentrating more and more of their communication efforts in controlled media, the uncontrolled variety occasionally can be useful. Uncontrolled media include the news or editorial components of commercial broadcast and publishing enterprises and not-for-profit entities such as the Public Broadcasting System.

News releases. All of those media supplement paid advertising with significant volumes of contributed information, most in the form of news and feature releases prepared by public relations professionals. News and feature releases differ from advertising in two respects. First, space and time they occupy is not paid for, as in the case of advertising. Second, their content is subject to change on the part of editors or news directors.

Media that use news and feature releases can be divided into two groups: mass media and specialized media. Managers of the mass media in print and electronic form consider most of the population to be among their prospective readers or viewers. Specialized media, in contrast, are oriented to the needs and interests of specific population subgroups. Most subgroups are readily identified as sharing special interests. They may be members of a specific business or professional group or may be interested in an avocation such as scuba diving or flying.

Media characteristics. Professionals seldom find mass media exposure of value in practice development. Several factors are involved. First, the mass orientation of media usually precludes their conveying sufficient detail concerning professional services to enable prospective users to make rational value judgments. Second, sale of many professional services, especially in the health care sector, are governed by needs that arise without warning. Prospective consumers cannot anticipate and prepare to become users.

Finally, and perhaps most importantly, services for which need can be anticipated seldom are of interest to mass media audiences or editors. Few audience members at any given moment will be interested in architecture, engineering, or interior decorating.

Communcation efforts involving the media and associated with practice development programs therefore are focused primarily on more selective media. They may be magazines catering to members of higher income groups, newspapers oriented to the business community in general, or trade journals that serve specific professions. Specialized television programs, most of them concentrated on cable channels, can be equally productive. More professional services are purchased or specified by readers and viewers of specialized programming than by members of other groups. Most of them fall in higher income groups, members of the business community, and, in many cases, members of other professions.

MESSAGE DELIVERY OPTIONS

Variation in media efficiency limits the ability of professionals to communicate effectively with groups of greatest interest to most of them: prospective clients and patients. A range of options nevertheless exists through which professionals can deliver messages through focused media to specific prospect groups.

Different sets of options are available in dealing with other groups with which professional practices are concerned. Existing clients and patients invariably are known and readily can be reached through controlled media. Those within the organization also are generally accessible. Vendors and subcontractors often are considered with employees as the organization's internal audience.

In each case, communicators turn to a finite set of media: interpersonal, electronic, and print. Other than in the interpersonal category, they exist in controlled and uncontrolled varieties. Each varies as to cost and efficiency in terms of each audience group.

Alternative Viewpoint

Professionals often comprehend cost-efficiency factors most readily in terms of cost-benefit relationships. Cost-benefit relationships relate cost of communication to potential benefit of communication. In merchandising organizations, for example, most communication expense is allocated to cost of sales. These often include such factors as package design, advertising, and other selling costs.

Selling costs cannot be adequately judged in a vacuum. No amount is inherently high or low. Instead, cost of sales varies with anticipated profit. High sales costs are acceptable where high profits are anticipated but are unacceptable where profit potential is low. This principle has a direct application to professional practices. Higher costs tend to be more acceptable where practitioners provide relatively expensive services for relatively few clients over extended periods of time. Gross profits per sale in these circumstances are higher than where relatively inexpensive services are provided infrequently to large numbers of clients. A costly personal sales call by an architect or advertising executive thus can be justified. Those in the healing arts, for economic as well as ethical reasons, must find alternative communication channels.

Greater than normal investments, in other words, can be justified only where expenditures can be expected to produce one of two outcomes: they will produce more durable results, or results will disproportionately influence the long-term welfare of the practice.

Durability of Results

Perhaps most striking in terms of potential for long-term results in professional practices are communication efforts that relate to personnel policy and procedure. Personnel behavior contribute disproportionately to practice success. Since their contributions—positive or negative—presumably will continue for years, superficially marginal improvements in their performance make major contributions to practice productivity.

These circumstances justify what otherwise might appear to be disproportionate investments in employee communication in several forms. Time and dollars necessary to design, install, and support performance-based compensation systems and supervisory and mangerial accountability systems are part of the process (see chapter 8). These systems only at first appear remote from the communication component of practice development. Performance realities induced by equitable application of personnel policy and procedure communicate practice quality more effectively to existing and prospective clients than any other factor. In other words, they communicate!

The same principle applies in terms of office locations, furnishings and equipment (see chapter 7). Practitioners considering acquisitions in each of these areas must look beyond cost estimates to potential results. A few pennies a square foot, or a few thousand dollars more or less in furnishing and equipping a waiting room, can communicate quality and concern to hundreds or thousands of clients for years. Cost must be weighed against those benefits; against contributions to sales that logically can be expected as the result of expenditures involved.

Alternative Media

The same principles apply in selection of communication channels or media to convey professionals' messages to personnel as well as clients or patients. Media must be chosen to produce desired results rather than for any intrinsic value or out of professional preferences.

Communication involves senders, messages, media or channels of communication, receivers, and responses. Of the five elements, the last is most important. Response, in fact, is the objective of communication. Success or failure of communication is measured accurately only in terms of response. All else is secondary.

Professionals occasionally may become enamored of fame, to which communication also can contribute. Fame and profit are not one and the same. Practice development is profit oriented. Communication cannot concurrently induce fame and profit with equal efficiency. By the same token, media vary in their ability to deliver messages and influence responses. Efficiency varies by audience, and their costs vary as well.

Media Selection

Practice behavior, message, and medium all must be focused on a single objective: audience response. Audiences may consist of practice personnel, existing clienteles, or prospective clienteles. The objective remains the same in any case, although message, media, and nature of response vary with audience.

Varying interests of practice personnel and existing and prospective clienteles necessarily require that they be addressed in different terms. Variation in the nature of the groups requires that different media or channels of communication be used.

Audience variation. Personnel in most cases are regularly on professionals' premises and can be readily reached through individual conversation, small group meetings, public address systems, memoranda, newsletters, bulletin boards, employee handbooks, and the like. On occasion, messages involving fringe benfits or other matters may be distributed in leaflet form on premises or by mail to employees' homes. The latter technique often is used where members of their families may be involved or especially interested in content.

Message delivery mechanisms for existing clienteles vary with the nature of professional practices. Some practices involve smaller numbers of clients or patients than others. Some involve more patient or client contact than others. Significant message volume can be conveyed in person where services involve frequent or regular contact. Where contact is infrequent or irregular, other communication channels must be used. Leaflets or brochures can be delivered by mail or distributed in waiting rooms. Periodic reminders of potentially needed services can be circulated by mail. Newsletters are becoming increasingly common as professionals assume responsibility for informing clients and patients of changes in the knowledge and technologies that underpin their practice specialties.

Practice variation. The nature of professional practices also governs selection of media used in reaching prospective patients or clients. Sizes of prospect groups, the extent to which they can be precisely identified, and the geographic scope of the practice are primary determinants in media selection. Dentists, for example, face far different circumstances than civil engineers. Virtually every individual is a dentist's prospective patient. Civil engineers deal primarily with govermental and quasi-governmental organizations that build roads, bridges, and water or waste treatment facilities. Dentists thus might seek to become known in their communities through civic or public service activities, while the civil engineering firm could successfully employ mail, in-person calls, brochures and other literature, and publicity in specialized media. Public speaking in several formats might be successfully used in either profession.

Unfortunately, however, media selection is but one of the several important remaining steps in the communication process. A critical last step remains: production of the materials in question. They may be as simple as invitations to an open house; as complex as an audiovisual presentation describing the firm's services. They can be produced in a broad range of forms and in a wide range of prices, and professionals must early decide precisely how production is to be accomplished.

Production Alternatives

Most professionals approach communication production through one of four alternative strategies. They range from do-it-yourself to use of highly sophisticated internal and external public relations and marketing organizations.

Organizations traditionally have seen their communication efforts progress through a logical series of developmental phases. Most begin by writing their own grand opening media releases in much the same manner that professionals use to announce opening of their offices. As organizations grow and communication needs increase, the typical organization will turn to an outside consulting firm. Consultants usually are used until communications tasks become so numerous as to justify creating an internal department.

In the relatively rare cases where organizations grow to become national or international in scope, the efforts of communication departments often are supplemented through intermittent consulting assignments. Consultants then are most often called upon to handle special events or projects of a magnitude that otherwise might interfere with ongoing communication activities.

IN SUMMARY

Communication involves a great deal more than the concepts that contemporary society attaches to that word. Communication occurs in many ways, and all of them are at work in every professional practice, for better or worse.

Messages concerning professional practices are delivered directly or indirectly to every patient or client, existing and prospective. Professionals can exert only limited control over those delivered indirectly, and these circumstances compound their need to control the remainder.

Direct-delivered messages are transmitted in two primary ways beyond the traditional. One set of messages is sent by practice environments: offices in which practices are situated, buildings in which offices are housed, and neighborhoods in which buildings are located. The other set consists of the behaviors, as opposed to the statements, of practice personnel. In most cases, these messages far outweigh those disseminated by design in the perceptions of recipients.

Clients and patients judge professionals by their offices and their staffs. Safe, convenient, and comfortable surroundings may indeed be relatively silent. Those seen as unsafe, inconvenient, or uncomfortable, however, are too often perceived to be the result of professional unconcern.

Behavior on the part of paraprofessional and clerical members of the practitioner's organization can be beneficial to professionals. They also, however, can be deadly. Personnel performance, good or bad, is perceived by clients and patients as being tolerated or condoned by professionals involved.

These circumstances require that professionals' first communication efforts be directed toward insuring that salutary environmental and behavioral messages are always being dispatched. Only when this objective has been accomplished should any effort be made to deal with more formal channels of communication.

The formal channels are readily sorted into two basic categories and a number of subcategories by order of efficiency. Interpersonal communication in one-on-one, small group, and large group form all are essentially superior to mediated communication. The mediated category includes electronic and printed communications, of which the first group tends to be more effective in contemporary society.

Professionals' ability to communicate with prospective patients and clients is limited to a varying extent by the efficiency and effectiveness of the three forms of mediated communication. In general, media should be selected on the basis of cost-efficiency ratios. Primary attention always should be given to practitioner cost per prospective client or patient rather than cost per recipient where messages are transmitted. Response is always the primary criterion for measuring the effectiveness of communication.

ADDITIONAL READING

Blythin, Evan, and Larry A. Samovar. *Communicating Effectively on Television*. Belmont, Calif.: Wadsworth, 1985.

Chambers, Wicke, and Spring Asher. *TV PR: How to Promote Yourself, Your Product, or Your Organization on Television*. Atlanta: Chase Communications, 1986.

Degen, Clara, ed. *Communicator's Guide to Marketing*. New York: Longman, 1987.

Gross, Lynne Schafer. *Telecommunications: An Introduction to Radio, Television, and Other Electronic Media*. 2nd ed. Dubuque, Iowa: Brown, 1986.

Hilton, Jack. *How to Meet the Press: A Survival Guide*. New York: Dodd, Mead, 1987.

———. *The New Television Technologies*. 2nd ed. Dubuque, Iowa: Brown, 1986.

Karlins, Marvin, and Herbert I. Abelson. *Persuasion: How Opinions and Attitudes Are Changed*. 2nd ed. New York: Springer, 1970.

Keil, John M. *The Creative Mystique: How to Manage It, Nurture It, and Make It Pay*. New York: Wiley, 1985.

7

Locating the Practice

A logical question arises after professionals have demographically and geographically identified markets they want to serve: what office location(s) will best serve the practice in meeting developmental objectives? The question is complex. It involves types of office facilities as well as their geographic location. It is pertinent regardless of the nature of the practice. An accounting firm with relatively little office traffic serving a six-state area, for example, might reduce operating costs and enhance visitor convenience by situating its offices near an airport rather than in a downtown high-rise building.

Professionals are free to open offices in any available location. They can elect urban or suburban sites, store-fronts or high-rise office buildings, high- or low-income areas. They are also free to relocate their practices in keeping with changing community conditions. Despite these circumstances, few consider carefully all of the available alternatives—or the implications of those alternatives in terms of practice development.

Careful periodic analysis of all available options is important to all professionals—newcomers to a community and those who have been in practice for extended periods of time. The word *periodic* is most significant for those in existing practices. Communities change. Professionals who fail to respond to change create unnecessary economic risks. Avoiding such risks requires that they instead constantly monitor community trends and reexamine their office options. While seldom amenable to immediate implementation, the options always include expanding or renovating existing facilities, relocating offices, or adding satellite offices.

Access, convenience, and safety are—or should be—among the primary criteria applied in site selection. Access refers to ease or difficulty that patients or clients experience in reaching the professional office. Convenience refers to site characteristics that may render locations more or less attractive to clients or patients. Safety includes neighborhood conditions and on-site security provisions.

Office locations also contribute to public perceptions of practices and practitioners. Some locations are considered "better" or more prestigious than others. Some also create a greater level of visibility. The impact of these attributes on the economic welfare of the practice usually varies with competitive circumstances and the relative stature of professionals involved. Competition makes them more significant other than for the preeminent few in any profession.

All of these factors are significant in selecting office locations, but in different ways to different groups. The nature of the practice—the extent of client exposure to office environments, for example—should determine the degree to which the interests of professionals, their personnel, and their existing and prospective clients influence the selection process.

COMPETITIVE STRATEGIES

Professionals whose practices are well established and who are well thought of in their communities enjoy distinct competitive advantages. These advantages are especially strong where practitioners involved are specialists and considered to be among the best in their fields. Clients are more tolerant of inconveniences encountered in obtaining the services of preeminent professionals.

Competitive circumstances, however, can quickly erode the relative advantage of even well-entrenched professionals. These conditions occur most often where communities are growing rapidly or are experiencing an influx of younger practitioners.

Rapid growth often results in relatively fast development of newer, more fashionable neighborhoods and office buildings. Long-established practices housed in older buildings and neighborhoods often are at a competitive disadvantge in attracting patients or clients from these areas.

Deterioration in older practices also can occur at an accelerated pace where growth attracts more professionals to the community. Newcomers tend to be younger and more aggressive. They become active in civic affairs to build their practices and often find themselves alone in these competitive arenas. More established practitioners seldom remain highly active in community affairs.

The relative importance of access, convenience, and visibility in different practice locations for these reasons varies with community and competitive conditions. Professionals should monitor developmental trends in their communities to avoid potential problems. Their decisions as to practice locations, however, also must be undertaken in light of a clearly defined practice strategy (see chapter 2). Practice locations should be selected to appeal as strongly as possible to prospective and existing client or patient groups.

ACCESS

Access to professional offices means different things to different people. The word generally refers to relative ease or difficulty encountered by those who must visit professional offices. Two primary groups are involved: office personnel and clients or patients. The latter group usually is the more important of the two from the practice development standpoint. Perhaps the only exception occurs where personnel are in short supply and are generally averse to a specific location or neighborhood.

Access means different things to different people. For the indigent, ease of access may mean an office within walking distance or on a bus line. For those in rural or suburban areas, the term may mean an office near an expressway or other major highway interchange. For urban residents, it may mean an office within a relatively short driving distance.

Access also involves two other factors, one general and one practice-specific, that influence decision-making processes among clients and patients. One is relative access, involving the perceptions of groups involved rather than objective realities. The other is group access, dealing with the geographic proximity of professional offices to specific patient or client groups.

Relative Access

Relative access refers to community patterns or standards. Those who have lived in communities of different sizes often notice significant differences among resident definitions of *near* or *far*. Those who work in major cities and live in adjacent suburbs, for example, often think little of commuting times of an hour or more between home and office. In smaller cities, thirty to forty-five minutes is the norm, while in villages and towns, anything in excess of fifteen minutes is viewed as a long commute.

These circumstances require that professionals remain sensitive to prevailing standards in their communities. The standards can be far different from those that prevailed in communities where practitioners grew up or went to school.

Geographic factors. Relative access also is a factor in weighing proximity of professional offices to client or patient groups. *Proximity* here refers to the fact that geographic distribution among these groups is a major variable. Variation occurs within communities and over time.

For some professionals, as in the case of attorneys or accountants, clients and prospective clients are concentrated in commercial and industrial areas. For others, such as dentists and physicians, patients and prospective patients are most often concentrated in residential areas. Among subspecialties, differences in residential neighborhoods can be important. A neighborhood consisting largely of the elderly is unlikely to support a pediatric practice but may be ideal for an attorney dealing in trust and estate matters.

Commercial and industrial areas tend to be relatively stable but residential areas change. Much of the residential change results from the aging process. Neighborhoods, like individuals, progress from infancy to maturity and ultimately decline. In some instances, usually over a period of decades or generations, as in some inner cities, neighborhoods may be reborn.

Changing populations. Populations change during the course of the aging process. Newer neighborhoods usually consist in large part of younger families with children. Over the years, the children grow up and depart, and neighborhoods become largely adult communities. The process repeats itself where neighborhoods are reborn.

The changes are slow but inexorable. They have little meaning for some professionals but are highly significant to others. The changes are significant beyond the health care professions. Rapid change signals opportunity for architects, engineers, accountants, and others. Neighborhood rehabilitation creates work for planners.

Changing Patterns

All professionals, but especially those in the healing arts, should be sensitive to change. Sensitivity is especially necessary in health care, where professionals traditionally have selected office locations on the basis of their own convenience more than that of patients or personnel. This practice has resulted in concentrations of physician offices near hospitals.

The tendency of physicians to locate adjacent to hospitals increased during the 1960s and 1970s. Physicians were relatively scarce during those years. Hospitals sought to assure high occupancy rates through aggressive physician recruiting. Many built medical office buildings adjacent to their premises to lure additional doctors.

The process worked to the benefit of both groups while the shortage persisted. By the mid-1980s, however, circumstances had changed. Suppliers of physicians were outgrowing demand for health care services. Medicare's cost-based reimbursement system had been changed, and hospitals more and more were competing with doctors to provide "nonprescription" services. What had been a seller's market became a buyer's market in physician services.

Market influence. Similar circumstances developed in law, accounting, and other professions. Lawyers had been relatively free to congregate around county and federal courthouses when they were relatively few in number. As the profession grew in relation to the population, more competitive circumstances developed.

Competitive factors first induced a relatively few younger professionals to locate offices distant from hospitals or courthouses and closer to prospective patients or clients. Their offices became, in a sense, the first "convenience stores" of the professions. Their practices grew relatively rapidly in an increasingly convenience-oriented society, and today's competitive battle lines were drawn in the process.

Competitive warfare became more heated with the emergence of storefront legal offices, minor emergency clinics, and tax preparation services. Each captured part of the potential clienteles of other legal, medical, and accounting practices.

Response patterns. Established practitioners sensitive to competition usually responded in one of three ways. Senior professionals nearing retirement and those in more esoteric specialties often elected to maintain previously existing practice patterns. They saw no need to respond to increasing competition. Others reacted by establishing satellite offices in areas more convenient to existing and prospective patients and clients. Still others simply relocated their practices. All of these options remain practical for contemporary practitioners.

Multiple practice locations have become commonplace where professionals find it necessary to maintain offices near courthouses or hospitals while responding to increasing competition. Multiple offices are most popular where group practices are involved. Professionals in these circumstances readily can divide their forces or rotate among multiple offices.

As multiple offices become more popular, professionals are also becoming more sensitive to collateral matters that influence client or patient patronage. Many relate to the convenience or inconvenience of environments in which professional offices are established.

CONVENIENCE FACTORS

Professional practices generally can be categorized by the extent to which patients or clients visit practitioner offices. In some professions, such as accounting, architecture, and engineering, client visits are rare. In others, such as dentistry and medicine, they are frequent and repetitive. Variation in client/patient traffic patterns determines the extent to which convenience of office locations influences practice development. Convenience may or may not be a critical factor in locating and relocating professional offices.

The convenience issue is complicated because practice locations also may be an asset or a liability in attracting professional, paraprofessional, and clerical personnel. Convenience to vendor and other groups also can be a factor in some instances. Advertising agencies, for example, often find locations near major vendors advantageous. Public relations firms frequently follow similar patterns.

Each of the primary groups with which professionals are involved must be considered in several contexts because convenience can be measured in several ways. Travel time and the physical characteristics of office sites usually are most significant. Time factors, as indicated earlier, must be viewed in terms of community norms rather than in the abstract.

Travel Time

Travel time creates cost—to a greater or lesser extent—for professionals, personnel, and clienteles. Costs vary with the nature of groups and types of practices involved.

Professionals are compensated for their time. Time spent in transit from one location to another usually cannot be charged to a patient or client. Many professionals therefore consider their own convenience paramount in selecting office locations. In competitive circumstances, however, professionals' preferences must yield to the needs of others.

Locations unattractive to prospective office personnel can create staffing problems. If clerical or paraprofessionals are in short supply, as demographic trends suggest will be the case through the remainder of the century, their interests also must be considered in making site decisions.

Practice variation. Travel time can be a major or a minor consideration for patients or clients. Architectural and engineering clients, who seldom visit professionals at their offices, find the locations of those offices to be of little consequence. The circumstances can be quite different, however, for physicians and dentists.

Convenience factors vary considerably within the healing arts. Among physicians, for example, radiologists and pathologists seldom need be concerned over patient needs. Most practice in hospitals, and their practices largely are limited to hospital patients. Obstetricians have a very different problem. Their patients visit them regularly for much of a year and may or may not tolerate extended travel times. The same principle applies in dentistry. Orthodontists, whose work can extend over months or years, find patient convenience more significant than colleagues who see their patients less frequently.

Competitive trends. Mounting competition in urban areas already is inducing significant numbers of practitioners to depart from traditional office patterns. While exceptions remain relatively few, significant potential for competitive advantage exists for those willing to reconsider earlier decisions.

Convenience in one sense extends beyond patients' or clients' ability to travel quickly from their residences or places of business to the professional's offices. The surroundings or physical characteristics of office sites can be of equal significance. They can make more remote offices relatively attractive, and the reverse can be true as well.

Site Characteristics

The term *physical characteristics* encompasses several elements. Some apply to almost every patient or client group. Others are group-specific. Availability, proximity, and cost of parking often are most important among employees as well as patients or clients. Professionals too often satisfy their own parking needs without adequately considering those of others.

Other factors that can be categorized as physical characteristics include ease of access for the handicapped, availability of related products or services, and similar elements. Each of these elements varies in its impact on practice growth potential. Some influence the welfare of all professions. Others are significant only within groups of professions. Still more are of concern only to specific disciplines. Access for the handicapped will be an increasing problem as the population ages. On-premises pharmacies make medical groups more attractive. Proximity to optical laboratories is helpful to ophthalmologists.

Other factors relate directly to the nature of client or patient groups. Orthopedists, for example, deal with substantial numbers of temporarily handicapped individuals. Attorneys who specialize in personal injury cases also may have disproportionate numbers of clients in this category. Like mothers of young children burdened with strollers or elderly individuals dependent on canes, they find such minor barriers as curbs and driveways to be major obstacles. The difference between downtown parking garages and suburban parking lots can be monumental to individuals in these circumstances.

Professionals often are insensitive to these needs and are too quick to accept rental agents' assurances that "plenty of parking is available." It may be plentiful, but it's often considerably more distant from professional offices than appears to be the case. Hospitals, for example, are notorious for providing extensive parking adjacent to professional buildings but relegating patients to the most distant and inconvenient areas.

Circumstances may be little better elsewhere. Developers dealing with high land costs tend to build as much building and as little parking as possible. Uncontrolled parking areas nearest buildings are quickly occupied by those who work within them, leaving the least accessible parking places to clients or patients.

Safety Concerns

The nature of parking facilities and the distances between them and buildings also influence perceptions of safety. Quality of lighting and the presence or absence of security systems also influence relative desirability of office locations. Dimly lit parking garages are discouraging to many, especially in less than desirable neighborhoods. Neighborhoods' reputations for safety—deserved or otherwise—also limit walking distances that clients and patients are willing to tolerate.

While varying in impact from one community to another, public perceptions of increasing criminal activity demand that professionals consider these factors in selecting office locations. Offices perceived to be in deteriorating neighborhoods or in high crime areas discourage patients or clients as well as employees.

These perceptions can be especially damaging from a practice development standpoint where professionals maintain late afternoon and evening office hours. Physical surroundings acceptable to clients and patients during daylight often are unacceptable after dark, especially in the absence of adequate security systems.

Other Physical Constraints

While patient or client impressions of professional practices may begin in the parking lot or parking garage, they also are influenced by many other physical elements encountered en route to the office door. The impact of each of these elements varies among individuals involved. Collectively, however, they contribute significantly to the success of professional practices. Although discussed here in terms of multistory office buildings, they are equally applicable in other settings.

Outside shelters, lobbies, building security systems, adequacy of elevators, access to telephones and restrooms, light levels, and a host of other factors contribute to overall impressions of professional buildings. At a minimum, they influence the attitudes and opinions of clients or patients. At worst, they can create "horror stories" to be shared with family, friends, and acquaintances to the detriment of the practitioner. "User-friendly" facilities, to borrow a term from the computer industry, enhance impressions of professional services. The opposite is equally true.

Weather problems. Perhaps the most lasting impressions created by buildings among patients and clients are those that develop in inclement weather. The most aesthetically pleasing structure often creates a very poor impression in adverse weather conditions. Presence or absence of a sheltered entryway is especially important. Most individuals are concerned over their appearances. Ability to close an umbrella without drowning in the process is important to them.

Problem potential increases where physicians' patients are involved. A canopy permitting drivers to discharge passengers at the building entrance may provoke no great applause. Absence of such facilities, however, can raise doubts as to whether professionals really care about those they serve.

Neglected lobbies. Lobby size is another factor often neglected among professionals. Lobbies superficially need be nothing more than passageways leading to stairways or elevators. Lobbies of inadequate size, however, can create problems. They should offer adequate space for those who may be waiting for rain to abate. Where adjacent to medical offices, they should be spacious enough to permit wheelchairs to maneuver.

Lobbies also should contain easy-to-read building directories. Like corridors, restrooms, and elevators, they should be adequately lighted and heated. Elevators and restrooms should be of sufficient size to handle building traffic and equipped to accommodate the handicapped. In limited access buildings, where visitors are required to register, security systems should present as few problems as possible. Where restroom facilities are not otherwise provided, they should be available off lobby areas and appropriately maintained. Telephones should be available for those who need them.

Some of these conveniences also can be made available in individual professionals' offices. Their presence or absence is viewed by visitors as an indication of professional concern. Practitioners should be certain that they are readily accessible.

TYPES OF OFFICE BUILDINGS

Professional offices usually are located in one of three types of buildings. High-rise office buildings long have predominated, but smaller multiple- or single-occupancy structures in office parks and elsewhere have been growing more popular. Each type of building has advantages and disadvantages.

All of the factors described above deserve consideration. Several others also require attention in selecting office locations. They include practice visibility, ancillary facilities, proximity to colleagues, and access to associated services. The latter factor is of concern to patients or clients as well as to professionals.

Practice Visibility

The term *practice visibility* refers to the extent to which office locations are visible to prospective clients or patients. Highly visible locations serve as ''ethical billboards'' for professionals. They are especially desirable among those establishing new practices.

Visibility is controlled by the type of building involved and by legal limitations on sign use. Signs in high-rise office buildings are usually limited to lobby directory listings and plaques on office doors. Smaller multioccupancy buildings often permit outdoor signs. These can range from relatively samll door or wall signs to space on illuminated, free-standing signs shared by building residents. Still larger signs often are permitted on or adjacent to single occupancy buildings. Professionals occasionally can defeat the limitations of high-rise buildings by acquiring ground floor offices opening to the street rather than to inside corridors. Even relatively small signs on or adjacent to doors then become visible to passers by.

Total sign area and types of signs usually are limited by municipal ordinance or restrictions in leases or purchase contracts. Large, internally or externally illuminated signs are permitted in many areas. In others, use of signs is relatively restricted. Since signs can be major components of professionals' promotional exposure, pertinent limitations should be examined carefully before lease or purchase contracts are executed.

Ancillary Facilities

Signs and other facilities may or may not be provided by building owners. Availability often is governed by the type of building involved. The extent to which ancillary facilities are available in any case influences professionals' out-of-pocket costs.

Common facilities such as lobbies and other service areas are provided for all tenants in larger buildings. Such facilities are usually limited in smaller structures and nonexistent in single-occupancy buildings. Where necessary, in other words, practitioners may have to provide them. Waiting areas then usually must be slightly larger than otherwise might be the case. Coat racks or closets and rest rooms consume most of the extra space.

Security services in smaller buildings also are usually provided by occupants at their expense. Utilities, janitorial services, and maintenance of parking areas and grounds almost always become occupant responsibilities.

Office parks and similar environments often appear to be blessed with extensive parking facilities, but appearances can be misleading. Much depends on the nature of professional practices and the businesses of other tenants. Some generate more office traffic than others. Office park developers are no more generous in allocating parking space than those who build high-rise structures. Professionals therefore must be certain that available space will be adequate to practice needs. Undue congestion can discourage prospective patients or clients.

Proximity to Colleagues

While investigating traffic potential among other office park tenants, professionals also should be sensitive to the presence or absence of other elements that may contribute to practice development. These include colleagues in associated professional disciplines and ancillary services relating to their own practices.

Proximity of colleagues in associated disciplines can be most beneficial in the medical profession, where one practitioner often refers patients to another. Their practices, in a sense, feed on one another. The effect of these circumstances is often enhanced where practices are situated conveniently to one another.

Obstetricians, for example, often find proximity to gynecologists beneficial where their practices do not overlap. Neurologists and neurosurgeons may enjoy similarly synergistic relationships. Pediatricians find locations near obstetrical practices potentially beneficial. Cardiologists may benefit from proximity to cardiovascular surgeons.

Availability of ancillary services produce similar synergies in medicine and beyond. Medical supply stores and pharmacies benefit where located with physicians. Many attorneys find access to title companies helpful. Optometrists and opticians, architects and engineers, and consultants in advertising and public relations often enjoy similarly synergistic relationships.

OFFICE ENVIRONMENTS

All of the practice development potential defined in the preceding pages pales, however, in comparison with that created by professionals' own office facilities. Waiting rooms, consultation rooms, and professionals' private offices all should contribute to the "user friendliness" of the practice.

The extent to which these environments enhance or detract from practice growth is a function of many small but significant attributes. Space, furnishings, and ancillary facilities that can contribute to client or patient comfort and convenience are primary among them.

Space

Office space is expensive. Cost per square foot, expressed in lease or rental rates or in construction or purchase prices, adds to professional overhead. These circumstances often encourage professionals to be conservative in deciding on office sizes. In general, private offices tend to be spacious. Waiting rooms too often are cramped. Consultation rooms vary in size with the nature of the practice.

Many professionals tend to undersize offices in the interests of economy. They incur considerable risk as a result. Successful practices usually grow more rapidly than professionals anticipate. Where this is the case, space limitations soon can choke off practice growth. In general, professionals find it far wiser to overestimate rather than underestimate when allocating office space.

Perhaps the only exception to this general rule occurs where no long-term lease or purchase commitments exist, permitting professionals to relocate when necessary. Relocation, however, can be costly and disruptive. Client or patient attrition can result when significant distances are involved.

Waiting rooms. Risks in underestimating space needs are greatest where waiting rooms are involved. Waiting rooms create an all-important first impression on patients or clients. The best of professional service will be undervalued if they are cramped and uncomfortable. Where waiting rooms are spacious and attractive, patients and clients are predisposed to respond favorably to the professional attention they receive.

Waiting room sizes are especially critical where professionals' schedules are subject to unexpected change. Where this is the case, or where practitioners prefer to "have everyone waiting" when they arrive, peak patient or client loads inevitably create problems.

Liberal sizing of waiting rooms then is preferable, despite a minor "downside risk." Near-empty waiting rooms may be interpreted as evidence of marginal practice success. The larger the room, the more empty it appears when few patients or clients are present.

Risk can be minimized by exercising care in office layout or by creating multiple waiting areas or rooms. A sense of emptiness seldom develops where waiting rooms or areas are other than rectangular in shape or divided by furnishings into conversational groupings. Multiple waiting rooms are advisable where practices involve significant numbers of children, as in dentistry or medicine.

Children at best are relatively noisy creatures. The volume of sound they create can be disturbing to others, creating conditions detrimental to the practice. This potential problem can be turned to advantage, however, if a play room or private waiting room is provided adjacent to the principal waiting room.

Acoustically insulated playrooms equipped with appropriate toys or a television set and separated from adult areas by glass partitions engender highly salutary responses from parents. One or two private waiting rooms where mothers can care for especially fretful youngsters also enhance the attractiveness of the environment.

Pediatricians, pediatric dentists, and other professionals who deal consistently with small children also would find it worthwhile to employ practical nurses to care for waiting youngsters. Such an approach would be costly, but resulting word-of-mouth advertising might more than offset the expense involved.

Consultation rooms. The nature of consultation rooms varies with professions involved. Those provided by engineers, architects, attorneys, and accountants usually take the form of conference rooms. They generally are relatively spacious and comfortable, perhaps because they are often used by staff members when not occupied by clients.

The latter circumstances seldom prevail in other professions. Physicians, dentists, optometrists, chiropractors, and others usually restrict consultation rooms to minimum sizes. As in the case of waiting rooms, small size alone is not necessarily detrimental. It can become a source of discomfort, however, when professionals are delayed for more than a few minutes.

Delays are not unusual among health care professionals. Many attempt to expand their ability to see patients by using multiple consultation rooms. Professionals may spend only a few moments with each patient. Amounts of time patients spend in consultation rooms, however, often is multiplied by the number of rooms in use. When delays occur, patients can find themselves alone for a half hour or more in relatively cramped and uncomfortable surroundings.

Professional practice on this sort of assembly-line basis can be economically productive, but only if practitioners make a special effort to adhere to their schedules. When frequent delays occur, client or patient discomfort levels tend to be counterproductive. Practitioners should consider carefully the balance between waiting room and consulting room space in their offices. More of the former and less of the latter usually produces a more favorable environment.

Private offices. While waiting and consultation rooms are often too small, the reverse frequently is true where professionals' private offices are involved. These circumstances occur despite the fact that many professionals use their offices very little and that clients or patients seldom are in them at all.

Where practitioner offices are designed primarily for work rather than appearance, adequate space is essential. Where primarily decorative or seldom used, minimal space should be involved. Professional firms can readily circumvent the potential for overallocating private office space by supplementing working offices with smaller spaces for client meetings.

Furnishings

A range of funishing styles is available for use in professional offices. Prevalent styles extend from the clinical austerity of chrome and plastic to the luxury of residential drawing rooms. Between the extremes are many relatively economical but still comfortable variations that often are neglected.

Too many offices appear to be furnished without regard for client comfort or for the nature of the clientele that professionals want to serve. The primary source of the problem appears to be a predisposition on the part of professionals to believe that quality of service is the only criterion by which they are judged. Unfortunately, this seldom is the case. Those who come to professionals for assistance only rarely are qualified to evaluate quality of service. They are more than competent, however, to assess the comfort of office environments. Their summary judgments therefore may be based more on comfort than on quality of service.

Waiting rooms. These conditions suggest that careful attention be paid to furnishings in the context of professional clienteles. Comfort should be the practitioners' primary criterion. In the absence of compelling reasons to the contrary, waiting rooms should be equipped with fabric-covered upholstered furniture, carpet or rugs, and lamps rather than fluorescent fixtures. These items should be neither luxurious nor flimsy. Ample examples of comfortable yet wear-resistant furnishings are to be found in public buildings, hotels, and similar environments in which visitors expect to be treated as guests.

Guest, in fact, should be a term that professionals bear in mind when specifying furnishings for their offices. Cost differentials involved in providing furnishings appropriate for a guest rather than an institutional inmate are negligible. They need add relatively little to the attractiveness of the practice and the professional to more than compensate for the dollars involved.

Perhaps the only acceptable exception to the approach specified above arises where small children or animals (in the case of veterinarians) are involved. Pediatricians, pediatric dentists, and others will be best served, however, by providing playrooms of the sort described earlier. Furnishings there can be of a more durable variety, permitting waiting rooms to be more comfortably furnished.

Consultation rooms. The same pattern should be followed, with perhaps one exception, in consultation rooms. The exception arises primarily in health care, where hygienic factors militate toward more austere examining room surroundings. Even here, however, the traditional chrome and plastic approach in some instances deserves careful reexamination.

Where patients are "warehoused" in examining rooms to facilitate assembly-line approaches to practice management, a modicum of comfort is indicated. An upholstered chair finished in a patterned vinyl, for example, is far preferable to the distinctly uncomfortable alternatives usually found in such settings.

Private offices. Those offices in which patients or clients are seen deserve as much care in furnishings as do waiting rooms. Fortunately, most professionals overfurnish rather than underfurnish their offices. Any excesses involved are acceptable, however, only to the extent that they do not detract from necessary and appropriate expenditures to insure client comfort elsewhere in the office complex.

Ancillary Facilities

Nowhere is the potential for competitive advantage greater in professional practice than in what might be called ancillary facilities. These are the extras (some might call them frills) that can distinguish a professional office in the minds of patients or clients.

An almost unlimited number of ancillaries or accessories can be provided inexpensively for patient or client use. Those that have proven most popular among clients and patients include telephones, coffee and soft drinks, and unusually appointed restrooms.

Telephones. Contemporary telephone technology has eliminated the single risk that once attached to client use of office telephones: unauthorized long distance charges. A telephone line allocated for client or patient use now can be configured to prevent its being used for long distance calls other than those of the credit card variety.

Provision of telephones for patients or clients creates multiple advantages. The greatest, of course, is the impression that the service makes on those involved. Professionals are perceived to be truly interested in and concerned for their clienteles.

Equally important, however, is a marked reduction in receptionist work load and inconvenience. When office schedules are running late, many patients or clients will have to postpone other appointments or notify others that they'll be delayed. Unless a telephone is readily available, they first have to ask to use a telephone and then must be admitted to the office containing the instrument. The more courteous among them then will pause to express their thanks, creating a further interruption in office routine at a time when interruptions are least desirable.

Refreshments. Access to soft drinks and coffee is equally welcomed by clients, especially when appointments are delayed. These amenities long have been provided by many business firms to their visitors and customers but are routinely offered by relatively few professionals.

Cost factors seldom are significant other than where large practices are involved. Even in these circumstances, per capita costs are moderate. Those concerned about expenses are not precluded from offering refreshments, however, in that a variety of vending devices can be used.

Restroom amenities. Restrooms should be readily available in every professional office. Ideally, they should be situated adjacent to waiting rooms where, as in the case of telephones, they can be used by clients or patients without having to make a special request of office personnel.

While welcomed in any form, restrooms create the best possible impression when furnished with supplies of headache remedies, antacids, mouthwash, sanitary napkins, and the like. Many professionals receive more than sufficient samples from vendors to stock patient restrooms. Others will find the minor expense involved far outweighed by the gratitude of their clienteles.

IN SUMMARY

Office locations can be major determinants of practice success. They are especially important where the nature of the practice involves frequent client or patient visits. Access, convenience, and safety are the primary location-related concerns of those who visit professionals. They therefore play a role in practice development and should be of concern to professionals as well.

Professionals in well established practices enjoy competitive advantages that can be enhanced or eroded by the locations of their practices. Erosion can occur when competitors establish offices perceived as superior by prospective clients or patients. Changing patterns of community development also can be damaging, especially in fast-growing communities that are attracting more practitioners.

Access to professional offices is a complex variable. The term refers primarily to time involved in reaching the office site. What some may consider a relatively brief drive, however, is a long one to others. Access also refers to the proximity between the professional office and specific patient or client groups—existing or prospective. For some, such as physicians and dentists, access in this sense is quite important. Visits to their offices are relatively frequent. For others, such as architects and engineers, access is relatively unimportant.

The increasing importance of access in competitive environments has been demonstrated in recent years by the efforts of many professionals to take their practices to prospective clients. Storefront law offices, in-store dental clinics, and minor emergency centers are examples of the trend.

Each of these facilities makes professional offices more accessible and convenient to clients or patients. Convenience involves a broader range of factors than access, however, and each of them deserves attention on the part of professionals examining alternative office locations. Convenience applies to paraprofessional and clerical staff members as well as patients and clients. It also may be of concern in context with colleagues and vendors. Professionals must balance the interests of all of these groups in terms of the economic interests of their own practices.

In many if not most professions, client or patient convenience is paramount. Staff convenience usually is the second factor to be considered. Proximity to colleagues and to a broad range of vendors also must be evaluated. Colleagues can be major sources of referrals and vendors can influence profitability through shortened delivery times.

Office sites and facilities require equal attention. Physical characteristics of sites, especially parking facilities, can be sources of difficulty to patients or clients. Professionals whose practices may involve the disabled also should be sensitive to the needs of those who are confined to wheelchairs or who use crutches.

Safety factors such as lighting and security services also can encourage or discourage enhanced patronage. So can availability of shelter in the event of inclement weather.

The nature of the several types of office buildings available in most communities also deserves attention. Each offers prospective advantages and disadvantages. Free-standing facilities often permit use of eye-catching signs, enhancing the visibility of the practice. At the same time, however, they also burden professionals with additional space requirements arising out of the absence of lobbies, public restrooms, and the like.

Parking conditions often appear more attractive in connection with free-standing buildings and office parks, but appearance and reality can be very different. The characteristics of nearby tenants' businesses or practices can cause shortages of parking spaces even where they appear to be in ample supply.

Perhaps nothing is more important from the standpoint of clients and patients, however, as the environments created by professionals within their office walls. Waiting rooms, consultation rooms, and private offices all should be designed with clients or patients in mind. Their sizes and furnishings should be specified accordingly. Thought should be given to such amenities as accessible telephones, refreshments, and the like, especially where the nature of the practice can produce unforeseen delays.

ADDITIONAL READING

Ackoff, Russell L. *Creating the Corporate Future*. New York: Wiley, 1981.

Block, Peter. *The Empowered Manager: Positive Political Skills at Work*. San Francisco: Jossey-Bass, 1987.

Cialdini, Robert B. *Influence: The New Psychology of Modern Persuasion*. New York: Quill, 1984.

Murphy, Robert D. *Mass Communication and Human Interaction*. Boston: Houghton Mifflin, 1977.

Weisbord, Marvin R. *Productive Workplaces: Organizing and Managing for Dignity, Meaning, and Community*. San Franscisco: Jossey-Bass, 1987.

8

The People Factor

Reputations earned by knowledge and skill are made productive for professionals by the behaviors of their subordinates. Successful professional practices require both elements; neither alone is sufficient. Paraprofessional and clerical personnel who staff the professional office personify practitioners in the eyes of clients and patients. Their actions and inactions are assumed to represent the wishes of the professional. If they are attentive, responsive, and sympathetic, professionals are assumed to be similarly disposed. If their behaviors suggest they are uncaring, unfeeling, and without understanding, opinion of the professional will move in that direction.

Office staffs, for these several reasons, are primary governors of the success of practice development programs. At worst, their behaviors destroy program effectiveness. At best, their commitments to the welfare of clients or patients as well as employers compound the benefits of practice development efforts.

Clients or patients readily can be made to believe, by performance, that professional organizations are truly committed to their welfare. The success of the practice development program is all but guaranteed when professionals insist that personnel behave accordingly.

Comfortable and convenient offices thus are necessary but insufficient to successful professional practice. Personnel skilled in handling people as well as clerical or paraprofessional tasks are essential. Clients or patients are relatively tolerant of inconvenience and minor discomfort. They are highly intolerant of cavalier treatment on the part of professionals' subordinates.

Professional knowledge and skill are probably less important to practice success than are staff behaviors. Reputations may be vital in recruitment of clients but dwindle in importance thereafter. Frequency and duration of clients' exposure to support personnel are almost always far greater than their exposure to professionals. Treatment received at the hands of these individuals, more than any other element, influences perceptions of and feelings toward the professional employers. Professionals' reputations, in other words, usually are the primary determinant in bringing patients or clients to the door. Paraprofessional and clerical behaviors determine how long they will stay.

THE ORGANIZATION TRAP

The typical professional practice, unfortunately, seldom is organized to reflect the reality described above. Productivity and efficiency almost invariably are primary criteria in hiring and rewarding staff members. These criteria usually are reflected in policies and procedures that encourage handling people and their problems in assembly-line fashion and as rapidly as possible. Human relationships become a secondary concern, if they are a concern at all. Anything that impedes the smooth functioning of the assembly line or interrupts professional routine is anathema.

Paraprofessional and clerical personnel long exposed to these conditions become practice liabilities rather than assets. They come to view clients and patients as products to be processed as quickly as possible. They see any departure from routine—even a question or a request for information—as an interruption to their routines or an imposition on the system.

Where patients or clients are viewed as intruding into otherwise smoothly operating practices, human problems grow at unprecedented rates. Telephones are answered brusquely. Questions are ignored. Professionals are "too busy to talk with you now" regardless of the nature of the call. Messages left for professionals may or may not be delivered promptly and accurately.

Behaviors of this sort once were generally tolerated by the clienteles of the best and the brightest practitioners in any profession. Idiosyncratic behavior also was more or less accepted as the price of excellence. Today's clients and patients are less tolerant. They expect to be treated with courtesy and respect. They are entitled to—and will accept—nothing less. Insuring that their expectations are met is one of the professional's primary responsibilities.

CREATING FRIENDLY ENVIRONMENTS

Professionals can assure optimal treatment of clients and patients in only one way: by obtaining total commitment to the welfare of the practice from every individual involved. Commitments of this sort can be obtained only by making the economic welfare of personnel as dependent on practice success as is that of the professionals involved. Interdependence, in other words, is the key to human resources management.

Interdependence is essential to assure practice success in competitive environments and in the face of natural tendencies toward self-serving conduct. The behaviors of paraprofessional and clerical personnel in professional practices, like those of every individual, are governed by two primary elements: self-interest and reward systems. Managerial failure to recognize and respond to these conditions has been responsible for many, if not most, of the economic problems suffered by organizations in recent years.

Productivity shortfalls that have plagued business and industry for the past decade and more are a direct result of systemic failures. Managers long have bemoaned their inability to induce greater productivity. At the same time, however, they have perpetuated management systems that reward attendance rather than performance. Their problems will persist until those systems are changed.

Reward systems should be designed to override self-interest, to induce behavior that serves the interests of the organization as well as the individual. Contemporary systems prevalent in the United States fall short of this objective. Close examination shows, in fact, that they are almost totally counterproductive.

Identical conditions prevail in professional offices. The size of professional practices, however, renders change easily accomplished. Paraprofessional and clerical personnel readily can be induced to perform in keeping with client needs if professionals carry out the following suggestions:

1. Establish reward systems based on individual and group productivity rather than on mere attendance.
2. Define productivity standards and assure that the standards are mutually understood.
3. Measure performance and assure that rewards are allocated accordingly.
4. Make every individual in the organization accountable for his or her performance and, more importantly, for the performance of his or her subordinates.

REWARD SYSTEMS

Functional reward systems are readily developed when professionals are willing to "share the wealth," when they are prepared to allocate predetermined percentages of *added* profits to the pocketbooks of those who create them. The concept involved is foreign to professional practices but has taken root rapidly in business and industry in recent years. Estimates compiled in 1988 indicate that performance-based compensation had already been introduced in some 25 percent of large businesses. Reward criteria vary radically with individual organizations, but the principles involved are readily applicable in professional practices.

Functional reward systems are based on a simple concept: substantial percentages of total worker compensation should be based on productivity. Employers seldom are resistant because of the mutual benefits that resulting systems afford. The process has come to be called gainsharing. Rewards increase only as worker performance improves. As performance improves, organizational productivity improves as well. Employers' commitments to reward systems thus involve nothing more than paying workers predetermined percentages of increased profits resulting from their efforts.

Design of performance-based compensation systems, as they often are called, is somewhat more complex but is readily accomplished. First, basic wage rates must be established for all positions, together with quantitative and qualitative definitions of work that must be performed to meet minimum acceptable performance levels. Second, accurate indicators of individual contribution to the economic health of the practice must be identified. Finally, rewards must be specified—and paid—for performance above minimum acceptable levels for each worker.

Basic Compensation

Traditional systematic approaches to compensating personnel seldom are applicable in professional practices. Most practices are too small to justify the time-consuming processes involved. The few large enough to use formal systems usually find them overly cumbersome. All compensation systems, however, must meet three criteria presumably met through formal systems. They must be fair, effective, and perceived as being both fair and effective by personnel. The first of the criteria usually are considered as having been met where compensation levels are comparable in three ways: among jobs within an organization, among similar jobs in different organizations, and for the same job within an organization.

Most organizations come to grips with the standards set out above in one of three ways. Some attempt to maintain compensation levels slightly above average. They assume this practice will enable them to recruit and retain higher caliber personnel. Others adopt a low wage strategy, accepting potentially high turnover rates in exchange for perceived savings in labor costs. Still others simply match the competition.

Performance-Based Systems

The alternative strategies described above are combined in performance-based compensation systems to accomplish two objectives. The first is to offer significant incentives for superior performance. The second is to abandon pay-for-attendance approaches to compensation in favor of pay for performance.

Weaknesses in traditional formal compensation systems are a product of their orientation toward attendance and seniority rather than performance and productivity. Most emulate the grade and step approach typified by the federal civil service system. The federal system categorizes workers by grade and advances them economically by seniority-oriented steps. The system proceeds on the basis of several tenuous assumptions. The first is a premise that all workers are alike. The second is that seniority can be equated with productivity. Few in business or industry would accept either assumption.

Compensation packages in performance-based systems consist of three components. The first is a base rate assigned on the basis of minimum acceptable performance for entry-level personnel. The second consists of one or more incremental supplements to the base rate granted during the first year of employment in recognition of experience-based improvement. The third is an incentive component based on individual employee performance.

Base rates. Basic compensation rates, regardless of strategies elected in calculating them, must be consistent in design. If management's philosophy is to pay slightly above going rates in order to obtain better candidates, for example, this approach should be used for all positions in establishing base or entry-level wage rates.

Where performance-based compensation systems are used, however, slightly below market base rates are often employed. Quality of candidates need not deteriorate as a result, provided only that performance incentives are clearly explained during preliminary interviews. These interviews also should serve to define for each candidate the minimum requirements of the job.

Every successful employer-employee relationship is based on mutual understanding of job requirements. No worker rationally can be expected to perform in keeping with organizational requirements unless those requirements are mutually understood when the worker is hired.

Automatic increments. New workers cannot be expected to meet minimum acceptable performance levels during the first days or weeks on the job. Considerable learning is usually required before workers are thoroughly familiar with practice procedures. In addition, qualitative performance standards usually must be conveyed by example rather than verbally. Words such as "clean" are necessarily ambiguous. Only supervisors or managers working with employees can tell them when their work meets the organization's definition of "clean."

Many employers recognize that workers become more proficient during their early months on the job if wages are raised at the end of probation periods. Raises usually are small, often bringing workers from below-market rates to prevailing rates for positions they hold. Nothing more is necessary. Some professional practices skip the end-of-probation increments in favor of higher starting wages.

Incentive compensation. The incentive component of the compensation system involves concepts that at first may provoke negative reactions among managers. They usually think better of the system, however, when they understand that it functions in much the same manner as commission systems popular in the sales field. No added compensation goes to workers until additional revenues already are in professionals' bank accounts.

Incentive compensation, however, should be open-ended. There should be no limits on what workers can earn. Remember, incentives are directly or indirectly linked to profits. Professionals necessarily earn more as staff compensation increases. After defining "minimum acceptable performance," employers need only specify qualitative and quantitative standards that must be met to earn additional rewards. The process, as will be discussed later, necessarily requires care. Professionals must be certain that increased productivity means greater profits, but that is seldom hard to accomplish.

Consider, for example, the architectural or engineering firm with three drafts-men or the medical practice with three laboratory workers. Where the performance of any two increases to the point at which the third becomes unnecessary, profits will increase even if compensation levels go up 50 percent. Owners of the practices would pocket the approximately 30 percent of salary that the typical employer today pays in fringe benefits.

Types of incentives. Incentive compensation in many cases can and should be offered to groups of workers rather than individuals. Group incentives, in fact, produce better results for professionals. They are especially helpful in situations where tasks are highly interrelated or where managers want to exert indirect pressure on laggards.

In a medical practice, for example, office staff members must work in close coordination to see that patients move swiftly through the office system. Clerical personnel, practical nurses, and registered nurses must work harmoniously to produce optimal results. Where group objectives are set and rewards are offered on an all-or-none basis, productive workers quickly drive out the nonproductive. Better workers' attitudes toward their colleagues seem to say, "We're going to get that bonus, and you can either grab an oar or get out of the boat." Peer pressure of that sort produces compliance more quickly than any direct intervention by superiors.

Timing of bonuses can and should be adjusted in keeping with the nature of workers involved. Most are granted on annual or semiannual bases. Where large numbers of clerical personnel are involved, quarterly bonuses may be preferable.

Additional benefits. Incentive-based systems also create major fringe benefits for employers while adding to the incomes of all involved. The benefits accrue in two areas. First, workers require significantly less supervision than otherwise would be the case. As a result, they enjoy relative freedom in achieving specified objectives, which in turn adds substantially to job satisfaction.,

Both of these factors produce salutary results. Reduced need for supervision is a natural outgrowth of the system. Workers who know what they must achieve are better equipped to accomplish their tasks than they otherwise would be. Professionals' administrative burdens decline as a result. Freedom to proceed on a self-starter basis enables workers to seek out for themselves the best ways to accomplish assigned tasks, creating a sense of accomplishment that psychologists have identified as essential to job satisfaction. Staff turnover can be expected to decline as a result.

Benefit-Based Systems

Incentives and satisfaction levels can be augmented when professionals also are willing to employ alternative benefit systems. Although to a limited extent, benefit systems can be structured to reward performance and to enhance economic results for workers and employers. Some benefits, such as unemployment compensation, are mandated by law. Most others, including vacations, sick leave, holiday pay, and insurance coverage, are another matter. Employers are free to provide benefits or cash. They often are better served by the latter than by the former.

Consider, for example, the rates of absenteeism and tardiness prevalent in the typical professional office. Sick leave too often is viewed by workers as the equivalent of vacation and is used accordingly. Abuse of this sort comes to a sudden halt when employers offer to pay in cash for all or a significant part of unused sick leave. Employers are creating such options in many organizations, making them work through formulas under which dollars saved are shared by workers involved.

DEFINING STANDARDS

While some benefits can vary with worker productivity, compensation is the primary component of performance-based systems. Workers functioning under these systems must be aware of employer requirements if they are to perform efficiently.

Managers and supervisors should be especially sensitive to the words, "but you never told me." Coming from an employee about to be terminated or disciplined, these words are incontestable evidence of managerial or supervisory error. Worker success in meeting organizational standards is governed by employer ability to precisely convey the meaning of job requirements. Misunderstanding, while perhaps in part the fault of a worker, is always the responsibility of a manager or supervisor.

Fulfilling the latter obligation is one of the major requirements of successful performance-based compensation systems. Employers seeking the benefits involved have no choice but to establish criteria by which performance can be measured. The system, in other words, requires that they address what often is the primary cause of worker failure, a condition more accurately described as managerial or supervisory failure.

Qualitative versus Quantitative

Worker performance criteria or standards must be expressed in two ways. The most obvious and least troublesome of them is quantitative: how much work must be done? Qualitative criteria are another matter. Rarely can professional practices substitute quantity for quality. Qualitative standards, however, are infinitely more difficult to define than their quantitative counterparts.

A maintenance worker, for example, can readily be told that he or she must clean one thousand square feet of corridor per hour to meet minimum standards. Defining the word "clean" is another matter. "Clean" means one thing in a drafting room, quite another in a surgical suite. The meaning can be accurately conveyed only where a supervisor can point to work successfully completed and declare, "That's what I mean by 'clean.'" Qualitative standards, in practical terms, must be demonstrated rather than merely expressed in words. Only where standards are demonstrated can supervisors safely assume that meanings have been accurately conveyed.

Quantitative requirements are more easily understood but nevertheless must be established with care. They should be logical and rational in the context of base wages and incentive compensation. Base wages should represent adequate compensation for minimum acceptable performance. Where base wages are low, minimum performance requirements should be comparable. Incentive compensation should begin at lower productivity rates. Where base wages are high, the reverse should be true.

Potential Pitfall

Job descriptions traditionally have been used by organizations to meet workers' needs for information concerning the requirements of their positions. These documents more often than not fail to accomplish desired results. Job descriptions are generic documents that list all tasks that may be assigned to any worker in a given category. Only rarely do they accurately reflect sets of tasks assigned by supervisors to individual workers.

Logic and supervisory discretion are responsible for mismatches between job descriptions and assigned tasks. Most workers function under what might better be called position descriptions. These consist of sets of tasks selected from those listed on the job description and assigned to individuals involved. Assignments are based on the contemporary needs of departments or other operating units and/or on worker knowledge and skill.

Mismatches between job descriptions and actual tasks occur most frequently when conscientious supervisors are involved. Their efforts toward productivity almost inevitably take into account differences in personnel. They recognize that skill and knowledge levels vary with individuals, that most workers perform some tasks better than others, and that most enjoy doing what they do best. Supervisors achieve highest possible productivity levels by assigning tasks accordingly, by permitting individuals to concentrate their efforts in areas in which they are most productive. The result, in any given situation, destroys the validity of job descriptions as bases for performance evaluation. Workers function under position descriptions defined by supervisors rather than under generic job descriptions. Their performance must be evaluated accordingly.

Basis for Evaluation

Since position descriptions are primary governors of worker assignments, they also must be the basis for worker evaluation. As such, they must be established as tasks are assigned rather than created on the eve of the evaluation process. The process imposes a burden, although a productive burden, on managers and supervisors. It requires that they examine their responsibilites in light of the talents and abilities of personnel assigned to them and that they allocate work accordingly.

The allocation process pays dividends by forcing managers and supervisors to better organize and delegate work. Tasks assigned to each worker readily can be defined, reduced to writing, and organized in order of importance during the assignment process. Resulting lists, on printed forms or unprinted sheets of paper, become position descriptions for workers involved. Position descriptions become the basis for initial communication and subsequent evaluation.

EVALUATING PERFORMANCE

Success or failure in performance evaluation—and in managing human resources in general—is a function of evaluator perspectives. Viewed and applied as an ongoing developmental process, evaluation brings continuing improvement in organizational productivity. Considered and used as an isolated, episodic process, evaluation at best contributes little to the organization. At worst, it engenders ill will, dissension, and employee turnover.

The evaluation process should contribute to achieving several organizational objectives. In order of importance from professionals' perspectives, evaluation should accomplish the following:

1. Improve organizational performance
2. Enhance individual performance
3. Insure equitable distribution of rewards

Process Steps

Performance evaluation thus is a multifaceted process that begins earlier than most consider to be the case. Managerial or supervisory decisions establishing position descriptions become the first step. Three others are essential, however, if performance evaluation is to be a constructive component of the management process.

First, position descriptions must be successfully communicated to personnel involved. Success here requires mutual understanding of assigned tasks as well as pertinent quantitative and qualitative standards.

Second, manager-worker understandings, as reflected in associated documentation, must be made the basis for subsequent evaluations.

Third, evaluations must lead to further understandings that in turn lead to subsequent evaluations. The process focuses equally on worker development and on rewards.

Performance evaluation thus is ongoing and cyclical in nature. The process also can and should be responsive to organizational and managerial needs. Task assignments are subject to change and, in most cases, change often as organizations respond to external pressures. Changes need not be troublesome as long as they are adequately explained to workers involved and made part of the performance evaluation system.

Evaluation forms in one of any number of formats are used where more formal systems are necessary. Perhaps most practical among them are forms printed on single 8 1/2–14–11-inch sheets and designed to be completed by supervisors prior to discussion with subordinates. The first of them is completed *when the worker is hired* and is used to establish, through discussion, mutually agreed bases for subsequent evaluation.

Evaluation forms of this type usually would include spaces or blocks in which immediate supervisors provide the following information:

1. Concise descriptions of each task together with quantitative and qualitative performance criteria.
2. Summary-ratings with point scales provided for supervisory use.
3. Supervisory comments, which must be both specific and constructive.
4. Interim review dates and notes as necessary.

Evaluations ideally are performed at six-month intervals. In each instance, supervisors complete evaluation forms in advance and discuss them with subordinates *before* they are made final and filed. Interviews focus primarily on techniques through which performance can be improved.

Each evaluation also permits supervisors to establish new performance criteria for the ensuing period. These may be elaborations of those previously used or wholly new criteria based in changing organizational and occupational needs.

Evaluation forms can be printed on one or both sides, depending on number of criteria to be specified. Criteria should be as few in number as practicable and, preferably, should relate directly to organizational and unit objectives. The latter linkage enables workers to better identify their roles and relate to the organization.

Most organizations attempt to establish and modify individual performance criteria not more than once a year. Interim performance appraisals then deal only with existing criteria. Annual appraisals generally are scheduled within 30 days of workers' anniversary dates. Interim sessions can be scheduled as deemed necessary by managers and supervisors.

Establishing Criteria

Forms used in performance evaluation are tools—nothing more, nothing less. They exist for only two purposes: to assist managers and supervisors in applying the process and to meet record-keeping requirements. Forms are containers for criteria and information by which employee performance is measured. Criteria must be established by managers or supervisors and must be defined in terms that insure mutual understanding.

Successful performance evaluation systems employ criteria developed in concert by workers and their supervisors. Supervisors in most cases develop tentative lists of workers' primary tasks for worker review. The two then meet to discuss the tasks and to establish criteria by which results can be measured. Care must be taken to insure that criteria are balanced to produce best results. Some necessarily emphasize speed and efficiency. These criteria must be counterbalanced, however, by others that focus on human values. Tasks or responsibilities incorporated into the evaluation process, in other words, should be equally divided between factors that influence the efficiency and productivity of the practice and those that influence patient and client perceptions of the practice. The bookkeeping department, for example, should be responsible not only for timely and accurate billing but for resolution of complaints on mutually acceptable bases. Professionals must collect monies owed to them without damaging the patient or client relationships on which ensuing months' revenues depend.

Performance measurement can be direct or indirect. Numbers of client contacts made by paraprofessional personnel can be counted, for example. The quality of those contacts and the extent to which clients are being satisfied can only be measured indirectly. Combinations of direct and indirect measurements are used to evaluate most workers.

Direct measurement. While usually most important in professional practices, qualitative factors are least amenable to direct measurement. The problem is compounded by the fact that the quality with which professionals are most often concerned can differ significantly from that perceived by clients or patients.

Consider, for example, the blood tests often conducted by paraprofessionals in medical practices. Where completed efficiently and accurately by personnel perceived as unfriendly or lacking in gentleness such tests can induce strongly negative patient responses. On the other hand, they may be carelessly performed by more caring technicians and be perceived as highly satisfactory.

Direct measurement of technician efficiency can be accomplished only by counting numbers of tests performed and, perhaps, by spot checking results. Patient responses, in contrast, can be judged directly only on those relatively rare occasions when patients compliment or complain. Indirect measurement thus becomes essential to adequate monitoring of technician performance.

Indirect measurement. Increasingly competitive circumstances make performance evaluation through direct indicators alone overly risky from the viewpoint of professionals. Highly efficient paraprofessional and clerical personnel literally can drive patients or clients away while meeting every technical performance standard.

These circumstances are leading more and more professionals to conduct regular patient or client satisfaction audits. Audits can focus on the humanity as well as the technical excellence of services the practice provides. They can assess client or patient reactions to receptionists as well as clerical and paraprofessional personnel. Perceptions of the convenience and comfort of professional offices also can be measured.

Audit data have two weaknesses, but neither are fatal to their use in performance evaluation. First, the data are indicators of overall impressions of practice personnel. Rarely will individual patients or clients be able to recall names. This apparent obstacle can be overcome by making audit results a factor in the evaluations of all personnel involved. Staff members in these circumstances have a strong tendency to police one another far more closely than would be the case with any manager or supervisor.

The second weakness in audit data results from people's tendency to more readily recall unpleasant than pleasant circumstances. Audit data, as a result, tend to show practice personnel in their worst light. The problem involved is readily overcome by conducting audits periodically and by evaluating personnel on degree of change between audits rather than on raw data generated by any single audit. Any efforts that induce improvement in patient or client perceptions between date A and date B is worthy of reward. Audit users also should keep in mind that further improvement between date B and date C will require still more effort on the part of those involved.

Changing criteria. Limited potential for further improvement, changing external conditions, or change in practice patterns often suggest changes in performance criteria. Such changes are to be expected and are readily made in keeping with guidelines outlined above. Most important among them is prior agreement between supervisor and worker as to criteria for measurement.

Changes in performance criteria most often result from changes in assigned duties. The mix of professional assignments in accounting and consulting firms, for example, can create expensive fluctuation in work loads. Sufficient work must be available to keep full-time personnel relatively busy throughout the year. Managers faced with these circumstances often change performance standards to shift practice development efforts toward those types of prospective clients that tend to generate off-peak assignments.

DISTRIBUTING REWARDS

Reward distribution is a critical component of performance-based compensation systems. The systems are designed to produce quantum change in traditional reward mechanisms. They must reward productive behaviors. To achieve productivity, as indicated earlier, organizations must reward productivity rather than attendance.

Professionals usually experience little difficulty in accepting the philosophy that underpins productivity-based systems. They often are confounded, however, by the mechanics of the process involved. They find it especially difficult to focus performance evaluation systems on practice components that, when changed, generate greater profits.

Difficulties are most readily overcome when professionals focus the performance evaluation system on sources of problems or profits. Practices necessarily become more productive as the first are eliminated and the second are strengthened. Each practice must be examined carefully, however, to determine how best to link outcomes to worker performance.

Worker behaviors that influence practice success are readily categorized. Each of them

1. generates profit or reduces expense,
2. can be measured quantitatively or qualitatively,
3. can be measured directly or indirectly, and
4. results from individual or collective behavior.

More important from professional perspectives, many if not most desired behaviors can be linked directly to practice profitability. To assure success, professionals need only be certain that most reward criteria are linked to behaviors known to generate profit or reduce expense.

Generating Profit

Profit in professional practices increases or declines in keeping with quantitative and qualitative variables. The primary quantitative variable is dollar revenue per unit of labor. In other words, profits necessarily increase with the productivity of paraprofessional and clerical personnel.

Productivity can be measured in several ways, none of them universally applicable in professional practices. Appropriateness in measurement devices varies primarily with the nature of professional compensation mechanisms. Some compensation systems are based on hourly rates. Others use fixed fees. Still others, as in the case of architects or engineers, may be expressed in percentages.

Where hourly rates are used, productivity of individual staff members is most often measured in numbers of hours for which they are paid that can in turn be billed to clients. Where fixed fees are applied, most professionals have calculated in advance the numbers of hours they expect to devote to projects involved. Productivity then can be based on comparisons of estimates and actual time expenditures. In professions using percentage compensation mechanisms, time used can be compared with practice or professional norms.

Calculating profit. In any of the circumstances described above, increased profits resulting from increased productivity are readily calculated: number of hours times hourly rate equals gross profit. Any number of hours billed in excess of established norms, any number of budgeted hours unused on a fixed fee project, and any number of hours used below norms on percentage fee projects all produce precisely measurable profit. Professionals need only decide what percentage of the increased profits should be allocated to reward those who create them.

The percentage should not be low. Every dollar saved in the circumstances described above goes directly to the bottom line. Overhead and other practice costs do not change. Human tendencies toward avarice must be controlled if the system is to continue to be productive. For most professionals, the primary question involved is a simple one: how many dollars are you willing to pay for each one hundred dollars in added net profit? The question must be answered in light of the fact that potential for continuation of increases in profits is governed directly by the level of rewards granted to those who produce them.

Indirect calculation. Increased profits are calculated with equal ease when productivity is a function of the combined efforts of multiple practice personnel. In the case of a medical or dental practice, for example, profit grows as the ratio of patients seen to staff hours expended increases. Incentive compensation thus can safely and logically be based on any growth in this ratio.

The same principle holds in any situation where hours of labor decline in relation to production of services that are billed to clients or patients. Increases in unit production on the part of medical or dental laboratories or radiology facilities, for example, necessarily produce greater profits. Since nonlabor overhead increases in the process, net profit is somewhat lower than where only labor is involved, but nevertheless it should be amenable to easy calculation.

When groups of workers are involved, as often is the case in laboratories and other more or less self-contained functional units, potential for increased profit can be compounded if those involved are permitted to control internal operations. Given latitude in such areas as personnel scheduling and work flow management, laboratory staffs often can produce more work at lower cost than professionals ever had believed possible.

Incentives in these circumstances must be managed on a group basis. Given equitable basic compensation rates, incentives usually can be allocated fairly on percentage bases in small group situations. In larger groups, immediate supervisors should control allocation of rewards. Fair, equitable allocation of rewards is essential to continued systemic success.

Reducing Expenses

While profits arising out of increased productivity may vary from one situation to another, savings in expenses always create equivalent increases in profit. Reductions in expense reduce overhead costs. Since net profit equals gross profit less overhead, the results are direct and obvious.

Other than those that may be passed along to clients, expenses in professional practices occur in two primary areas: materials and time. Materials are supply items that may be handled carefully or carelessly by personnel. Time involves minutes lost or wasted in the course of a day or week by personnel who are not accountable for results of their efforts.

Wasted time. Most time wasted in a typical professional office occurs in the form of late arrivals and early departures at the beginning and end of the day and during lunch and break periods. The problem is made worse by abuse of attendance and sick leave policies. Combined losses contribute to what some have estimated to be an average loss of 40 percent of the typical worker's time each year.

Tendencies to waste time are discouraged among most personnel by productivity-based incentives described above. They can be almost eliminated by changing benefit programs to create incentives for attendance rather than absence.

Wasted materials. Cost of wasted materials is a variable across professional practices. Supplies used in medical, dental, and optometric practices, for example, are more expensive than those used in architecture, engineering, advertising, and public relations.

Savings are most easily calculated on a per patient or per client basis. Dividing the average number of clients served per month into total supply expenditures will produce a valid indicator of savings. Control is most readily accomplished by allocating a portion of prospective savings to bonuses for personnel who handle supplies.

ESTABLISHING CONTROLS

Control is an especially critical factor in medium- to large-size practices where professionals delegate significant responsibility to managerial and supervisory personnel. In any organization, but especially in professional firms, managers and supervisors potentially are a major obstacle to success. Seldom are they adequately educated or trained in management. Most are senior personnel who have been promoted to positions of responsibility as a result of extensive experience. That experience seldom adequately equips them for management roles.

Absence of necessary knowledge and skill often results in abdication of responsibility. Management expectations are inadequately defined. Personnel are permitted to function with little direction. Performance appraisal and reward systems almost inevitably malfunction.

Failures in the latter areas are a natural result of human tendencies to avoid confrontation, which is likely to develop when worker deficiencies must be discussed. Avoidance of confrontation usually results at best in generally favorable and approximately equal performance appraisal reports for all personnel. At worst, favoritism may creep in to further distort the process.

Failure in performance appraisal destroys any potential for effective productivity-based compensation programs. Workers quickly perceive that performance is not rewarded and revert to traditional responses. They do little more than enough to prevent being fired.

These conditions can be avoided in only one way: by holding managers and supervisors accountable for the performance of those they supervise. Accountability is best imposed by making managerial and supervisory rewards a function of worker performance. When this is the case, multiple benefits accrue.

First, performance appraisal and reward systems are applied as designed to encourage subordinate performance.

Second, tendencies toward discriminatory conduct quickly disappear. Any such behavior would discourage worker productivity and, in the process, would erode supervisory economic potential.

Third, and perhaps most important, accountability requires professionals or senior managers to apply the same performance appraisal and reward systems to their immediate subordinates as are applied to rank-and-file personnel. They must develop position descriptions and performance standards to guide productive behavior and then reward productivity.

Performance-based compensation systems in this manner can and should be applied at every organizational level. Accountability for results requires that every superior first inform every subordinate of performance expectations and allocate rewards accordingly.

The nature of the system controls the reward mechanism to a point at which it can be safely delegated to subordinates. Individuals' rewards are established by their superiors, who also earmark lump sums that subordinates use in rewarding their subordinates. Accountability, in other words, creates an unparalleled economic interdependence among members of the organization. The point involved was perhaps best made rather crudely by a senior human resources executive: "When you've got them by the pocketbooks, their hearts and minds will follow."

IN SUMMARY

Professional proficiency is the primary attribute that attracts clients or patients to professional practices. The human relations skills of practice personnel, however, are at least equally important in retaining their patronage, since typical clients or patients experience more person-to-person contact with paraprofessional and clerical personnel than with the professionals who first attracted them. Professionals' preoccupation with the technical aspects of the services they offer nevertheless often leads them to neglect the all-important behavioral patterns of their personnel.

Responsiveness to client or patient needs on the part of practice personnel can be assured in only one way: by linking the economic welfare of those involved to the performance of the practice. Professionals can be certain that their personnel will behave in keeping with the needs of the practice, in other words, only to the extent that those workers are equally dependent on the success of the practice.

Interdependency can best be assured through use of performance-based compensation systems. Such systems have become increasingly popular in business and industry in recent years and are equally applicable in professional practices. They are most successful where

1. rewards are based on individual and/or group productivity rather than on attendance,

2. productivity standards are clearly defined and mutually understood by all involved,

3. performance is measured in keeping with defined standards and rewards are allocated accordingly, and

4. every individual in the organization is accountable for his or her performance and the performance of his or her subordinates.

Reward systems are most productive when much of individual workers' compensation is based on performance and provided as bonuses rather than as wages. Many successful professionals divide compensation into three components: basic salary for entry level workers, small increments in recognition of early increases in efficiency gained through experience, and periodic bonuses based on organizational productivity. Incentive or bonus compensation may be granted to workers individually or on a group basis, depending on the nature of their work.

To best serve professionals' needs, benefits must be linked directly to performance. These circumstances require that performance standards be precisely defined in qualitative and quantitative terms. Workers must understand the meaning of "minimum acceptable performance" on which wages are based as well as the extent to which superior performance will be rewarded.

Understanding is easily achieved when employers substitute position descriptions, consisting of sets of tasks assigned to specific workers, for more generic job descriptions. Specific requirements then can be attached to assigned tasks to provide precise guidance for all involved. Precise definition also renders evaluation processes more productive for individuals as well as the organization by assuring equitable distribution of rewards.

Worker success in meeting performance criteria can be measured directly or indirectly. Direct measurement usually serves well where quantitative factors are involved but indirect approaches often are necessary where qualitative criteria are to be measured. Criteria may be changed from time to time in keeping with the needs of the practice but must be balanced to insure appropriate results. Criteria dealing with volume of work, for example, should be counterbalanced with qualitative standards. Formal research procedures such as practice audits often are used to assess patient or client perceptions.

In general, performance standards should be (*a*) designed to generate profit or reduce expense, (*b*) amenable to quantitative and/or qualitative measurement, (*c*) subject to direct or indirect measurement, and (*d*) be controllable through individual or collective behavior. In most cases, improvement in performance criteria should influence practice profits. Professionals then need only assign portions of realized profits to reward the efforts of those whose efforts produce the improvements involved.

Control of performance-based compensation systems is necessary to assure that rewards are appropriately allocated and desired results are achieved. These conditions are most easily met where managerial and supervisory personnel are held accountable for the performance of their subordinates and rewarded accordingly. Accountability of this sort insures that the economic rewards of every member of the organization are linked directly to organizational success.

ADDITIONAL READING

Dowling, William F., Jr., and Leonard R. Sayles. *How Managers Motivate: The Imperatives of Supervision*. New York: McGraw-Hill, 1971.

Hall, Richard. *Dimensions of Work*. Beverly Hills, Calif.: Sage, 1986.

Macarov, David. *Worker Productivity: Myths and Reality*. Beverly Hills, Calif.: Sage, 1982.

McCaffery, Robert M. *Managing the Employee Benefits Program*. New York: American Management Association, 1972.

Miner, John B. *People Problems: The Executive Answer Book*. New York: Random House, 1985.

Morgan, Gareth. *Images of Organization*. Beverly Hills, Calif.: Sage, 1986.

Weiss, Carol H., and Allen H. Barton, ed. *Making Bureaucracies Work*. Beverly Hills, Calif.: Sage, 1980.

Wetmore, Edward Jay. *Mediamerica: Form, Content, and Consequence of Mass Communication*. 3rd ed. Belmont, Calif.: Wadsworth, 1987.

9

Employee Communication

"Inside-out" communication logically begins with the innermost and most volatile groups with which professionals are concerned: their personnel. Paraprofessional and clerical personnel should be practitioners' first targets because their behaviors strongly influence client and patient satisfaction. Few service organizations fail when clients are satisfied with their services. Few experience lasting success if their services are deemed inadequate.

The critical importance of employee-employer relationships dictates pertinent professional behaviors and content of associated communication programs. A few basic principles are applicable to both. Two are most important among them: honesty and equity. Successful employee-employer relationships are based on mutual understanding and are created for mutual benefit. Understanding is vital to the usually unwritten social contracts that underlie employment situations. Benefits must accrue to both parties.

The latter principles at first appear so basic as to require no elaboration. Appearances are more than a little deceiving. Stripped of mythological facades, occupational environments have been essentially exploitative rather than mutually beneficial for decades. With few notable exceptions, any semblance of equity found in employer-employee transactions has been a product of legislation rather than of fairness.

These conditions are becoming increasingly troublesome in the typical professional office. *Typical* here refers not to the megapractices of metropolitan America but to individual and small group situations found across the nation. Other than under unusual competitive compulsion, theirs has been a paternalistic world, with all of the weaknesses the word implies. "Father knows best" cultures are not readily changed. More and more are yielding, however, to the economic pressures that also encourage professional development programs. As practice cultures become more collegial, and gainsharing becomes the primary economic model, communication processes tend to change as well.

Change may be too mild a word to describe contemporary developments in internal communication in professional practices. Elaborate communication systems are being installed where communication earlier had been all but non-existent. Patterns vary with professions and practice sizes, but five basic communication techniques are almost universally involved.

The five techniques embody the primary methods through which human beings communicate individually and in groups. They are behavioral, interpersonal, electronic, print, and hybrid. All are applicable in employee communication. One is essential.

The essential one is the behavioral technique. Professionals' behavioral characteristics and the nature of organizations they create transmit messages to practice personnel as efficiently as to other groups. The behavioral messages involved support or contradict those transmitted interpersonally or through other communication channels. Consistency in messages is vital if the objectives of communication are to be achieved.

FOCUSING ON OBJECTIVES

Consistency requires more than is readily apparent. Communication long has been narrowly viewed as transfer of information. The process has been seen as involving a sender, a receiver, a message, and a channel of communication. Communication was considered accomplished when messages were successfully delivered, when they were received or understood.

Two major changes in this construct have occurred in recent years. First, the process has come to be viewed more broadly than earlier had been the case. Individuals and organizations alike now are perceived to be "making a statement" in the way they decorate homes or offices, in the way they dress, and even in the types of vehicles they drive. Second, the objective of the communication process has been restated. Effectiveness in communication now is viewed in behavioral terms and measured in the level of response the process evokes among intended message recipients.

Breadth of Communication

Effectiveness in communication requires attention to all the ways in which the process is carried out. Environmental factors, ranging from the neighborhoods and structures in which professional practices are maintained to the nature of offices involved, have been addressed in earlier chapters. These attributes or characteristics of the practice speak as loudly as any other.

Behaviors communicate even more strongly, for better or worse. Messages involved may be affirmative or negative, intended or unintended. They are transmitted with or without the conscious approval of professionals. The messages may contribute to or detract from the effectiveness of more formal communication efforts.

The content of environmental and behavioral communication may or may not be consistent with messages transmitted through interpersonal or other channels. Consistency magnifies the impact of all messages involved, while inconsistency produces the opposite result.

Successful Communication

Level of consistency is a governor of communication success. Those who doubt need only refer to their own everyday experiences in such mundane areas as shopping. Consumer research indicates that any inconsistency in consumer perceptions of product-related messages impedes decision-making processes. It takes only one negative comment, in other words, to make most individuals hesitate.

The same conditions prevail in consumers' decisions concerning professional relationships. Strength of reputation can be viewed as the sum of everything prospective clients or patients have heard about the practitioner and the practice. *Heard* here refers to knowledge of neighborhoods in which practices are situated as well as comments originating with friends or mass media.

BEHAVIORAL COMMUNICATION

Consistency is especially important in behavioral communication, a process at least as effective in dealing with practice personnel as with existing or prospective clients. Behavioral communication refers to the behaviors of professionals and the manner in which those behaviors influence their organizations.

Organizations are influenced by three sets of messages. One set consists of the behavior of professionals in dealing with subordinates as well as with patients or clients. Another encompasses the office environments professionals create and the messages those environments convey to all exposed to them. The third consists of verbal and written messages delivered to personnel and others.

In each case, behavioral communication with personnel involves greater constructive or destructive potential than communication with any other group. Professional practices for the most part are small, close-knit organizations. The nature of their "outputs," unlike those in manufacturing or distribution, permits them to operate in relatively confined spaces. Their productivity is more a function of the abilities of all involved to work harmoniously together than of any other factors.

Professional Behaviors

The manner in which professionals treat their personnel, individually and as groups, sets the tone for their organizations in much the same manner that a tuning fork sounds a tone for an orchestra. Consciously or unconsciously, practitioners are role models for their organizations. Consciously or unconsciously, their behaviors are emulated by subordinates. When professionals' policies are designed to make paraprofessional and clerical personnel feel a part of organizations, those involved are apt to make similar efforts toward clients or patients. Professionals' concerns over the welfare of their associates, as expressed in such diverse areas as office environments and reward systems, tend to produce similar predispositions among workers. They become more concerned over their employers and the patients and clients with whom they deal.

Emulation can create as many problems as benefits in professional organizations, however, for two reasons. First, practitioners often are few in number in relation to paraprofessional and clerical personnel. Any unfortunate example thus is followed by disproportionate numbers of subordinates. Second, professionals traditionally have been installed as near-deities in their disciplines. To the extent that this syndrome persists, it encourages subordinates to follow blindly in the footprints of their mentors.

Problem scope. The scope of the problem is greater than many professionals perceive to be the case. A number of damaging circumstances can arise out of professionals' unthinking behavior in dealing with personnel.

Consider just a few examples. When practitioners gossip about clients and patients among themselves, subordinates feel free to do likewise, perhaps outside the office as well as within its walls. Where personnel are treated with rudeness and discourtesy, they are far more prone to similar behavior in dealing with clients or patients. Where professionals are dilatory in responding to telephone calls and letters, the same tendencies usually will develop on the part of others in their organizations.

The list could go on at length. Professionals who are careless or uncaring in any respect should expect no better behavior from those around them. The contrary, in fact, is apt to occur. Research has demonstrated that those who are—or who feel—abused are likely to be similarly abusive to those with whom they deal. It is precisely this mechanism, in fact, that tends to make social misfits of abused children.

The reverse, however, is equally true. Workers made to feel a part of the organizations that employ them reciprocate by acting and speaking in support of those organizations. The benefits of "psychic ownership," in other words, are very real. They are readily obtained, moreover, when professionals recognize that practice success is composed of individual successes on the part of every member of the organization. Practice reward systems then need only be structured to equitably and consistently distribute the rewards of success.

Consistency necessary. Consistent behaviors are necessary if professional practices are to grow and prosper with the support of their personnel. Consistency must exist, in fact, in two respects. It must apply across as well as within groups.

Consistency across groups means that behaviors directed toward personnel must match those directed to outsiders. Both must be treated with dignity and respect. Professionals otherwise risk having personnel visit on patients or clients the same treatment they receive from superiors.

Consistency within groups means that signals professionals may send behaviorally must match those transmitted by policy, procedure, or otherwise. Inconsistency within groups produces conflict, uncertainty, and inefficiency.

Conflict across groups usually is considerably more destructive. Consider, for example, the professional who treats patients or clients with the utmost respect while dealing abusively with personnel. As differences of this sort become known in the community—as inevitably is the case—practices necessarily suffer. The principle involved is a simple one. Personnel in many ways serve as "two-legged billboards" for professionals who employ them. The messages they transmit are shaped more by the behaviors than by the words of their employers.

Office Environments

The nature of office environments—internal and external—in a sense are extensions of professionals' behaviors. These environments are viewed by personnel as having been deliberately shaped, for better or worse, by their employers.

This perspective may be somewhat extreme in the case of external environments. Practitioner control over the buildings in which they practice and in the surroundings of those buildings is quite limited. Professionals exercise direct control, however, over the internal environments. They usually are responsible for the design of their offices and for the equipment they contain.

External factors. Workers' concerns with the external environments of the offices in which they work arise primarily in two areas: safety and convenience. Safety especially is a source of concern where much of the office staff is female, the neighborhood is less than wholly desirable, and office hours begin or end during hours of darkness. Convenience is a related factor of most concern in connection with distances between parking areas and office buildings.

Employers can eliminate workers' concerns to a substantial extent by taking all practical steps to assure their safety and convenience. Close-in parking occasionally can be found or made available through employer efforts more readily than is the case when workers are required to negotiate individually. Security services also can be provided if workers are required to arrive early or depart late for professionals' convenience.

Visible effort in each of these areas ultimately may be more important than tangible results. Effort implies concern for worker welfare, even when no good solutions are available. Effort usually is accepted at face value if internal environments also attest to employer sincerity.

Internal factors. Worker and employer concerns logically should be identical concerning internal environments. Supportive environments contribute to optimum productivity. Where environments detract from worker efforts, the reverse is equally true. In either case, two factors are primarily involved: office attributes and equipment characteristics.

Office attributes include temperature, ventilation, lighting, and sound levels that should be controlled for maximum comfort. Equipment characteristics include furnishings and production equipment that can add to or detract from worker efforts.

This book, for example, was written on a computer equipped with a larger-than-normal monitor mounted on an adjustable base. The fourteen-inch screen (as opposed to the traditional twelve-inch model) showed all characters in slightly larger form than otherwise would have been the case. The adjustable base permitted the screen to be angled downward so as not to reflect light from a nearby window. Difference in cost between this and the least expensive unit available was less than thirty dollars.

Expenditures of a few dollars or several hundred dollars per employee to insure maximum comfort produces disproportionate returns for professionals. First, such efforts enhance productivity. More important, they serve as constant reminders to individuals involved that "the boss really cares."

Demonstrated caring, then, should be the primary objective of behavioral communication. Actions involved speak louder than any words that may be conveyed to workers through interpersonal or mediated communication. No misleading statement or commitment, no matter how strongly expressed, withstands the test of behavior over time. Affirmative behavior creates the credibility that controls the effectiveness of all other forms of communication. Negative behavior produces the opposite result.

INTERPERSONAL COMMUNICATION

Behavior is a significant component of interpersonal communication. The relative strength of the process in comparison with other forms of communication is created by personal delivery of words involved. Recipients are able to weigh speakers' inflections, read their body language, and otherwise form far more accurate opinions as to levels of honesty and sincerity supporting the statements involved.

Interpersonal communication is approached in comprehensive fashion only rarely in dealing with professional practice personnel. Most employers seldom think beyond traditional small group meetings in considering use of interpersonal techniques to enhance organizational productivity. Much more can and should be done.

Interpersonal communication in professional practices is divisible into several broad categories, most of them readily identified in chronological fashion. One consists of those interviews, formal or informal, that accompany the preemployment and employment processes. Another encompasses communication that occurs in the course of performance appraisal processes. Group meetings and casual day-to-day communication also can be considered separate categories.

Each creates opportunities to enhance or detract from the vital relationships involved.

Employment Processes

Major pitfalls in interpersonal communication involved in the employment process arise out of human frailties that usually afflict prospective employers and their employees. First, there is a tendency on both sides to oversell, to make the product more attractive than realistically is the case. Second, once tentative agreement has been reached, the parties tend to gloss over any negatives in order to "close the sale."

As pools of available manpower become smaller through the remainder of the twentieth century, tendencies to oversell will become progressively more dangerous. This especially will be the case among prospective employers seeking to attract personnel in highly competitive markets.

Gilding the lily. The oversell process traditionally begins with "help wanted" advertising that often is highly misleading. Competition in phraseology produces the sort of hyperbole that presents entry-level jobs with little potential for advancement as "career opportunities."

These conditions probably will grow more dangerous with the passage of time. The courts already are interpreting the content of organizational personnel policies as creating contracts between workers and employers. Only one small step would be necessary to produce judicial recognition of the content of help wanted advertising as contractual in nature.

Problem potential will remain high, however, whether or not these circumstances develop. Workers hired for "career positions" only to find themselves in dead-end jobs seldom become productive organization members.

Interview process. Avoiding these pitfalls requires special care in the conduct of interviews during the hiring process. Interviews or parts of interviews fall into two categories. The first involves selling on both sides. Prospective employers are selling the merits of their organizations and their jobs. Prospective employees are selling themselves. (Overtly misleading claims during the interview process have been more dangerous in the late 1980s than the content of advertising has been, especially on the part of employers. The courts have made significant progress toward redefining employee-employer relationships as contracts and toward granting employees vested interest in their jobs.)

Potential legal problems readily can be overcome during second interviews, or second parts of initial interviews. At this point, general agreement has been reached and the parties are attempting to "close the sale." The process *must* be made to yield mutual understanding. Workers must know precisely what is expected of them and what they can expect in return.

Performance Appraisal

Mutual understanding is critical to performance appraisal. The appraisal process is designed to (*a*) measure what has been accomplished, (*b*) produce a valid basis for rewards, and (*c*) provide guidance to induce greater productivity and justify still greater reward. It will produce desired results only if job requirements are mutually understood.

Understanding ideally can be reached during interviews. Otherwise, it must be accomplished belatedly during initial performance appraisals. Workers and employers both suffer as a result of any delay. Employers lose in terms of productivity. Workers lose in subsequent rewards. Both consequences can be avoided if quantitative and qualitative performance standards are agreed upon during initial interviews.

Establishing standards. Quantitative and qualitative standards are based on specific tasks assigned to workers. Major tasks consequently must be discussed by workers and their immediate superiors. Minimum acceptable performance levels must be specified, and workers must be made aware of performance levels at which rewards will increase.

Quantitative standards usually are more readily communicated to workers. They establish the volume or quantity of work that must be accomplished to achieve minimum acceptable performance. Qualitative standards are more difficult to convey. Supervisors often find it necessary to demonstrate or otherwise provide examples of quality levels that meet organizational requirements.

Appraising performance. Establishing standards is necessarily time-consuming. The investment involved pays off, however, when performance appraisal begins. When standards have been clearly defined at the outset, appraisal becomes a process of mutual assistance in which workers and supervisors *together* attack problems for *mutual* benefit.

Performance-based compensation systems induce this result because they impose accountability on managers and supervisors for the performance of their subordinates (see chapter 3). The mechanism involved is simple but effective. Managerial and supervisory rewards are based on collective subordinate performance. Senior managers thus are assured that their immediate subordinates are working consistently to improve performance.

Group Meetings

Functional appraisal and performance-based compensation systems also enable managers to produce improved results when using other forms of interpersonal communication. Two factors are involved. One is the nature of the systems themselves. They motivate workers.

The second factor is far more important from a communication standpoint. Performance-based compensation and appraisal systems clear communication channels that otherwise can become "clogged" in much the same manner that floating debris can collect in a stream.

Motivation and communication. The motivational element inherent in performance-based compensation is quite simple. The system creates circumstances in which managers and supervisors succeed or fail with their workers. Neither can win without the other.

These conditions arise out of the accountability mechanism described earlier. When managerial and supervisory performance is judged by measuring worker output, linkages involved immediately become as clear as they are inescapable.

These linkages quickly make it apparent to the parties that game playing in any form is counterproductive for all involved. Favoritism on the part of superiors and malingering on the part of subordinates become equally unacceptable to those who otherwise might be tempted in these directions.

Channel clearing. The process essentially neutralizes any temptation to sacrifice the interests of colleagues or the organization for personal advantage. Concurrently, and more importantly, it eliminates in all eyes the possibility that others might be pursuing personal advantage to the detriment of the group.

Requests of any sort made of any individual under these conditions bring more rapid and affirmative response than otherwise would be the case. Instructions are more readily followed, assistance is more quickly given, attention to the needs of others is enhanced. Communication channels are clear because those to whom messages are directed want to receive, understand, and respond.

Group efficiency. Attitudes involved are more readily evident in group communication than in most other situations. Problems brought to groups for attention are approached positively rather than with reluctance. "Turf problems" involving individuals and groups are readily disposed of in the interests of mutual productivity.

Moreover, and perhaps most important, the spirit of mutuality that arises within the organization also strengthens impersonal communication vehicles. Messages packaged in printed or electronic form produce more rapid and more affirmative responses because all parties are predisposed toward the affirmative. Recipient knowledge that message senders are pursuing no hidden or manipulative agendas destroys barriers that otherwise all too readily arise.

The system essentially minimizes group and individual insecurities that too often can be removed only through interpersonal communication or over extended periods of time. Need for consistent reassurance is eliminated when parties to communication processes have confidence in one another. All involved are quick to recognize that some messages are more readily transmitted in printed or electronic forms and that communication processes become more efficient as a result. They also recognize that efficiency contributes to the productivity that all are seeking and, as a result, more readily accept the limitations inherent in mediated communication.

ALTERNATIVE CHANNELS

Mediated communication supplants or supplements interpersonal communication in any of several sets of circumstances. In general, print or electronic channels increase in use with audience size and geographic dispersal. These changes also are used in support of interpersonal communication and in a number of special circumstances.

Printed forms of communication usually are employed when information involved must be available for future reference, when precise understanding is necessary, and when the transfer of knowledge rather than skill is involved. Electronic communication is more prevalent when messages are intended to motivate rather than inform and when content is designed to assist in acquisition of mechanical skills.

Printed Communication

The nature of employer-employee relationships usually brings workers first into contact with printed information and only later with the electronically-delivered variety. Members of organizations are first introduced to organizational messages in printed form early in the employment process. Many will have been attracted by advertising or other recruiting materials. All ultimately will be exposed to job descriptions, personnel manuals, policy and procedure manuals, and a host of other documents. Once inside the organization, employees are exposed to a broad range of printed material. Most organizations use memoranda, letters, bulletin board postings, and newsletters of various kinds to communicate with personnel.

Effectiveness in printed communication varies with several factors. Some are message-related, while others involve audience characteristics. Most important among message-related factors are source credibility and content consistency. Age and educational level are the primary audience characteristics with which communicators should be concerned.

Message-related factors. Source credibility refers to variation in confidence levels among audiences confronted with different speakers or message sources. Workers are prone to accept information from individuals or organizations only to the extent that those involved have demonstrated their reliability.

Credibility is produced by reliability. A history of messages supported by subsequent behavior, of promises met through later action, creates credibility. In organizations, credibility also is partly a function of consistency in message content. Credibility increases where messages are consistent across sources and communication channels. The reverse is equally true.

Audience-related factors. The extent to which credibility is created by any communication channel or group of channels also is controlled to some extent by audience characteristics. A number of indicators of relative effectiveness are often available. They include but are not limited to age, occupation, and educational level.

Age is a factor because television has produced generations of individuals progressively more conditioned and receptive to electronic communication. The extent to which younger age groups may be predisposed toward videotape, motion pictures, and slide-tape presentations may be modified, however, through prior exposure to printed communication.

Exposure to printed materials varies to some extent with occupation and substantially with educational level. Level of acceptance to information in printed form necessarily varies with prior exposure.

Variety in Application

Use of the alternative communication techniques should be governed by organizational need and audience characteristics in combination. Personnel policies and procedures should be reduced to writing, for example, even if first conveyed verbally or, in the case of larger organizations, by videotape. Other than where legalities are involved, written or printed materials prove most useful if the information they contain must be readily available for reference. Electronic records are more difficult to handle.

Success in applying communication channels also varies, however, with process objectives. Printed and verbal forms usually are relatively efficient where knowledge is to be transferred. Electronic and verbal channels have proven superior in conveying skill-related information and in motivating message recipients.

Written records with dates of issue and revision are essential in maintaining protective "paper trails" in a litigious society. This means that almost every organization must maintain appropriate documentation. Documentation need not be elaborate. Mimeographed sheets serve as well as printed brochures or booklets in meeting legal requirements. Videotape might serve as well, but the nation's traditionalist legal system has a predilection toward paper, and videotape is more readily tampered with than is paper.

Electronic Communication

Most individuals think first of videotape when electronic communication is mentioned because of the intense television orientation of today's society. Closer examination of electronic media use in contemporary organizations suggests, however, that videotape is far from being the only significant medium.

Use of electronic channels in employee communication once was largely limited, other than in very large organizations, to unsophisticated slide-tape presentations. Rapid advances in technology in recent years have produced much different circumstances. New technologies, and improvements in those earlier in use, are becoming common in organizations of all sizes. Potential value in all cases is limited, however, by the same content constraints that apply in the print area.

Improved technologies. Improvement has been greatest in the audiovisual sector. Where slide-tape and motion picture presentations once dominated quantitatively and qualitatively, respectively, videotape has become the primary medium. Since its introduction in commercial television production several decades ago, videotape equipment has improved in sophistication and has declined in price to the point that it is within reach of virtually every organization.

Videotape is most often used in two applications, one well established and the other relatively new. Teaching is the well-established application. From orientation programs to on-the-job training, videotape has become the medium of choice. The new application involves using video equipment in personnel development programs, especially in service industries. Development programs most often deal with human relations skills and frequently involve use of videotape equipment to enable individual employees to see themselves as others see them and to improve performance accordingly.

Ease in duplication also permits inexpensive use of videotape in delivering complex messages to multiple locations. Chief executives' annual messages, detailed descriptions of new procedures, and similar information often can be more efficiently and economically disseminated in this way than in any other manner.

New technologies. Duplication and distribution of videotape can be improved upon through one of the newer technologies, but only at considerable cost. Satellite-based videoconferencing occasionally is used nationally and internationally by large organizations such as Federal Express Corporation to keep personnel apprised of organizational progress.

Other relatively new technologies are more often used, however, in professional practices of all sizes. Most involve computers, and many link computers together through telephone lines or intraorganizational networks.

The several forms of telecommunication, ranging from conventional telephones in their several applications to networked and modem-equipped computers, have become progressively more pervasive. Improvements in computer technology permit their inexpensive use as employee bulletin boards and in interoffice mail systems. These systems readily can be extended to encompass multiple locations through use of modems and appropriate software programs. More sophisticated computers linked to satellite transmission systems permit international distribution of words and illustrations on a nearly instantaneous basis for broadcast to entire populations.

National and international organizations such as the 3M Company have long maintained sophisticated data banks or bulletin board systems for internal and external use. Codes are provided to news media representatives, for example, to give them access to those portions of the system dedicated to news, new product releases, and other public information. Multiple data libraries are available to personnel in keeping with their positions within the organization. Bulletin boards also provide immediate access to current information for all members of the organization anywhere in the world regardless of time zone differences.

Rapidly improving technical capabilities in microcomputers during the 1980s also spawned a new breed of printed products generated through what has come to be called desktop publishing. The desktop publishing process enables firms or individuals to combine what once were four functions in the writing and printing process into a single step. Writing, layout, typesetting, and composition now can be carried out by the same person on a computer screen in a minimum of time. Electronic files then can be printed by laser printer in a form suitable for duplication by copying machine or printing press.

BENEFITS AND DRAWBACKS

Collectively, the new technologies have created benefits and problems for every professional. They have made most tasks easier than ever before. Computer-assisted design, for example, has multiplied the capabilities of architects, engineers, and designers beyond what once were the limits of human capabilities. Computers permit attorneys to conduct research from their desks. Patient and client records are more easily maintained by computer than in any other form. Computers enable every professional to better maintain billing records and to more easily prepare monthly statements.

At the same time, however, the new technologies have created communication problems. Ease of communication has induced more communication. With the exception of daily newspapers, numbers of mass media continue to grow at an unprecedented rate. Technology has made every organization a video producer, a desktop publisher, or both. The efforts of the novices involved can readily produce ineffectiveness or worse.

Communication necessarily becomes ineffective or unproductive where communicators fail to deliver messages to intended audiences. Breakdowns in delivery systems probably are the most common causes of communication failure. Most occur for one of two reasons. Messages either are not received by intended recipients or are ignored or neglected by those involved.

Nondelivery of messages results from breakdowns in communication channels, as in the case of undelivered memos or letters, speeches unheard, or bulletin board postings unheeded. Nondelivery is relatively rare in organizational communication. Employees are readily identified. Most appear regularly on employer premises. Communicators are not at the mercy of consumer decisions as to whether to read today's newspaper or watch the evening news on television.

Recipient neglect after messages have been delivered is a very different type of problem. Neglect occasionally can occur under pressure of day-to-day problems or client/patient demands in the best of professional practices. Chronic neglect, however, usually is symptomatic of major communication problems.

Employers' messages seldom go unheeded. Where communication systems are weak, the so-called grapevine in most cases gets the job done. Neglect usually occurs only when employees believe messages to be wholly self-serving on the part of senders or when past performance has destroyed sender credibility.

Ineffectiveness in communication created by lack of audience response is the most common failing in communication. Sender weaknesses that lead to ineffectiveness can become even more troublesome, however, when legal problems arise. They are most prevalent in employee communication in two areas: copyright infringement and labor law.

LEGAL CONSTRAINTS

Whether dealing with communication verbally or through the media, professionals should be ever alert to changing legal and social trends that bear on the process. Potential for problems has increased in recent years with worker-oriented court decisions, proliferating legislation, and a growing worker predisposition toward litigation.

Improved technological capabilities in the hands of novices also have become a problem. Microcomputers equipped with optical scanners have made copyright infringement more readily accomplished than ever has been the case before. Scanners enable computer operators to import graphics as well as words at the flip of a switch. Results are not necessarily readily identified as plagiarism by supervisors.

Court decisions concerning the legal implications of communication arguably are more threatening from an employer perspective. Through the 1980s, the courts increasingly have bound employers to statements contained in promotional materials as well as in policy and procedure manuals. Coupled with decisions in some jurisdictions that workers have vested interests—ownership rights—in their jobs, communication-related rulings require special attention.

No message containing any promise, explicit or implied, today should be delivered without legal advice. Most employers have become sensitive to potential risks relating to such formal documents as personnel and procedure manuals. Relatively few recognize, however, that identical risks occur in connection with other printed and audiovisual materials as well as the content of interpersonal communication.

IN SUMMARY

Employee communication is the only logical starting point in developing programs designed to capitalize on added strengths inherent in inside-out strategies. These strategies require involving practice personnel in programs designed to enhance relationships with clients or patients, who in turn become practice ambassadors in the communities in which they live and work.

All of the five methods or techniques through which humans communicate individually or in groups can be applied in employee communication. One of the five, for better or worse, is always applied. The five are behavioral, inter-personal, electronic, print, and hybrid. The one that is always applied is behavioral.

Professionals' behaviors in dealing with employees communicate more effectively than any alternative approach. Consistency of messages across communication methods is essential, however, if credibility is to be developed and maintained. Credibility, in turn, is vital if employees are to be made a part of the practice development program.

Message consistency must exist within and across groups with which professionals communicate. Information contained in behaviors and other messages to employees must be in agreement. Information conveyed to employees also must be consistent with that delivered to existing or prospective clienteles.

Professionals communicate in the manner in which they treat personnel and others and in the environments and facilities in which they elect to practice as well as in words and gestures. Where personnel are concerned, communication often begins with classified advertising that too often is misleading. The employment process too readily can result in misunderstanding about the nature of jobs and their economic potential.

Further vulnerability usually exists in performance appraisal systems used within professional practices. They, too, communicate. Performance appraisal requires mutual understanding of performance criteria, accurate measurement of individual performance, and fair and equitable distribution of rewards.

Performance appraisal and reward systems can support or undermine other communication systems. Well-designed reward systems encourage open communication that enhances performance to the benefit of all involved. Weak systems encourage game-playing and other destructive behaviors.

Mediated communication supplants or supplements interpersonal communication in larger and in geographically diverse practices. Printed communication predominates where transmitted information must be available for future reference. Electronic systems are most popular where messages are intended to motivate or to enhance mechanical skills. Most communication programs use multiple communication systems for mutual reinforcement and optimum results.

In all circumstances, communication systems must be designed in keeping with changing technologies and their impacts on society. As channels of communication proliferate, no individual medium serves as efficiently as it might have in earlier years. In general, print media decline in popularity and acceptance while the electronic media become more popular. Communicators must adjust to this reality as well. Programs at all times must be tailored to the needs and interests of message recipients in order to induce appropriate responses.

ADDITIONAL READING

Brookfield, Stephen D. *Developing Critical Thinkers: Challenging Adults to Explore Alternative Ways of Thinking and Acting*. San Francisco: Jossey-Bass, 1987.

Deutsch, Arnold R. *The Human Resources Revolution: Communicate or Litigate*. New York: McGraw-Hill, 1979.

Fulmer, Robert M. *Practical Human Relations*. Homewood, Ill.: Irwin, 1983.

Kellogg, Marion S. *What to Do about Performance Appraisal*. New York: amacom, 1975.

Kouzes, James M., and Barry Z. Posner. *The Leadership Challenge: How to Get Extraordinary Things Done in Organizations*. San Francisco: Jossey-Bass, 1987.

Schramm, Wilbur, and William E. Porter. *Men, Women, Messages, and Media*. 2nd ed. New York: Harper & Row, 1982.

10

Practice Communication

Professionals' behaviors and the realities of their practices communicate more effectively and persuasively with clients or patients than any contrived effort. The extent to which behaviors and realities meet client perceptions of quality service governs ability to retain their patronage and attract that of others. Professional success, in other words, is primarily a function of the extent to which professional services and consumer expectations match one another. Objective qualitative or quantitative standards are secondary.

A number of alternative professional communication strategies can be applied to bring consumer perceptions of services into conformity with their preexisting expectations. All require inducing change in one of three elements: perceptions, realities, or expectations.

Development of practice communication thus requires knowledge of client perceptions and expectations of the practice. Necessary information can and should be obtained through appropriate research using one or more of the several techniques described in chapter 4. Thereafter, practitioners must address a series of questions:

1. What are patient or client expectations of the practice?
2. To what extent do clients or patients perceive their expectations are being met?
3. To what extent is the practice really meeting those expectations?
4. How can false perceptions best be modified?
5. To what extent can expectations be modified?
6. To what extent can realities be modified?

These questions must be addressed and, in some instances, responses must be in place before effective communication programs can be designed. Perceptions and expectations can be changed through communication. Realities can be changed only through tangible action. Professionals almost always find it most productive to first address the realities. Only when realities have been made as attractive as possible should efforts be made to explain why they must be as they are. Only after the waiting room has been made as comfortable as possible, for example, should patients or clients be told that it is impractical to provide separate facilities for patients with young children.

CREATING REALITIES

All of the realities discussed in chapter 9 in terms of practice personnel are applicable to patients or clients. Interpersonal relationships, however, are most important among them. No effort toward changing client or patient perceptions of a professional practice will be optimally effective until professionals have first resolved existing intrapractice problems and have gained the commitment of personnel.

Practitioners alone, other than perhaps small consulting practices, are incapable of creating the sort of realities most valued by patients and clients. They spend too little time or, in the alternative, members of their staff spend too much time with the individuals involved. Attitude and opinion in those individuals are shaped accordingly. Professionals' best intentions are at the mercy of their subordinates.

Development Rationale

These conditions create the practice development rationale presented here. Practitioners who would succeed in increasingly competitive environments must conform to patient and client requirements. To meet their demanding standards, professionals often must make changes in practice environments, internal and external. Tangible and durable change in internal environments seldom can be accomplished without wholehearted commitment on the part of colleagues as well as paraprofessional and clerical personnel. Only when these changes have been accomplished, only when professionals are confident they have created wholly friendly environments, are they ready to proceed to communication in the conventional sense of that word.

Environments communicate. Behavior communicates. Professional practice environments and the behaviors of practitioners and members of their staffs are the loudest voices patients and clients hear while in contact with professional practices. Conventional communication techniques can be effective in expanding upon, enhancing, and amplifying messages generated by environment and behavior. These techniques usually range from the valueless to the counterproductive, however, if applied in efforts to contradict environmental and behavioral realities.

The latter circumstances largely explain why the communication disciplines—

public relations, advertising, and marketing—have not been uniformly productive for professionals. Some professional practices have been significantly improved, while others have experienced little or no results. The differences in most cases result from the nature of the practices involved rather than from consultants' communication skills. Communication cannot change reality, and consumers today are highly sensitive to conflicting messages.

Satisfaction and Expectations

Message conflicts, in fact, often are at the heart of the expectation problem discussed earlier. Satisfaction with professional services is a function of the extent to which services meet consumer expectations. Public relations, advertising, and marketing campaigns therefore must depict professional practices as they exist rather than as practitioners might like them to be perceived. Failure to do so widens rather than narrows any gaps that exist between expectation and experience, with devastating results.

Devastation is produced when patients or clients amplify dissatisfaction rather than satisfaction. Professionals can be confident only that their clienteles will, indeed, serve as amplifiers. Messages they will be amplifying can be controlled only by altering the environments and behaviors from which message content originates. The key to successful communication in practice development thus is to be found in creating superior realities.

DEFINING OBJECTIVES

When client or patient expectations are met to as great an extent as practicable, communication techniques can be applied successfully to modify expectations as well as false perceptions. The most efficient of program strategies, however, seldom conforms to the expectations of the typical professional and almost never meet the stereotypes harbored by the more traditional among them. Communication efforts associated with strategies oriented toward existing clients or patients rarely are promotional in nature. They almost universally are designed to educate, inform, or explain. Neither persuasion nor promotion will overcome perceived weaknesses in professional services.

Using communication to educate, inform, or explain, in contrast, is logical and appropriate for two reasons. First, patients and clients will not be long deceived by the sort of strategies associated with aluminum siding or used car sales persons. Second, and more important, most practice development difficulties encountered in any profession are caused by misunderstanding.

Every professional, for these reasons, develops formal or informal mechanisms through which clients or patients can be educated, informed, or given explanations. The processes are separate and distinct, but all are designed to anticipate and avoid misunderstandings that can undermine practitioner relationships. Misunderstandings develop most frequently where patients and clients are not knowledgeable or adequately informed on subjects with which professionals or members of their staffs consider everyone to be conversant. Resistance and resentment are almost inevitable when professionals or their staffs fail to explain why a procedure is necessary.

When need for education, information, and explanation have been adequately defined, professionals can proceed to specify communication techniques most appropriate to their practices. Applicability of techniques varies with several factors. Most important among them are the nature of clients or patients and the frequency with which they experience need for professional services.

Roles of Communication

Education, information, and explanation are complementary but separate and distinct components of the communication process in professional practices. Education deals with the nature of the discipline, the types of services it offers, and the benefits that can accrue to clients or patients. Information is provided as to the policies and practices that the professional has adopted to govern his or her own practice. Explanation usually applies to specific problems that clients or patients bring to the professional. They may or may not be so specific in nature as to require handling in interpersonal communication between professional and client.

Education, information, and explanation efforts should function concurrently in practice development programs. These circumstances seldom prevail because professionals usually permit communication programs to grow on an ad hoc basis rather than encouraging consistency and productivity through logical design and implementation. These circumstances are neither unusual nor unexpected among individuals trained in disciplines in which communication often is expected to take care of itself. Results are no less damaging, however, in competitive environments.

Education. Expectations of existing and prospective clients and patients are most amenable to change through early education. The process, from the professional standpoint, should introduce members of clienteles to professions in much the same manner that early childhood education introduces youngsters to the educational system. No prior knowledge should be assumed on the part of professionals or their personnel.

Educational procedures should be used to define the scope and nature of the professional practice. They should deal with what is done and not done as well as what kinds of results to expect. Architects, for example, should be careful to clearly delineate the borderline between their discipline and engineering. Ophthalmologists and public relations practitioners, in like manner, should define the limits of their work in relation to opticians or advertising specialists. No client or patient should be permitted to harbor any misconceptions over precisely what the professional intends to accomplish on his or her behalf.

Differences in types of results produced among superficially similar practitioners also can create potential for misunderstanding. Consider, for example, the efforts of chiropractors in what has become an age of instant gratification. Patients preconditioned to headache remedies that act in seconds or antibiotics that cure in hours readily can become disenchanted with the relatively slow pace of recovery that often occurs in chiropractic practice. Resulting problems in large part can be avoided, however, if practitioners or members of their staffs act early to modify client expectations.

Information. Those expectations encompass every aspect of the practice. They deal not only with results but with patient or client treatment, with the speed with which calls are answered, and with scheduling of appointments and the manner in which billing problems are handled. These and a host of other factors, varying by profession, should be viewed by practitioners, as they are by clients and patients, as constituting a sort of social contract. The term *social contract* is not too extreme given the economic sensitivity of contemporary professional practices to client and patient expectations. Few of them will be so bold as to state those expectations or to inquire as to professionals' policies. The burden thus shifts to professionals or, at minimum, to those who would maintain salutary relationships in increasingly competitive environments.

Consider, for example, the damage potential evident in the various ways in which dentists can handle emergency calls. Dentists may or may not be available to patients other than during office hours. They may or may not use back-ups when they are out of town. They may or may not charge premium rates for emergency or other services (the two are not synonymous) rendered other than during regular office hours.

Precisely expressed policies covering these variables and clearly conveyed to all patients are essential to avoid misunderstandings. Policies need not be complex but must be comprehensive. For example, in the case above, an appropriate policy might read: "Services will be provided at prevailing rates outside regular office hours only to patients seen at least twice annually for preventive or other services. Special additional charges otherwise will apply."

Explanation. Policies such as the after-hours service policy readily can and should be explained in detail in a leaflet, or brochure distributed to all patients. Explanation, however, should go beyond mere elaboration of fiscal or business policies. It is most necessary and, unfortunately, most often neglected in context with professional services.

Services best meet and exceed consumer expectations when recipients understand why services are being rendered. Those under physicians' care, therefore, should be told why specific tests are being administered, what information the results will provide, and what that information will mean in terms of treatment. Engineers' clients, in like manner, should be told why test borings are necessary before building footings can be designed. Accountants' clients should be made aware of the nature of accounting tests applied during audit procedures. Professionals too often assume that clients and patients have been through a process many times before and have long since obtained answers to all questions that might arise where novices are involved.

The opposite assumption is preferable from a practice development standpoint. What patients and clients do not know may not hurt them. The absence of information they want, however, can go far toward destroying confidence in relationships with professionals.

Specifying Techniques

Information delivery techniques vary with the nature of professional practices and practitioner development strategies. The nature of a practice influences numbers of active clients, average longevity of professional relationships, the extent to which further professional services may be needed, and other factors that govern practitioner communication needs. Practitioner development strategies involve the three primary sources of professional patronage discussed earlier: additional services provided to existing clienteles, new services provided to existing clienteles, or existing services provided to new clienteles.

Practice variation. Some professionals, such as accountants and dentists, see their clients with some degree of regularity. They can transmit considerable information during those meetings. Others, such as chiropractors and dental surgeons, seldom see patients beyond the end of courses of treatment that often are of relatively short duration.

Variation among types of patients or clients within professions also can influence volume of in-person contact. Clienteles of attorneys in general corporate law practices, for example, probably change little over time. Those who specialize in mergers and acquisitions, on the other hand, may experience high rates of client turnover. Successful corporate attorneys also are apt to earn more consistent patronage from clients than is the case with their colleagues in mergers and acquisitions.

Strategic needs. Professionals seeking to develop their practices necessarily select one or more of the strategies specified above. Each strategy implies a different set of communication objectives. The nature of the objectives dictates the extent to which practitioners seek to communicate with existing clienteles.

A great deal of communication is indicated where professionals are seeking to enhance their practices by providing new services to existing clients. Significantly less communication is indicated where developmental strategies focus on prospective rather than existing clienteles.

Relatively few professionals find existing clienteles to be valid prospects for more of the services they already are purchasing. Opticians occasionally may be able to market new eyeglass frames. Plastic surgeons catering to aging and affluent populations may find that one procedure leads to another. Architects, engineers, and most other professionals find little repetitive work within existing clienteles.

Many professionals find, however, that satisfied clients or patients can become major sources of referrals. Referral potential often can be realized, however, only where those making referrals are frequently reminded of professionals' names and the nature of their services. Gratitude, appreciation, and memory in most individuals appear to wane at approximately equal rates. A minor professional miracle performed last week therefore may be highly stimulating of referrals while that of last month or last year yields little direct benefit.

Where the nature of the professional practice generates only irregular personal contact with patients or clients and where these groups directly or indirectly can influence practice development, personal contact must be supplemented with mediated communication. Communication can be maintained through any of several channels: electronic, printed, and interpersonal. No one of them, however, is universally applicable in all situations.

SELECTING CHANNELS

Several criteria always are employed in selecting channels of communication. Primary among them is cost, but not in the abstract sense. Dollar totals are less important than two other criteria, both economic: cost per prospect and revenue potential per prospect.

Channels of communication and, in fact, communication itself are costly only in relation to their potential productivity. The most expensive is readily affordable where profit exceeds cost. The least expensive is too costly where it produces no results. These considerations demand that communicators focus first on reach and response in making value judgments concerning channels of communication. When reach and response potential have been evaluated, the media selection focus then shifts to production costs.

Reach and Response

Reach refers to the extent to which any medium or channel conveys messages to target populations. Response refers to levels of measurable reaction within those populations. Each of these elements requires attention in professional development programming.

Evaluating reach. Attaching a value to the reach of a specific medium or communication channel can be approached in either or both of two ways. One involves calculating the percentage of the target audience captured by the medium. The other requires measuring potential of one medium in comparison with others.

An engineering firm, for example, might find a community's weekly business and legal newspapers more productive channels than the local daily newspaper because they are better read by those who decide on engineering services. The weeklies' circulations doubtless would be minuscule in comparison with those of the daily, but larger percentages of their circulations are apt to be members of target groups.

A cosmetic surgeon similarly might find the local city magazine superior to all newspapers. His or her first priority, however, well could be a daytime television talk show with high ratings among women. Still greater potential might be found in an audiovisual presentation to participants in country club women's golf or tennis tournaments.

Weighing response. Exposure generated for a product or service, through communication media or otherwise, is not equivalent to sales. Sales ultimately may result, but level of results often varies with type of exposure. Differences in reach often account for the variation, but a great deal of the variation is never satisfactorily explained.

The latter circumstances produce continual experimentation on the part of communicators. Over time, they will use virtually any medium experimentally on the chance that it might "click." A major Florida resort, for example, once found the nation's most prestigious magazines outclassed by *TV Guide* in advertising productivity. The resort used a system that permitted the advertising manager to track numbers of inquiries received, numbers of reservations arising out of those inquiries, and numbers of sales dollars generated by the reservations. *TV Guide* proved no better than average in generating inquiries and reservations but outperformed every other medium in dollar return.

The key point here is a simple one. Exposure does not equal sales. Professionals must make every effort to track the origins of new clients and patients in order to continually assess the relative effectiveness of communication channels.

Production Costs

Analyses of cost incurred in communication processes often are distorted in professional practices by a sort of false logic that attaches no value to the time of staff members involved. The logic is best expressed in words typical of managers involved: "If it doesn't add to direct expense, it doesn't cost anything." The attitude involved too often leads to unnecessarily high cost and less than optimal efficiency levels.

The efficiency problem is compounded by a tendency on the part of professionals to believe that their expertise applies in almost any field of endeavor. Few will readily concede, for example, that communication professionals may be better able to convey information concerning their practices than they can do themselves. Their attitudes are based on a largely valid assumption that they can communicate as well as a professional. The logic is valid to the extent that most professionals have the basic mental and mechanical capabilities to perform any task. It is invalid in that a great deal more than basic effort may be required in successful completion of the task.

Before proceeding to examine components of production cost, professionals are well advised to pause and consider one cogent question: "Can I earn as much on the time I'll spend doing this as I can earn in pursuit of my own profession?"

Few can respond in the affirmative. Those who can should examine production processes as consisting of three basic components: the creative, the mechanical, and the administrative. Each process can be handled by practice personnel or subcontracted to others. Some, especially in the mechanical sector, almost always are subcontracted.

Creative elements. Creativity, and the element of persuasion it is supposed to add to communication, is an overrated component of the process. No amount of communication can substitute for organizational performance. No mere message, no matter how finely crafted, can successfully fill in the blank in "Come to us for professional service because _____." Where communication succeeds, reasons almost invariably have been supplied by professional performance before words are put on paper.

Putting words on paper nevertheless is the beginning point in preparing to use most formal communication channels. Someone, or some several individuals, must develop articles for newsletters or news releases and scripts for speeches or audiovisual presentations. Two different sets of skills are involved. Few writers have mastered the different writing techniques used in print and electronic media. Those seeking professional assistance therefore should be cautious in selecting writers.

Mechanical elements. Writers' first products—draft texts or scripts—are required by printers and audiovisual producers in preparing production cost estimates. Neither script nor text need be in final form, but the draft length should be a close approximation of the finished version.

Length of presentation, whether in print or audiovisual form, is a major governor of production cost. Length depends on number of words and illustrations, each of which must be converted from original form to printed pages or audiovisual media. Multiple vendors may be involved, although their number varies with production techniques.

Administrative elements. Production of printed or audiovisual materials can be contracted or subcontracted. Professionals can select a single vendor for each product or can deal with those who supply vendors. Printers, for example, often subcontract typesetting and color separation work. Audiovisual producers usually subcontract graphic design, typesetting, and music.

Size of professional practice and scope of communication program usually are primary factors in determining how to administer communication programs. Professionals often elect to serve as their own administrators for occasional projects, using a contractor or subcontractors. As practices grow, public relations or marketing firms usually are called upon for assistance. Still further growth often prompts professionals to establish their own communication departments.

Labor Costs

Production costs associated with printed and audiovisual materials can be considerable. Professionals should remember, however, that they essentially are buying time in using these media. They are investing in alternative channels of communication to insure that patients or clients receive necessary information without human intervention.

The only alternative to these delivery systems, in other words, is embodied in professionals' office staffs. Their time almost universally is too costly to permit them to personally convey information to patients of clients on any lengthy and consistent basis. Some exceptions to this rule exist, as will be discussed below, but they are becoming fewer rather than more plentiful.

Time costs at all organizational levels are the primary overhead factor in professional practice. Every technique that can be employed to reduce time required in serving patients or clients without sacrificing quality of service is important. As average time requirements decline, more patients or clients can be served without increases in personnel.

Most professionals, for reasons of economy, attempt to give the appearance of providing more personal attention while reducing time investments. This objective can be accomplished only where other practice personnel or impersonal communication channels can do the job without disturbing professional relationships.

Human substitution. Professionals use an exceptionally broad range of techniques to provide less while appearing to provide more. Physicians and dentists, for example, attempt to limit in-office time with patients to an irreducible minimum but then make it a point to call them—or have staff members call them—after office hours. Telephone calls take less time and demonstrate real interest more effectively than would be the case if comparable amounts of time were added to office visits.

Professionals also can and should demand more of their personnel in supporting a caring approach to clients and patients. Receptionists and those who answer telephones should be required to emulate the approach taken by AT&T, which has every operator thank every user of operator-assisted services. "Please," "thank you," and "we're glad you selected us" are a small price to pay for greater client or patient satisfaction and loyalty.

Substituting technology. A few words can be applied quickly and economically in building practice relationships. Detailed explanations are another matter. Professionals have only two alternatives in dealing with patients or clients who need or require a great deal of information or explanation. They can provide the service with human beings and raise rates accordingly, or they can use alternative techniques.

Print and audiovisual techniques both can be appropriate. Virtually no professional office, for example, should be without an inexpensive leaflet designed to accomplish two objectives. First, it should briefly describe all professional services offered. Second, it should explain what patients or clients can expect of the practice and what the practice expects of them. The rules of the game, in other words, should be clearly defined for all involved.

At the opposite technological extreme, audiovisual and print channels can be used together to provide detailed information on complex subjects to patients or clients who require clear explanations and who will subsequently want to refer to the information involved. Larger medical practices, for example, in recent years have started using extensive videotape libraries to convey detailed information concerning diagnoses and courses of treatment. Patients view the tapes in small but comfortable rooms designed for that purpose and receive leaflets summarizing the content for future reference.

Professionals reap two major benefits. Demands on their time are radically reduced and every patient receives complete and accurate information without human intervention. So popular has this approach become that it has been adopted by others in the healing arts and by many in other professions.

Selection Processes

With all of these factors in mind, media selection processes proceed within individual professional practices on the basis of communication need. Two questions must be answered. How much information must be conveyed? How frequently must contact be made? The second question can be answered only in light of normal levels of in-person contact on the part of individual professionals with patients or clients. In other words, how often does the client come to the office or does the professional visit the client?

Answers to these questions must reflect varying conditions across the several professions. Answers are essential, however, in selecting communication channels and, ultimately, deciding on frequency of use.

Information needs. Volume of information to be conveyed varies with the needs of professionals and their clients or patients. Professionals' needs relate to their interests in providing more or additional services. Client or patient needs are another matter.

Professionals more and more are perceived by patients or clients as obligated to provide information concerning new products or services. This especially is the case where new technologies may have resulted in new products or services or radical improvements in those that previously existed.

Development of superconductivity resulted in creation of more powerful magnets that enabled dentists to successfully apply them for the first time in holding dentures in place. Laser technology, in like manner, expanded the horizons of surgery, while computers and satellites enhanced the economics of public relations and advertising practices.

Frequency of contact. Where visits to professional or client offices are relatively frequent, as in the case of dentists' patients or auditors' visits, a great deal of information can be delivered verbally. Verbal communication can be supplemented with material also amenable to use as what communicators call "leave-behinds." These may be printed materials or copies of magazine or journal articles.

Where visits are infrequent or unpredictable, as with interior decorators, plastic surgeons, architects, and the like, alternative communication channels must be considered. These can be relatively simple devices such as newsletters or more sophisticated literature delivered by mail. They also can be information concerning professionals and/or their practices disseminated through the mass media.

Unfortunately, no general guidelines exist as to appropriate frequency of contact between professional and patient. Contacts should be sufficient in all circumstances to serve the interests of both parties. They should meet client or patient needs for reassurance that professionals are indeed interested in them. At the same time, they must meet practitioner needs from a marketing standpoint.

Types of contact. Only where necessary frequency of contact and usual frequency of contact have been established can the final step in the channel selection process be completed. That step requires professional response to more questions: What types of contact are necessary or appropriate? Is interpersonal contact vital? Will telephone calls suffice? Can printed or audiovisual messages adequately serve?

Most professionals find that contact can be most readily maintained on a cost-effective basis by using several channels of communication. Formulas vary, however, with type of practice. In general, volume of interpersonal and telephone contact increases with the size of typical fees. Volume of contact through impersonal channels grows as typical fees decline. Architects, engineers, and landscape designers usually emphasize interpersonal contact, while dentists, investment counselors, and insurance agents more often use impersonal techniques. Not coincidentally, use of impersonal media tends to decline with the extent to which the practice of each profession requires frequent interpersonal contact.

One Added Concern

As professionals prepare to make their decisions as to communication channels, one final variable requires consideration: the extent to which each channel might be applied to multiply overall communication effectiveness. Two "multiplier" techniques often are employed. The costs that professionals incur in developing communication programs suggest that both be carefully considered.

The multipliers involve using one communication channel to reach multiple audiences or applying one channel to reinforce another. One method of reinforcement, combining printed material with interpersonal contact, was mentioned earlier. Others exist as well.

Printed materials, for example, often are distributed in conjunction with audiovisual presentations or in small group settings. Audiovisuals reinforce group presentations as well. Reprints of information disseminated by printed mass media are equally useful and relatively economical.

Extending the use of any channel of communication reduces relative cost because preparation expenses are amortized over larger groups. Printing costs decline as order sizes increase. Additional showings of audiovisuals involve no increase in production costs unless they are used so frequently that they wear out.

In addition, printed and audiovisual materials often are readily prepared for use with multiple groups. A practice brochure describing scope of services and expectations, for example, often can be successfully distributed to prospective as well as existing patients or clients. A newsletter developed primarily for patients or clients readily can be used with prospects and, with little modification, may be applicable in communicating with personnel as well.

Practice personnel should receive at a minimum all information generally disseminated to clients or patients. They must be adequately equipped informationally to provide interpersonal support when presented with questions.

IN SUMMARY

Successfully communicating with existing practice clienteles in the context of practice development requires more effort than may appear to be the case. Practice development programs are designed to accelerate growth in the practice and the economic rewards that growth can produce for all involved.

Growth and rewards are most readily induced where two other prerequisites are met. First, as described in chapter 9, practice personnel must be made a part of the process in their own interests as well as those of professionals. Second, developmental efforts must be based on complete understanding of patient or client perceptions of the practice.

Perceptions—good or bad—are created by two elements. One consists of client or patient expectations of the practice. The other is the extent to which those expectations are perceived as being or having been fulfilled. Client or patient satisfaction is produced only when expectations are consistently met. Anything less creates dissatisfaction in varying degrees. That dissatisfaction, as conveyed to friends and acquaintances throughout the community, reduces the effectiveness of practice development programs.

After enlisting the support of practice personnel, successful development programs then turn to existing clienteles and the extent to which they are satisfied with professional services. Any existing dissatisfaction must be eliminated before the development process can proceed.

Dissatisfaction can be successfully addressed in one or both of two ways: through improved performance or through altered expectations. In most cases, both techniques are used. Professionals attempt to meet patient or client standards that can reasonably be met or to educate them to the fact that some of the standards are unrealistic.

The circumstances are not unlike those in effect during airline deregulations in the late 1980s. The deregulation process and increases in air traffic created untold problems for passengers. One of them involved schedules created more in keeping with the carriers' need to attract customers than in keeping with their mechanical capabilities. Within weeks of implementation of a Federal Aviation Agency plan to report on carriers' performance in meeting published schedules, arrival and departure times were modified to reflect reality. Aircraft departed and arrived no more swiftly than earlier had been the case, but passengers no longer expected the impossible.

One of the first practice development steps that should be applied in dealing with existing clienteles thus involves creating as attractive a reality as possible and correcting any conditions that may lead to overly optimistic consumer expectations. The process almost inevitably involves a great deal of communication designed to educate, inform, and explain rather than to promote or persuade.

Education efforts usually predominate where professionals want to meet client or patient need for information concerning services they need or desire. Scope of services always should be precisely defined. Explanation usually is necessary where professionals deal with such matters as emergency services. Clients or patients must be told how to obtain such services, costs involved, and other factors that otherwise might produce confusion or misunderstanding if not conveyed in advance. Information concerning the professional or the practice also may be necessary to insure that those involved comprehend why specific policies or procedures have been established.

Techniques used in delivering information to clienteles vary with the nature of professional practices and practitioners' developmental strategies. Frequency of contact between professionals and patients or clients is a primary practice variable. A great deal of information that can be transmitted during practitioner visits to clients or patient visits to professionals' offices must be conveyed by other means where such contacts are irregular or infrequent.

Alternative developmental strategies also play a role in selecting communication techniques. More frequent communication usually is indicated where professionals are attempting to induce greater use of practice services by existing clienteles. This especially is the case when the practice is introducing new or expanded services.

Other factors that require attention include the reach and response potential indigenous to available media. *Reach* refers to the extent to which a specific medium will convey the professional's message to a given group of individuals. Media usually are selected in keeping with their reach.

Response is an important but secondary consideration. Reach and response are not synonymous. Messages delivered through some media apparently are more persuasive than others, although no one totally understands how such differences come to exist. These circumstances lead to a great deal of experimentation on the part of professionals in the communication disciplines.

In considering experimentation with alternative media, professionals must carefully analyze costs involved. Production of a videotaped presentation, for example, usually is more expensive than a comparable slide-tape presentation but far less costly than a motion picture. Considerable variation in cost also can occur in dealing with different printing techniques. In general, creative aspects of media development are relatively consistent. Costs associated with message synthesis differ relatively little within the major media categories.

What appear to be relatively high costs that arise in development of communication vehicles usually prove otherwise when examined carefully. Messages usually can be communicated in any number of ways. Interpersonal communication during the course of a client or patient visit, for example, can be used to convey a great deal of information. Such communication is costly in personnel time, however, even when contact with patients or clients is relatively frequent. Alternative communication channels therefore are used as cost-efficient substitutes for interpersonal communication.

New technologies are making the alternatives progressively more efficient and less expensive. Desktop publishing, for example, has reduced the cost of newsletters, while videotape has produced radical reductions in audiovisual costs. Professionals should monitor changes in the technologies in order to keep production costs at minimum levels.

ADDITIONAL READING

Bivins, Thomas. *Handbook for Public Relations Writing*. Lincolnwood, Ill.: NTC Business Books, 1988.

Brody, E. W. *The Business of Public Relations*. New York: Praeger, 1987.

Desatnick, Robert L. *Managing to Keep the Customer: How to Achieve and Maintain Superior Customer Service throughout the Organization*. San Francisco: Jossey-Bass, 1987.

Kakabadse, Andrew, and Christopher Parker. *Power, Politics, and Organizations: A Behavioral Science View*. New York: Wiley, 1984.

Lesly, Philip. *The People Factor: Managing the Human Climate*. Homewood, Ill.: Dow Jones–Irwin, 1974.

Londgren, Richard E. *Communication by Objectives: A Guide to Productive and Cost-Effective Public Relations and Marketing*. Englewood Cliffs, N.J.: Prentice-Hall, 1983.

Miller, Ernest C., ed. *Human Resources Management: The Past Is Prologue*. New York: amacom, 1979.

Nolte, Lawrence W., and Dennis L. Wilcox. *Effective Publicity: How to Reach the Public*. New York: Wiley, 1984.

Schoenfeld, Clarence A. *Publicity Media and Methods: Their Role in Modern Public Relations*. New York: Macmillan, 1963.

Zander, Alvin. *Making Groups Effective*. San Francisco: Jossey-Bass, 1982.

11

Reaching Out

All the time, effort, and money that professionals invest in creating salutary environments—internal and external—start producing returns as the practice development program turns toward prospective clients or patients. While necessary and beneficial in and of themselves, the productivity of the preliminaries usually is relatively low. Enhanced employee relationships make only small direct contributions to practice profitability. Resulting improvement in personnel performance contributes significantly to efforts to limit client or patient attrition. Benefits implicit in those efforts are augmented, however, as developmental efforts turn outward.

The ultimate objectives of practice development are growth and prosperity. As personnel come to view the practice as their own and as potentially restless patients or clients settle in for the long run, professionals are free to exploit the internal strengths they have developed. *Exploit* may be too strong a word, but the meaning is appropriate. Practice development is a building or rebuilding process. The process begins internally in orienting or reorienting facilities and personnel to better serve clients and patients. Better service, in turn, increases their satisfaction and loyalty, slamming shut the back door through which too many otherwise escape.

At this juncture, practice development departs, to a greater or lesser extent, from the traditional reputation-building path to prosperity. Departures can be conservative or radical, but nevertheless they are departures. They are tactics applied to enhance the visibility and attractiveness of practices to prospective clients or patients by whom they might otherwise be overlooked.

At the conservative pole, practice development techniques embrace activities such as public speaking, writing for professional journals, and involvement in civic and community affairs. All these devices can be productively applied while meeting the most stringent of traditional ethical standards.

At the liberal extreme, professionals can advertise in the mass media—television, radio, and daily newspapers—and can go so far as to offer discount coupons through direct mail advertising. Coupons good for free consultations or examinations are common among opticians, podiatrists, chiropractors, and a host of others in whose specialties competition long has been a painful fact of life.

Appropriateness of specific developmental techniques, especially their communication components, is a function of the profession and the practice involved in any given situation. Variation across professions and across practices within professions make practice development a highly individualized process. Variation among channels of communication makes them appropriate in some practice settings and inappropriate in others.

VARIATION ACROSS PROFESSIONS

Each of the sets of differences specified above must be considered in creating practice development programs. Strategies and tactics that are highly productive in one profession may be valueless in another. The same circumstances also may occur, although for different reasons, within professions.

Differences across professions occur in six primary areas, all involving their clienteles, as follows:

1. Numbers of clients or patients
2. Consistency and predictability of needs
3. Frequency of professional contact
4. Geographic distribution
5. Identity of primary decision makers
6. Client/patient demographics and psychographics

Each of these variables requires careful examination in designing professional development programs. Each influences the success potential of every communication strategy.

Differences in Numbers

Practices in most professions fall into one of two basic categories in terms of client or patient bases. Practices are broadly based, as in the healing arts, real estate, banking, and insurance, or they are narrowly based, as in architecture, engineering, accounting, marketing, advertising, and public relations.

A few professions may first appear to occupy a middle ground between the two extremes. Closer inspection, however, usually permits their inclusion in one category or another. Attorneys, for example, usually orient their practices to broad or narrow bases through specialization.

Broad-based practices differ from narrowly based practices in several significant respects. Primary among them are average numbers of clients or patients served and the average economic value of individual patients or clients to the practice.

Practitioners in broad-based professions usually serve larger numbers of clients or patients who individually account for relatively small percentages of practice revenues. In narrow-based professions, the reverse tends to be true. Numbers of patients or clients are fewer and their individual contributions to the economics of the practice are larger.

Investment per prospective client or patient in communication programs almost invariably is higher in narrow-based then in broad-based professions. The former require a more customized approach, often involving personal letters, telephone calls, and personal sales calls (see chapter 14). The latter usually rely primarily on newsletters, direct mail promotions, and other less individualized tactics.

Variation in Need

Consumers' need for services also varies from one profession to another. Factors that vary across the professions include frequency, extent, and predictability of need. Each factor influences professionals' communication programs.

Frequency of need is relatively low for architects, engineers, interior designers, and real estate professionals. Physicians and dentists generally are needed more often, but specialists among them—such as neurosurgeons and orthodontists—are called upon infrequently by most individuals.

Volume of service. Extent of need refers to the volume of service required when needs arise. Volume of need tends to be relatively high in interior design or architecture, relatively low in real estate, and highly variable in law and medicine.

In some professions, volume of need varies with frequency of need. Engineering or architectural commissions tend to be relatively large and time-consuming. They are placed relatively infrequently, however, by the average individual or organization. Complex legal and medical problems, which also occur relatively infrequently, similarly require larger volumes of service but over broader time spans.

Need for professional services also varies in predictability. Demand for accounting services, for example, is highly predictable and relatively cyclical. Need for marketing, advertising, and public relations services tends to vary with national and international economic cycles.

Function of need. All these factors are significant in professionals' efforts to induce practice growth because of a basic principle of communication: message effectiveness increases with recipient need and interest levels. Interest in information concerning architectural services increases, for example, as prospective owners move from first consideration of a building project into economic feasibility studies, site selection, and so forth. Interest in public relations services usually grows as share of market declines or problems occur. And interest in health care services increases with the severity of medical problems involved, usually as indicated by level of pain experienced.

Professionals must design practice development programs to insure that as many prospective clients or patients as possible are aware of them and their services when purchase decisions are imminent. Early or late awareness, too often the case, produces no beneficial result.

Geographic Distribution

Distribution of prospective patients or clients is no less challenging than their need patterns in shaping professional development programs. Broad-based practices generally tend to serve smaller geographic areas, while narrow-based practices serve larger areas. Physicians, attorneys, and accountants tend to practice in individual communities. Architectural and engineering practices, in contrast, more often are regional and occasionally become national in scope.

Professionals seldom find their practice areas—existing or proposed—to be ideally suited to their communication needs. The nature of available media is the principal problem involved. Professionals with clienteles concentrated in small areas, such as the suburbs of large cities, find few channels of communication ideally suited to their needs. Mass media generally encompass too great a population to be beneficially employed, while more selective media tend to be costly.

The opposite circumstances can be equally troublesome. Few channels of communication adequately fit those whose practices cover broad geographic areas, as often becomes the case with specialization and subspecialization. Regional and national media usually are excessively costly, and their audiences may or may not meet professionals' needs.

Frequency of Contact

Potential for difficulty in achieving communication objectives increases where the nature of a profession encourages infrequent, irregular, or episodic contact between practitioners and their clients. Contact here refers to face-to-face encounters, whether on professionals' or, as in the case of accountants, clients' premises. Strength of interpersonal and interprofessional relationships in part is a function of volume of contact. Loyalties also tend to be stronger where contact is frequent.

Greater frequency and regularity of patient or client contact in the normal course of events enhances interpersonal communication. The contacts involved reduce professional need to use alternative communication channels. The converse also applies. Those seeking to maintain relationships established by frequent contact must employ still stronger communication programs.

Accountants generally are best positioned to maintain client contacts on continuing bases. Most of their services necessarily are ongoing. Attorneys, other than in organizational settings, usually are called upon only as needs arise. Many people go through life with little professional contact with the legal profession.

Between the extremes, as represented by accountants and attorneys, are a host of other professions. Optometrists usually recommend annual eye examinations. Dentists usually see patients twice a year. Physicians in general practice and internists frequently schedule annual examinations for their patients. Marketing, advertising, and public relations consultants' contacts with their clients can range from weekly in the normal course of events to daily during periods of special need.

Those who would displace incumbent professionals must expect to encounter greater difficulty where personal contact levels are high. Most new patients or clients are recruited only through effort over time. Limited research suggests most attrition in professional clienteles is produced by a combination of dissatisfaction with existing relationships and knowledge of attractive alternatives.

Decision Maker Identities

Level of difficulty encountered in displacing incumbent professionals also is significantly affected by variation in decision-making processes. Complexity in these processes can make communication difficult. Some organizational decision-making processes are simple and direct. Others are indirect. Still others involve committees or boards rather than individuals.

Levels of simplicity or directness encountered by practitioners vary with the nature of professions involved. Complexity tends to prevail in organizational decision making. Seldom will a president or chief executive officer unilaterally and without consultation select an architectural, engineering, or accounting firm.

Superficially simple decision-making processes, however, often are more complex than they appear. Selection of specialists in the healing arts, law, and other areas, for example, often are strongly influenced by previously retained colleagues. Architects often influence the selection of engineers and designers. Internists are instrumental in patients' choices of surgeons, who in turn often name anesthesiologists. Marketing, advertising, and public relations professionals frequently are instrumental in selecting their colleagues.

Parents obviously make decisions for minor children, but few recognize that, as parents age, these roles often are reversed. Guardians make decisions for their wards. Trustees often act for beneficiaries of estates.

The list could go on, but the point by now should be well made. Decision-making processes in the selection of professionals extend far beyond consumers of their services. Successful practice development programs must deal with all parties to the process.

Demographics and Psychographics

Dealing with all parties requires close attention to communication channels. Channel productivity varies with audiences and the appeals contained in messages transmitted. Effectiveness and productivity are functions of the extent to which channel and message match targeted audiences. Professionals therefore must concentrate their efforts in channels that reach their prospective clienteles.

Matching channel, message, and audience usually is readily accomplished where professionals can define the groups they serve or want to serve. Definitions are most logically cast in demographic or psychographic terms. Demographics encompass the geographic, social, and economic characteristics of the group. Psychographics deal with their lifestyles and, by inference, their buying habits.

Demographics. Some basic demographic characteristics already have been mentioned. Others are readily extrapolated. Among the basics are age, family status, and economic status. Educational level and economic status generally are close correlates of one another.

Most organizational decision makers are members of higher demographic and socioeconomic groups. They are older because experience is a prerequisite to promotion and wealthier because rewards usually accompany progress through the organizational hierarchy. They are more apt to be male than female, although this characteristic is changing.

Those who make decisions to purchase personal rather than organizational services are another matter. They necessarily constitute more diverse groups. They often can be characterized to a large extent, however, in keeping with the services professionals offer. Levels of age, education, and wealth are apt to be high among those who use the services of architects, plastic surgeons, and tax attorneys. Obstetrical practices cater to the relatively young and exclusively female. Orthodontists deal in large part with school children.

Psychographics. The nature of client groups is highly indicative of messages and communication channels to which they will be most attuned and responsive. The advertising of plastic surgeons, for example, often resembles that of cosmetics manufacturers and appears in the same media. The reason, as expressed by a cosmetics industry executive in the course of a television interview, is simple: "We manufacture cosmetics; we sell hope." Those who specialize in plastic (as opposed to reconstructive) surgery are essentially in the same business.

Architects and engineers working with business clients can readily find themselves similarly positioned but for different reasons. Their clients not infrequently are as interested in immortality as expressed in monumental buildings as they are in providing space for their organizations. Those preparing to build homes seldom are similarly motivated. While requiring architectural services, they are more prone to seek status than immortality.

Professionals must psychographically attune themselves to their constituencies. They must understand, to use contemporary vernacular, where prospective patients and clients "are coming from." Knowledge of the demographic and psychographic origins of these groups is critical to successful practice development programs.

VARIATION ACROSS PRACTICES

A somewhat different set of variables is involved in examining practices within professions. Practices vary in the following ways:

1. Level or degree of specialization
2. Community and practice demographics
3. Client/patient socioeconomic status
4. Frequency in client/patient need and contact

Individually and in combination, each of these factors must be considered by individual professionals in determining how best to establish practice development strategies. All of the four directly or indirectly influence the makeup of audiences toward which practice development efforts must be oriented.

Degree of Specialization

Most professionals ultimately specialize their practices to a greater or lesser degree. Some become quite restrictive by design, as in the case of pediatric surgeons or criminal trial lawyers. Others become restrictive in less conscious fashion, by exercising personal preferences or otherwise. Still others elect to enter professions in which practitioner selection is controlled more by third parties than by users of services involved.

All of these contingent circumstances must be considered in developing communication strategies for practice development programs. For optimum economy and productivity, all strategies must be designed in keeping with two parameters. First, they must result in delivery of messages to as many prospective decision makers as possible, Second, they must exclude those who are not decision makers, especially where cost is a function of audience size, as in the case of promotional mailings.

Specialization. Personal preference often plays a larger than evident role in practice development. Professionals, like most individuals, tend to do best what they like to do, and vice versa. Referrals therefore are apt to be most numerous from those who use services that practitioners prefer to provide. Over time, professionals' reputations for experience and expertise in the areas involved grow disproportionately.

These developments readily can produce a relatively specialized general practice. Communication efforts usually should reflect the extent to which such informal specialization exists in order that reputation support communication and vice versa. Potential conflict between reputation and communication should be tolerated only when new services are being introduced or when circumstances dictate change in existing practice development trends.

Specialization also should exercise a strong influence in professionals' communication strategies. Their efforts should concentrate on delivering appealing messages to those they prefer to serve, to the exclusion of all others. Messages delivered to others are wasteful and expensive. Cost of the waste varies with media but always exists.

Message strategies. Messages from pediatric surgeons, for example, would produce little response if disseminated in the retirement communities of Arizona and Florida. Such messages would be more productive in metropolitan areas but probably would be most beneficial in suburban communities populated largely by couples under the age of forty. Message delivery costs may be no greater in one community than another, but results can be very different.

Potential for variation expands in cases where decision makers and consumers of professional services may not be one and the same. Decision making is a shared process in some professions. In engineering and interior design, for example, decision making may be shared by consumers and previously selected architects. Communication strategies in these circumstances must address both groups. In other situations, such as anesthesiology, radiology, and pathology, decisions almost always are made by third parties. Messages then must be directed exclusively toward decision makers rather than consumers.

Demographic Factors

Efficiency in message delivery is a function of two factors. One consists of the communication channels available to professionals. The other involves the nature of the groups with which practitioners are seeking to communicate. The nature of groups—their demographic and psychographic characteristics—influence their use of communication channels. Messages can reach them only to the extent that they are "tuned in" to channels that professionals select.

While vital in selecting message delivery channels, demographics are even more important in another sense. The demographics of practice clienteles are a major determinant of the nature of the practices involved. Office locations and other factors play a part, but practices are more amenable to characterization through descriptions of clienteles than in any other way. Virtually every practice can be identified along a demographic spectrum ranging from "carriage trade" to "welfare." At one end of the spectrum, relatively small clienteles expect and pay for first class service. At the other end, large clienteles expect and pay for "bargain basement" services. The spectrum, in other words, ranges from class to mass.

Professionals must select channels of communication in keeping with the nature of practices, existing or desired. This is not to say that mere selection of communication channels can change the nature of a professional practice. Reputation, credentials, practice location, and a host of factors all play a part. What is important here is that channels to which opera goers are attuned will not reach the country music crowd, and the reverse is equally true.

Put another way, demography and socioeconomic status go hand in hand. Education and income levels are highly correlated. Practice development strategies must take these facts into account. The process is necessarily discriminatory. Guidelines for successful practice development are as follows:

1. Practice development must be focused on specific groups. There is no "general public," only a very specific public or set of publics of interest to individual practitioners in specific communities.

2. Development must be designed to elicit specific responses from those groups by concentrating on their needs and interests to the exclusion of others. No professional can be all things to all groups.

3. Development must be organized around themes and messages that are created to evoke desired responses and that are delivered through communication channels that will reach target audiences.

Socioeconomic Differences

Different practice development techniques tend to attract different clienteles in much the same manner that different clothing styles or different types of music are attractive to different groups. Those who are attracted to Chopin and Bach are unlikely to become enamored of acid rock or heavy metal groups. Those who select Patek-Phillip timepieces are not likely prospects for Timex.

In the same manner, those who would accept an attorney's "first consultation free" offer probably are unlikely to become clients on continuing bases. Podiatrists' "free examination" and opticians' "second pair free" offers are similarly unlikely to attract affluent clientele.

Superior services delivered in superior environments work to the benefit of all professionals under all circumstances. Each also must ultimately decide, however, just what kind of professional he or she wants to be; what kind of clientele he or she wants to serve. These decisions dictate the nature of clienteles and, by inference, the channels of communication that will best serve in delivering messages that will appeal to them.

Frequency of Need

Channel selection also must be examined in light of the informational needs of practice clienteles. Frequency in use of professional services varies within and across professions. Most individuals, for example, use the services of dental surgeons far less frequently than they do the services of dentists. Industrial real estate services usually are needed less frequently than those of the residential variety.

The variations involved should go far toward influencing selection of communication channels. The reason is a simple one: it is impractical for professionals to communicate continuously with those who may require their services on only a few occasions in a lifetime. In part for these reasons, one of two other sets of circumstances is also common. Selection of professionals is influenced by third parties, as with dental surgeons, or practices broaden geographically, as with industrial realtors. In either case, viable communication channels change apace.

Third parties. The term *third parties* thus involves more than parental influence on children or children's influence on aged parents. Significant numbers of professional assignments originate to a greater or lesser extent with other professionals. In the healing arts, radiologists and anesthesiologists usually are selected by surgeons rather than by their patients. Pathologists are employed by hospitals, and neither patients nor their physicians are involved in decision making where pathology services are necessary.

Lesser levels of third-party control arise where the services of surgeons, dental surgeons, engineers, interior designers, and other specialists are involved. Recommendations of primary care physicians and dentists usually influence the selection of surgeons. The same conditions apply for specialists in law and accounting. Engineers and designers often are selected by architects or on their recommendation.

These selections or recommendations may or may not lead to durable relationships. Patients often return to medical or dental specialists of their own volition when specialized services are required. Limited data suggest that this pattern is less prevalent in other professions. Few specialists therefore can afford to depend on returners for practice growth. Communication programs necessarily must focus on primary sources of referrals—colleagues rather than prospective patients or clients.

Practice geography. Somewhat different conditions develop in communities where numbers of potential clients or patients are so few as to frustrate conventional practice development efforts. These circumstances readily can develop in law, accounting, and other professional firms seeking to specialize in specific industries or types of clients. Practitioners in those disciplines who want to develop practices in the financial industry, for example, seldom find sufficient numbers of banks or savings and loan associations within their own communities to meet developmental needs.

Promotional efforts then must encompass larger geographic areas and different channels of communication. Traditional mass media—daily newspapers, television, and radio—seldom are productive where professionals are attempting to develop statewide or regional rather than municipally based practices. These media lack the reach to cover the pertinent geography. Radio and television signals seldom are strong enough to cover an entire state, and newspaper circulation patterns are similar.

Questions of cost versus efficiency would arise even if mass media reach was adequate to professionals' needs. Most questions would involve numbers of prospective clients or prospects among media audiences. Metropolitan newspapers today seldom reach more than 60 percent of the households in their communities. Radio and television penetration is lower still.

Professional development efforts require greater media selectivity, as usually can be achieved through one or both of two alternatives. The first consists of professional journals. There are journals to serve virtually every profession and many professional subspecialties. The second involves specialized forms of direct mail advertising. Newsletters and similar devices are most common among them.

EVALUATING COMMUNICATION CHANNELS

Most of the communication channels that conceivably might be used by professionals in pursuit of practice development have been mentioned in the foregoing pages. Situations in which some of them are especially applicable have been specified in general terms. Generalities, unfortunately, are inadequate to provide guidance to those unfamiliar with communication techniques and technologies. Professionals must instead be equipped to evaluate alternative communication channels in light of their own needs and situations.

Knowledge of communication channels necessary in practice development embraces several basic concepts as well as the variables that must be compared in evaluation processes. One of the basic concepts outlined earlier is worthy of repetition here: everything communicates. Another is equally important in comparatively examining channels of communication: costs arise in forms other than dollars.

Channels of Communication

The term *channels of communication* encompasses more than is readily apparent. Communication requires neither words not illustrations. Behaviors communicate. Environments communicate. People communicate. Other forms of communication are necessary in practice development, but the first three always exist and should never be forgotten. They communicate silently but with great effectiveness.

The word *silently* is appropriate because few professionals pause to consider the extent and effectiveness of behavior, environment, and people in planning practice development programs or their communication components. People and offices, from their perspectives, are merely there. These elements make no obvious contribution to practice development and too often are assumed to make no contribution. The reverse is true. The three perpetual communicators, as they might be called, inevitably compound or dilute the effectiveness of formal communication activities.

Dilution can be so great as to render formal communication ineffective. At the extreme, realities conveyed by the three perpetual communicators can be so strong as to overpower conflicting messages distributed through formal communication channels. The real nature of the professional practice, in other words, can communicate so effectively, for better or worse, that contradictory formal communication is counterproductive.

Formal communication. Formal communication activities can be sorted into two basic categories and a number of subcategories. The basic categories are interpersonal and mediated. The interpersonal category includes individual, small group, and large group components. The mediated group is more complex. Mediated communication generally is accomplished in printed or electronic form.

Within each of these subcategories there exist two others: controlled and uncontrolled. Controlled communication in the print area includes leaflets, brochures, mail materials, and other devices in which messages are controlled by senders. In the electronic areas, controlled communication includes slide-tape presentations, film strips, and other audiovisual communication. Uncontrolled communication encompasses messages prepared for dissemination through the news media, print and electronic. These include news, features, and product releases of all kinds.

New concepts. Many formal communication activities traditionally are associated with specific environments. Interpersonal communication especially is thought of primarily as organizational or internal communication rather than as a channel to reach groups outside an organization or practice. Today's communication environment requires, however, that no potentially productive device be discarded out of hand. Interpersonal communication therefore has come into common use externally as well as internally, as will be described in subsequent pages.

Technological advances similarly have brought traditionally external communication channels into common use within organizations. Audiovisual techniques are most prominent among these, especially in the form of videotape technology. Videotape cameras and associated equipment have increased in sophistication and declined in cost at such rapid rates in recent years as to be within the reach of virtually any organization. They are used extensively in patient and client communication as well as in educating, training, and motivating practice personnel.

Cost Factors

The onset of the new technologies—ranging from video to desktop publishing equipment—has resulted in quantum change in application of communication channels. The change has not significantly influenced costs, although contrary appearances are common in many organizations.

Contrary appearances can take the form of apparent increases or reductions in cost. Changes in cost usually occur where organizations change provider arrangements, often to establish more sophisticated internal operations. Communication responsibilities also can be shifted to external vendors, and apparent inconsistencies in cost can arise in either case.

Inconsistencies typically occur when managers fail to accurately assess all of the factors that contribute to cost in communication or other organizational functions. These factors include labor, facilities, equipment, and supplies. Developing sophisticated internal communication functions necessarily increases payroll and other costs. These increases often are offset, however, by declines in use of external vendors. The reverse can occur as well.

Professionals often take advantage of new technologies to enhance communication capabilities internally. They assume that costs will be significantly lower than costs of services obtained from external providers. Savings indeed may be achieved, but caution must be exercised in evaluating the alternatives. Labor costs especially must be carefully allocated internally if communication expenses are to be accurately reported. Do-it-yourself approaches, in other words, may or may not produce real economy.

The problem described above can arise in any organization but seems to develop with unusual frequency in the professions. The cause may be relatively high educational levels in the professions that can encourage practitioners to believe that they and their colleagues can do virtually anything. This indeed may be the case. Often neglected in the ''I-can-do-it-myself'' equation, however, is the amount of time required and the associated cost.

Any professional can learn enough accounting to keep an accurate set of books. Writing news releases or audiovisual scripts also involves acquired skills. Professionals should consider carefully, however, whether their economic interests are best served by a do-it-yourself philosophy. Is it ever possible, in other words, for one to save as much as he or she can earn by practicing his or her own profession?

IN SUMMARY

Extensive preliminaries necessary in creating practice development programs become optimally productive as those programs begin to reach out to prospective clienteles. The preliminaries are only marginally productive in and of themselves, in other words, but make major contributions to overall program success.

With preliminaries complete, professionals depart, to a greater or lesser extent, from activities designed exclusively as exercises in reputation building. Reputation, in professional practice, traditionally has produced its own rewards. Tradition, unfortunately, no longer is adequate to support a practice. Competitive contemporary environments demand more.

Practice development techniques can be created in conservative fashion or otherwise. They can remain within more or less traditional parameters or can go far beyond those boundaries. Traditional activities include public speaking, writing for professional journals, and involvement in community affairs. The nontraditional can involve advertising in all of its forms, from radio and television to direct mail coupons.

The appropriateness of any of these techniques varies with profession and practice. Some professions, especially the younger among them, have been more liberal than others in defining the boundaries of promotional propriety. Others have been more conservative. Development programs recognize these differences as well as a number of others at least equally significant.

The others include numbers of patients or clients, consistency in client or patient need, frequency of professional contact with typical clients or patients, geographic distribution of clienteles, nature and identity of decision makers and the demographic and psychographic characteristics of clienteles. Each of these factors influences the nature of the development program.

Numerically, practices can be categorized as broad-based or narrowly based. The bulk of healing arts practitioners are in the former category, while most other professionals are in the latter. Those in the latter category usually deal with infrequent needs of greater magnitude, while others are called upon more frequently but for less intensive services. Professionals whose services are needed with relative frequency tend to concentrate their practices geographically, while others often cover broader areas. Finally, broad-based practice clienteles tend to be socioeconomically diverse while narrowly based practices usually focus on more affluent clients.

A similar set of variables is to be found within individual professions. Practices vary in level of specialization, community or practice demographics, client/patient socioeconomic status, and frequency in client/patient need and contact with professionals. Each of these variables requires professional attention during the formation of practice development strategies.

Practices tend to become specialized for any of several reasons. Some specialization is created by design. In other cases, practitioners merely gravitate toward those activities they prefer and, as a result, do well. Practice demographic characteristics change accordingly. So does the nature of services delivered by professionals and the relative efficacy of alternative communication channels in reaching prospective clients. Demography and socioeconomic factors go hand in hand, as do education and income levels. These factors, coupled with the frequency with which professional services are required by existing and prospective clienteles, govern the selection of practitioner communication channels.

Communication channels include far more than the traditional media channels. Professionals must always remember that environments and behaviors communicate far more strongly than messages. Existing and prospective clienteles always will be influenced more strongly by environments and behaviors than by messages. Messages conveyed through media appropriate to specific audiences can do no more than magnify or diminish those delivered silently through associated environments and behaviors.

Formal communication activities, as opposed to the behavioral and environmental, can be sorted into two categories: interpersonal and mediated. The interpersonal include individual, small group, and large group communication. The mediated can be categorized as electronic and printed, controlled and uncontrolled. Controlled includes such media as audiovisual programs in the electronic sector and brochures in the print area. Uncontrolled includes news and feature releases, news conferences, and other activities designed to induce delivery of messages by print media editors or broadcast media news directors.

Recent technological developments, from the miniaturization of the videotape system to the microcomputer-based desktop publishing technologies, have expanded professionals' communication horizons in recent years. Costs in many cases have declined, although benefits have been realized more often in improved communication programs than in direct savings.

ADDITIONAL READING

Atway, Robert, Barry Orton, and William Vesterman. *American Mass Media: Industries and Issues*. 3rd ed. New York: Random House, 1986.

Baus, Herbert M. *Publicity in Action*. New York: Harper, 1954.

Connor, Richard A., Jr., and Jeffrey P. Davidson. *Getting New Clients*. New York: Wiley, 1987.

Hanan, Mack. *Consultative Selling*. 3rd ed. New York: amacom, 1985.

Katzen, May, ed. *Multi-Media Communications*. Westport, Conn.: Greenwood, 1982.

Marcus, Bruce W. *Competing for Clients: The Complete Guide to Marketing and Promoting Professional Services*. Chicago, Ill.: Probus, 1986.

12

Channel Variables

Whether conducted interpersonally or through alternative channels, communication essentially is a personal process. Results are personal even when the communicator is inanimate or behavioral. The impact of the process, moreover, is influenced by the extent of personal contact involved. For these reasons, professionals should direct every effort toward making communication as personal as feasible.

Level of personal involvement is a function of two factors. One consists of the frequency and duration of individual contact and the extent to which contact affords opportunity for communication. The other is the extent to which members of intended audiences can be identified. The extent to which professionals can apply interpersonal communication in practice development is dictated by the circumstances in which personal contact takes place. The manner in which alternative media can be applied is governed by professional ability to identify existing and prospective clients and patients.

Feasibility of use varies among channels of communication, interpersonal and mediated. Cost is the major variable in determining feasibility. Factors contributing to communication cost include out-of-pocket expense, developmental time requirements, extent of applicability across audience groups, channel-related factors, and durability of finished products.

Out-of-pocket cost results from purchase of products or services necessary to the communication effort for which professionals ultimately will receive bills. Developmental time includes all time required of professionals and members of their staffs that otherwise might have been devoted to other purposes. Cross-audience applicability refers to the extent to which a communication vehicle used with personnel, for example, might also be employed with patients or clients. Durability of finished products refers to obsolescence, while channel-related factors include such matters as reach and credibility.

All these elements must be examined in light of the fact that communication in professional development is a cumulative process. The cumulative result of communication in practice development consists of attitudes toward and opinions of professional practices. A great deal goes into construction of those attitudes and opinions, and the process must be understood by those who would successfully use the communication techniques involved.

CUMULATIVE COMMUNICATION

The cumulative or layering process that occurs in communication between individuals and organizations consists of five components. Three become operational before clients or patients come into direct contact with professionals. As such, they are subject only to indirect control. The remainder are or should be controlled by practitioners.

Different environments control the three sets of impressions created before prospective clients or patients come into contact with professionals. The first is reputation, that intangible mixture of fact, hearsay, and rumor concerning professionals that individuals seemingly absorb by osmosis. The second consists of reports elicited of friends and acquaintances before initial contacts are made. The third involves first impressions of practices created by their environments— the neighborhoods in which they are situated, the buildings in which they are located, and the offices in which they are housed.

Superimposed on these precontact impressions is another set created by the behaviors of practice personnel, including telephone operators and receptionists as well as paraprofessionals and professional staff members. Each, for better or worse, is a representative of the practice. And each is viewed by patients or clients as a conscious agent of the professional.

Finally, intermixed with the impressions created at these two levels is a third set intentionally created by professionals to influence practice development. Impressions involved cannot be considered a level in the usual sense, in that they are created during precontact as well as postcontact periods. Where aggressive practice development programs are used, they may include interpersonal as well as mediated communication during both periods.

Practitioner understanding of the concepts described above is important in that professional development programs are designed to influence the overall impressions of the practice in the minds of prospective clienteles. The cumulative process exists and operates with or without practitioner assent. It becomes operational wherever and whenever individuals and professionals come into contact with one another. The process consists of the construction—in part uncontrollable and in part controlled—of individual opinion toward practitioners. Its existence challenges professionals to influence the process in order to enhance the productivity of their practices.

INTERPERSONAL COMMUNICATION

Few professionals fully comprehend the potential productivity of interpersonal communication in practice development. That potential can best be understood by examining a long-standing principle of marketing communication: people prefer to deal with those they know *or think they know*. Excessive familiarity conceivably may ultimately become counterproductive. Faced with a need for professional services, however, most individuals tend to be more comfortable in calling on those with whom they have come in contact earlier. Contact, in this sense, may have been nothing more than attendance at one of the professional's speaking engagements. Behavioral results are the same. Other factors being equal, audience members subsequently will be better disposed toward speakers than toward their competitors.

These circumstances need not necessarily suggest that all professionals should become after-dinner speakers. As with most communication devices, the interpersonal variety is not an unalloyed blessing. The process must be viewed, with alternative techniques, in light of the factors specified earlier: out-of-pocket expense, developmental time requirements, extent of applicability across audience groups, channel-related factors, and durability of finished products.

Cost Factors

Interpersonal communication is the most effective method used by humans in the transfer of ideas. The term *interpersonal* applies to one-on-one and small-group and large-group communication. Effectiveness tends to decline inversely with audience size, but interpersonal communication nevertheless remains more effective than any mediated alternative.

The reasons involved are simple. Interpersonal communication permits direct contact between the parties. Speakers can "read" and respond to nonverbal as well as verbal audience responses. The objective of communication—successful interchange of ideas—is enhanced as a result.

Interpersonal processes are undertaken, however, only at relatively high real cost. As applied here, the term *real cost* refers to time as well as dollars—to the dollars that practitioners might have added to their revenues had time devoted to interpersonal communication been dedicated to the practice of their professions.

Relative cost may be low for professionals just starting out in practice because their waiting rooms are not full. These circumstances usually encourage practitioners to be more liberal with their time in dealing with individual clients or patients and otherwise. Their liberality is not misplaced. Strong client and patient relationships pay dividends. Time devoted to existing and prospective clienteles, whether in extended conferences or in public speaking, ultimately will pay dividends.

In successful practices, however, time becomes progressively scarcer. Office hours become precious. An hour away from the office involves progressively larger economic sacrifices as months and years pass. Professionals can and must find adequate time for interpersonal communication with staff members but this can be accomplished before or after office hours. The extent to which practitioners can productively dedicate time during office hours to interpersonal communication outside the office, however, is a function of individual circumstances.

Time Factors

Time required in interpersonal communication varies with the level at which the process is conducted. Relatively little preparation is necessary before conducting a performance evaluation or a staff meeting. A great deal may be involved in preparing a speech, especially if visual devices are to be used.

Once written, however, speeches can be used more or less repetitively with different groups. This especially is the case if professionals choose topics with care. "New Techniques in _____" is always a prime topic. Professionals need only plug in the hot new area of interest in their own practices. Speechmaking quickly becomes routine, requiring little preparation, when this approach is taken. Effectiveness requires, however, that speakers keep one point in mind: always focus on *the audience's* interest in the new development of which you're speaking. Answer, for the audience at hand, that ever-present question, "What's in it for me?"

Cross-Audience Applicability

The content of a speech, or any other message container can be used in multiple settings when professionals are willing to take time to fully exploit the products of their efforts. In many cases, in fact, the ultimate value of a communication effort is not found in the initial outcome but in the sum of several outcomes derived from multiple message applications. Overall potential is readily seen by examining the manner in which speeches can be exploited, although the technique involved can be applied to any communication effort.

The first question that logically occurs to those preparing to give speeches deals with media coverage. "Will the newspaper (or television station) cover the speech?" Perhaps, and perhaps not. Professionals can compound potential for coverage by providing advance copies of the speech to editors and news directors. That should be only one of many steps taken to exploit the process.

Preliminaries. It is always advisable to field test speeches with members of the professional organization. They are more comfortable audiences from speakers' perspectives and no doubt will be hearing questions from patients or clients concerning the speech soon after it is given. After testing, availability of the program should be made known to the program directors of professional, civic, and fraternal organizations. Each of these people is responsible for filling twelve to fifty-two program slots annually. That is no easy task, and the professional's speech often will be viewed as an answered prayer.

Each potential talk creates an opportunity for further exposure. First, there are the broadcast and print media in the local community. Copies of the speech should be provided to them in advance—far enough in advance to make coverage easy for the editors or news directors involved. Advance copies also should be circulated to magazines or professional journals relating to the audience involved. If it is a civic club, send speech copies to related state, national, and local organizations. If it is a professional group, send copies to all professional journals.

Follow-up. Appropriate follow-up measures should be taken as soon as the speech has been given. Letters should go to magazine or journal editors following up on the speech copies sent earlier and inquiring as to whether they would prefer content be rewritten to conform to editorial specifications. If radio or television representatives were present, arrange immediately to obtain copies of their tapes. Remember, those tapes often will be discarded in a matter of days if not hours. Videotapes especially may be amenable to reuse later.

Where magazines or professional journals print speeches, or articles adapted from speeches, authors can obtain a further promotional tool at little or no cost: reprints. Most magazines provide them at negligible cost and they can be used in many ways in practice development. Reprints can be mailed to existing or prospective clienteles, kept in waiting rooms to impress visitors, or distributed in the course of speaking engagements. Magazine or journal use of professionals' speeches constitute implied endorsements that should be exploited to the fullest.

The same principle can apply with the electronic media. A videotape of the portion of the professional's speech captured by a television station can be tastefully rerun ad infinitum on a continuous play projector in his or her office lobby. Alternatively, the speech might be commercially videotaped by prearrangement for use in other settings. Professionals can exploit program chairpersons' needs for programs by having audiovisual presentations available to them. The advantage here occurs in that principals in the professional firm need not always be in attendance. Taped or otherwise mechanized presentations can be played by paraprofessionals sufficiently experienced in subject areas to answer audience questions.

Durability and Obsolescence

Two other related factors require evaluation in assessing the value of interpersonal communication in professional development: durability and obsolescence. The two are not alike. Durability refers to the longevity of the medium or container in which information is placed. Obsolescence refers to the longevity of the content or message.

Durability factors were addressed in part above. The durability of interpersonal communication is a function of professionals' ability or willingness to see that messages are captured in electronic or printed form or both. Where either of the latter tactics are successful, messages originally contained in speeches gain almost unlimited durability.

Obsolescence is another matter. Obsolescence is a function of content and audience rather than packaging. The latter variable is especially noteworthy. The value of information deteriorates with age, especially in the professions. Today's state of the art procedure or technology is obsolete tomorrow. To a varying extent, however, the very fact that the professional's thoughts have been published or broadcast will impress audiences.

The latter point deserves attention. Reprints of articles containing information long obsolete continue to impress in many circles. Reprints therefore remain deserving of prominent positions in waiting rooms long after their content has become valueless. They tend to be even more valuable in the hands of professionals in those disciplines that require making personal sales calls on prospective clients.

Personal or sales calls are most effective where tangible evidence of expertise can be left behind in one form or another. Brochures are most often used. A brochure necessarily is less credible, however, than a reprint from a business or professional journal, no matter what the cover date. The reprint is especially effective where multiple individuals or groups are involved in decision-making processes. With business cards attached, reprints pass from hand to hand within prospect organizations long after brochures have been discarded or shuffled aside.

Cross-Channel Applications

The techniques described above represent what might best be identified as cross-channel applications, a process by which professionals gain more for their money in practice development. The objective always is to produce maximum exposure by extending the life or applicability of communication tools.

Few professionals readily recognize the many ways in which cross-channel application can enhance practice development efforts. Only a few have been pointed out above. Discussion to this point essentially has dealt in speeches and the ways in which they can be made more useful. The same principles, it should be remembered, can be applied in making interviews and other interpersonal and mediated communication devices more productive.

Consider, for example, use of reprints of journal, magazine, or newspaper articles in conjunction with a speech to any organization. This process gives each audience member something to take away with him or her. Many copies are discarded but others are retained for future reference or passed along to members of recipients' organizations.

Cross-channel application of communication techniques is a reinforcing mechanism that professionals ignore at considerable expense, and at what might be viewed as willful disregard for their own economic welfare. Expense arises in that large portions of the potential productivity of communication efforts go unharvested, with obvious negative economic consequences.

ELECTRONIC COMMUNICATION

Points emphasized above lead directly to what should be the first concern of those considering electronic communication: how can the results be used for greatest effectiveness across audience groups? Responses vary with the nature of groups, but most electronically packaged messages can be successfully employed with multiple groups given adequate preparatory planning.

Planning is the most needed and most often neglected component of communication. Need relates primarily to potential for cross-channel applications, but other factors are involved as well. Cost and time are interrelated in electronic and printed communication. Costs tend to increase or decline with the amount of time available to complete any project. Ability to anticipate communication needs and opportunities thus enables professionals to control costs and increase effectiveness in practice development programs. As was the case in terms of interpersonal communication, the following elements—out-of-pocket expense, developmental time requirements, extent of product applicability across audience groups, channel-related factors, and durability of finished products—must be examined in evaluating the electronic sector.

Cost Factors

Range of potential costs in packaging messages in electronic form is considerable. At one extreme are motion pictures that can involve production costs in the tens of thousands of dollars per minute. At the other extreme, as indicated earlier, is the duplicate of a television newsman's tape of a message delivered in speech form. In between are a nearly limitless number of variations.

Ranged from least expensive to most costly, audiovisual production generally would progress along the following continuum:

Slide-tape packages

Filmstrip presentations

Do-it-yourself videotapes

Professionally produced videotapes

Motion pictures

Any or all of these processes also can be combined with live telephone or satellite-based transmission when simultaneous real-time access is necessary on the part of relatively large groups at distant points. When small groups need to exchange information, as seldom is the case in professional development programs, telephone and computer-based conferencing also may be an option.

Cost factors in all cases are difficult to pinpoint. Slide-tape presentations usually can be produced on a do-it-yourself basis at costs in the tens of dollars per minute of finished material. Conversion to filmstrips adds little to total cost. Cost of do-it-yourself videotape usually moves into the hundreds of dollars per minute of finished material. Difficulties often are encountered requiring retakes, and editing adds to time burdens involved. Professionally produced videotape can involve costs in the thousands of dollars per minute of finished tape.

All of the foregoing are gross estimates. They assume availability of ample time to handle projects involving no special technical problems in cities of moderate size. Production costs can skyrocket in major metropolitan areas.

Time Requirements

Audiovisual production involves developing several basic components. Development processes usually begin with preparation of a script. When scripts are in near-final form, producers begin planning visuals to accompany scripted scenes. When visual planning is complete, photography or videotaping begins.

Each of these processes is time-consuming. Weeks or months can be involved in developing and fine tuning a script. Time requirements vary with complexity of subject material, anticipated running time for the finished product, quality level required, and proficiency of personnel involved. The latter elements are most important. "Quick and dirty" videotape production can be accomplished in hours. Broadcast quality presentations can require weeks or months.

The process is fraught with pitfalls, most of them self-induced as practitioners yield to the temptation to become personally involved in production. Practicing professionals usually have mastered the English language. As such, they are quite capable of writing. Writing and scriptwriting, however, are two very different things. Practitioners usually find the scriptwriting process challenging, interesting, and excessively time-consuming. In other words, it is best left to professionals, as is necessary camera work. Like scriptwriting, videotape camera work looks easy. Indeed, it is neither difficult nor exceptionally time-consuming in the living room or the back yard. Again, however, professional quality requirements can make the process far more complex.

Contemporary technology has made slide-tape, filmstrip, and videotape production less time-consuming in most circumstances than are the necessary preliminaries. Assuming no great technical problems, the transition from script to videotape is more rapid than the writing process. Editing of the videotape and adding sound track can extend the time requirements. Total elapsed time necessary in production is considerably greater, however, where motion pictures are involved. Technical processes are far more complex and more equipment-intensive. Although still used in some situations, motion picture production seldom is a viable option in professional practice development.

Cross-Audience Applicability

Of the techniques specified above, those involving videotape tend to be least costly over time. Two factors are involved. First, videotape presentations are readily edited, perhaps even more so than their slide-tape counterparts. Second, and more significantly, segments of one videotape are readily copied for inclusion in another without disturbing the original.

Flexibility of this sort permits videotape to be quickly edited for use with multiple audiences in accomplishing diverse objectives. Videotape of a complex medical procedure prepared for presentation at a professional meeting, for example, quickly can be converted for use in training, in orientation of patients and their families, and perhaps for mass media as part of an electronic news release.

Architects, engineers, decorators, and a host of others can use videotape in much the same manner. Perhaps the only practical limitation that persists in using videotape technology arises in terms of playback equipment. Until playback equipment becomes more portable, or until it becomes common in the offices of existing or prospective clienteles, use of videotape as a component of sales presentations will remain difficult. Slide-tape and some filmstrip equipment, in contrast, has been reduced in scale to the point at which it is transportable if not portable.

Regardless of these limitations, professionals always will be well advised to consider carefully the applicability of audiovisual technology in terms of all of their message-delivery needs. Contemporary society, with few significant exceptions, is becoming so visually oriented that electronic delivery of messages is preferable in most circumstances to printed alternatives. Only interpersonal communication usually proves superior, and that superiority persists most strongly only when the process is reinforced through electronic devices.

Durability and Obsolescence

Professionals usually view durability and obsolescence in audiovisual products more as a matter of audience than of technical factors. From a technical or obsolescence standpoint, the longevity of virtually any audiovisual presentation is apt to extend beyond the durability of its content. Technology has advanced to a point at which slides, tape, and motion picture film are, for practical purposes, indestructible. Other than as historical records, content usually becomes valueless long before container deterioration causes any concern.

Professionals' concerns in developing audiovisual presentations thus are more logically focused on content durability. Is the state of the art in the profession relatively stable, or is it advancing at a pace that will render presentations obsolete in weeks or months rather than years? Most professions change at rates that make motion pictures of questionable merit. Professional videotape may or may not be another matter. Comparison of production cost estimates with estimated useful life factors should be the professional's primary basis for comparison.

The useful life concept is best applied in keeping with sizes and numbers of audience members who will be exposed to messages contained in finished products. By estimating numbers of individuals who will be exposed to the message, professionals can gain quick insight into message cost on a per recipient basis. This indicator of productivity usually best serves in making production decisions.

Cross-Channel Applications

Perhaps the only significant drawback in electronic communication in comparison with the interpersonal variety develops in terms of product flexibility. Difficulties involved are not readily evident. Speeches are more easily adapted to audiences beyond the original than are audiovisual materials. When speeches are converted to audiovisual form, changes can be more complex, especially in videotape and most especially in film.

Segments of visual components of audiovisual communication nevertheless can often be used to strengthen presentations to other groups. This is especially the case if the originals were designed primarily for professional groups. Community organizations thereafter are apt to be impressed by portions of the original presentation, even though they may not thoroughly understand the content. As in the case of speech reprints, impressions left on lay people often are greater than the product merits.

Visual segments also are often adaptable for use in educating professional staff members or clienteles, although significant changes in scripts usually are necessary. Scripts must be written for individual audiences for maximum effectiveness. Seldom are those designed for use at professional meetings adequate for client or patient education purposes.

Overall cost and productivity of audiovisuals can be enhanced consistently only when professionals plan multiple applications in advance and adjust production processes accordingly. When scriptwriters are aware that their work may go before several audiences, for example, they can often adjust language accordingly. The result can be radically reduced variation across audience-specific scripts. The same benefit often develops, although usually to a lesser degree, in preparing the visual components of the product.

PRINTED COMMUNICATION

The multiple application concept is as productive in print as elsewhere. Despite videotape's flexibility, in fact, multiple applications in print today are equally economical. The effective cost of printed messages has been radically reduced and continues to decline under the pressure of the new technologies.

Net cost of printed messages in many cases also has declined in recent years. Introduction of the computer and the laser printer first spawned desktop publishing. More recently, word publishing, a somewhat less sophisticated but simpler process, has been introduced by computer software publishers. These techniques together have reduced the per recipient cost of printed messages to an unprecedented extent. Cost reductions have not been apparent only because their existence has resulted in increased use of print in the communication world.

Cost Factors

Average cost of printed materials probably has declined between 10 and 20 percent. Most of the savings have occurred in less sophisticated forms of printing, but the economies are nevertheless real. Disproportionate distribution in savings results from the nature of the printing process. The process involves three parts: typography and composition, preparation of negatives and plates, and transfer of ink from plates to paper. The advent of the computer and laser printer permit eliminating must of the labor earlier required in the typography and composition processes.

Pragmatically, savings in printing begin before typography and composition. Most writing and editing involved in preparing message content now are done by computer rather than typewriter. No retyping is necessary. The completed electronic file is printed on a laser printer, creating camera-ready copy from which negatives and printing plates will be made.

Variation in this process occurs only when finished printed products are to be printed in multiple ink colors or demand especially high quality levels. Savings persist even then. Writers' electronic files are fed into computer-based typesetting devices to provide higher quality type without further input.

While reducing printing cost, the new technologies have brought less expensive printed materials within the reach of virtually every professional. Statement inserts, leaflets and folders for on-premises use and mail distribution, newsletters, and a host of other items now can be produced more quickly and economically.

Precise cost estimates on specific products are difficult to project, primarily because of variation in labor cost. Newsletters directed by surgeons to anesthesiologists, or by engineers to architects, might well be written by professionals involved. Their knowledge of each other's perspectives are so akin to one another that understanding is virtually assured. Circumstances can be far different, however, when dentists or plastic surgeons want to use similar vehicles to communicate with patients or prospective patients. Additional skill then is needed to translate professionals' technical language into English comprehensible to the average individual. Translation costs, in other words, must be added to final prices.

Time Requirements

Computers and laser printers also have influenced time requirements in printing, especially where simpler projects are involved. A few hundred leaflets for a waiting room often can be completed in a matter of hours by using the laser printer as a printing press. Unit costs in laser printing are too high for projects requiring more than a relatively few copies, however, and most laser printers are limited to 8 1/2-by–11-inch sheets. Obtaining finished printing in so short a time nevertheless was unknown before the advent of the new technologies.

Newsletters, leaflets, brochures, and other products usually require larger paper sizes and may demand professional writing and editing assistance. Time required in their production increases apace. Still more time is needed if multiple ink colors and other "bells and whistles" are involved, but the printing process generally has been rendered shorter by advancing technologies.

In general, professionals should expect to be able to have a newsletter comfortably produced in a week to ten days; a brochure printed in one ink color in two to three weeks; and something as sophisticated as an annual report in a matter of two to three months. The major variable in these products is not in production time requirements but in the time necessary to avoid error. A few thousand newsletters can be thrown away and reprinted in the event of error without tremendous expense. Circumstances are far different where more sophisticated printing is involved. Consumers therefore usually are asked to check type proofs, composed proofs, color keys, and, perhaps, press proofs during the preparation process. Progress toward completion of the work is suspended while materials are taken to consumers, reviewed, and returned. If changes are made, time spans grow proportionately.

Cross-Audience Applicability

Time and cost factors in printing are a greater influence in cross-audience applicability of finished products than is the case when other channels of communication are involved. While reuse of electronic materials requires no additional investment and interpersonal communication adds only the cost of time involved, reprinting is disproportionately expensive.

Economy of scale makes the difference. Printing costs decline as quantities increase, because preparation costs, from writing to the moment the press begins turning, are amortized over quantities involved. Preparatory costs often account for one-third to two-thirds of total cost. This means, for example, that only one hundred dollars of the three hundred dollars cost of a job can be attributed to printing. Cost, in this case, for one thousand copies would be thirty cents each, but five thousand copies, all run at the same time, would cost only fourteen cents each.

These circumstances add urgency to the matter of cross-audience applicability. When five thousand copies of a product, to extend the analogy above, can be beneficially used by the professional, cost will drop significantly. It thus becomes logical to consider, for example, whether prospective clients or patients can be added to a mailing designed primarily for existing clienteles.

Cross-audience applicability probably is more extensive where printed products are concerned than in other situations provided appropriate precautions are taken at the outset. As in the case of audiovisual materials, preparation of content for printed items becomes more critical where multiple audiences are contemplated. The effort is worthwhile, however, to extend product usefulness and to reduce unit production costs.

Durability and Obsolescence

Printed materials present a somewhat different problem than electronic in terms of durability and obsolescence. Shelf life for printed materials is almost limitless if quality papers are used and storage conditions are good. Obsolescence, however, is another matter.

Rarely will the content of printed materials survive unchanged for twelve months in fast-changing technological, social, and economic circumstances. Professionals thus are positioned precisely on the horns of a dilemma. They must balance the economies of long-run printing against the potential waste that occurs when large quantities of material must be discarded as obsolete.

Other than such staples as checks, statement forms, and similarly mundane items, few printed products should be prepared in quantities sufficient for more than twelve months. Virtually every item used in practice development, with the possible exception of greeting cards, falls into the latter category. Where small numbers of clients or patients are concerned, even greeting card orders should be limited. Greeting cards preferably should not be used repetitively.

Cross-Channel Applications

Somewhat offsetting the obsolescence problem of printed materials is the potential for use with multiple groups, as indicated above, and in multiple applications. Multiple applications are most readily envisioned in terms of three basic distribution methods: mail, on premises, and off premises.

Each item to be printed should be examined beforehand to determine the extent to which it can be productively applied in other settings. Potential for further use often surprises many professionals. Productivity potential in additional applications often is even more surprising.

Consider, for example, the many ways in which a reprint of an article published in a professional journal can be used. Copies can be distributed in the waiting room and to practice personnel; mailed to colleagues, existing clienteles, and prospective patients or clients; and distributed in the course of speaking engagements. A reprint, in addition, in all likelihood can continue to be used in this fashion for years.

Other printed materials are equally adaptive. Those designed for use in waiting rooms usually can be used in connection with speaking engagements. Those designed for mailing to clients or patients often can be used both internally and at speaking engagements. Return on investment is compounded where professionals take advantage of this potential.

IN SUMMARY

Communication is a personal process. The impact is personal and results are personal. The process therefore is most effective where undertaken on as personal a level as possible.

Ability to personalize communication is limited by a number of factors. These include the extent to which practice requirements expose professionals to clients or patients and the extent to which prospective clienteles can be identified.

Within limits imposed by the factors specified above, cost becomes a controlling element in selecting communication channels. Cost variables include out-of-pocket expense, developmental time requirements, breadth of product applicability, channel-related factors, and durability of finished products. All of these elements must be considered in light of the fact that communication between organizations and the groups with which they are involved is cumulative in nature.

Three sets of factors contribute to the communication process that exists before prospective clients or patients ever arrive at practitioner doors. Reputation is the first of them. Reports of friends and acquaintances constitute a second. The third is the impression created by practice environments.

Behavioral communication on the part of practice personnel is added to the prearrival mix before traditional communication techniques can be applied. The latter include interpersonal and mediated forms of communication. The mediated include print and electronic.

Interpersonal communication arguably is the most powerful and most costly approach to practice development. No mediated technique can create the level of communication that interpersonal contact provides. Interpersonal techniques— one-on-one, small- and large-group communication—nevertheless are costly in terms of communicator time as well as dollars. Time demand varies with techniques selected.

Costs associated with interpersonal communication can be controlled by augmenting results. This objective is most easily accomplished by applying messages prepared for interpersonal delivery through other media as well. Speeches, for example, can be readily recorded for other applications. Advance copies distributed to the news media can generate exposure before and after delivery in the mass media and in trade and professional journals.

When speeches are recorded, they often can be integrated in part into other presentations. They also can be used for internal purposes, as in lobby or waiting room exhibits. Finally, materials generated for other applications, from article reprints to brochures and newsletters, can be used in conjunction with speeches to enhance mutual productivity potential.

The same principle applies, of course, in terms of mediated communication, print and electronic. Multiple applications, as in the case of interpersonal communication, help justify professional investment in electronic and print media. The electronic media yield audio or videotapes that can be used in whole or in part in many applications, provided adequate planning occurs in advance. Cost of electronic production can be considerable, however, ranging from tens of thousands of dollars per minute for motion picture film to hundreds of dollars for an uncomplicated slide-tape presentation.

Audiovisual production is relatively time-consuming. Most forms of the art require more skill than is readily apparent to produce a quality result, and practitioners are best advised to delegate responsibilities to qualified personnel.

Durability and obsolescence exert a negligible influence over the audiovisual sector. Flexibility in application of finished products enables users to achieve sufficient productivity to justify costs involved.

The multiple application concept is equally useful in the print sector. While one set of technologies has enhanced flexibility in electronic production in recent years, another set has reduced costs in many print applications. Desktop publishing has produced substantial economies—in terms of dollars and of time—in producing less sophisticated printed products. Use of printed products in conjunction with audiovisual and interpersonal communication can amortize costs incurred in their production, although care must be taken in determining printing quantities. Few products should be ordered in quantities greater than their anticipated annual consumption rates.

ADDITIONAL READING

Bretz, Rudy. *Media for Interactive Communication*. Beverly Hills, Calif.: Sage, 1983.

Brody, E. W. *Public Relations Programming and Production*. New York: Praeger, 1988.

Greenberger, Martin. *Electronic Publishing Plus: Media for a Technological Future*. White Plains, N.Y.: Knowledge Industry Publications, 1985.

Kindem, Gorham. *The Moving Image: Production Principles and Practices*. Glenview, Ill.: Scott, Foresman, 1987.

Knapper, Christopher K. *Expanding Learning through New Communication Technologies*. San Francisco: Jossey-Bass, 1982.

Maas, Jane. *Better Brochures, Catalogs, and Mailing Pieces: A Practical Guide with 178 Rules for More Effective Sales Pieces That Cost Less*. New York: St. Martin's, 1981.

Rice, Ronald E., and associates. *The New Media: Communication, Research, and Technology*. Beverly Hills, Calif.: Sage, 1984.

Van Nostran, William. *The Nonbroadcast Television Writer's Handbook*. White Plains, N.Y.: Knowledge Industry Publications, 1983.

13

Strategic Communication

Successful communication efforts in practice development are built on dual foundations. One is knowledge of alternative communication techniques. The other is a clearly defined practice development strategy. Developmental strategies provide direction for communication as well as development. They specify the intended scope of the professional practice. They describe, by implication, the nature of groups whose behaviors will influence practice growth. Collectively, developmental strategies guide every communicative aspect of the practice, including the behavioral and environmental.

All of the foregoing should underscore a single point: promiscuous communication at best is wasteful and at worst can be economically disastrous. Communication, like practice development, is a purposeful effort. It is a process designed to support professionals seeking to move their practices from where the practices are to where they want them to be. Communication and practice development strategies, in other words, are mutually dependent. Strategic decisions as to practice development must precede decision making necessary to implement supporting communication programs.

PRACTICE STRATEGIES

Most professionals deal with relatively few variables in determining how they want their practices to develop. Variables most often used in defining strategies include the following:

1. Socioeconomic status or businesses of clienteles
2. Geographic scope of practice
3. Scope of services to be offered

4. Office location(s)

5. Extent of specialization

6. Optimum size of practice

    These variables are interrelated. Professionals' decisions as to optimum practice size often are reflected in the nature of clienteles they seek to serve. Smaller practices can be as lucrative as their larger counterparts if confined to more affluent socioeconomic groups. Level of specialization is similarly related to the geographic scope of practices and the range of services they offer. In general, the more specialized a practice, the narrower the range of services and the broader the geographic area.

    Professional decision making in the practice strategy arena, however, usually is more a function of market conditions than of practitioner preference. Consciously or unconsciously, professionals proceed through a relatively simple sorting out process in identifying areas of optimum economic potential. Variables that can and should be considered during the process include community developmental trends and alternative market niches. The practitioner's first objective in professional development, in other words, should be a comprehensive strategy. Creating that strategy requires two preliminaries: information gathering and market analysis.

Information Gathering

    Outsiders' perspectives of any market tend to be far different from those of insiders. Neither of the viewpoints involved, in addition, is apt to be wholly accurate. Professionals contemplating establishing practices or in the process of reevaluating practice strategies should examine all available insights in order to reach informed decisions.

    Insights in most cases can be obtained from multiple sources. The sources include clienteles, colleagues, associated professionals, and vendors. The several sources of demographic and psychographic data described earlier should be consulted as well. Professionals' efforts in each case should be oriented to determine as precisely as possible the breadth and depth of demand for services that is likely to exist over the ensuing two to three decades.

    Practice information. Those already in practice will find their first rich lodes of information within their own records. The data involved, dealing with such variables as patient age, longevity, and so forth, may be easy or difficult to obtain. Information may be readily available from computer records or may have to be extracted manually.

    Whichever may be the case, professionals must identify prevailing practice development trends and the reasons why those trends exist. They may favor further exploitation of existing practice patterns or changes in strategy.

    The primary questions at hand are relatively simple: what will be the economic potential of the practice over the ensuing decades, and how can that potential be enhanced by adjusting one or more of the variables mentioned above?

Colleague information. A great deal more information exists, and usually is available, through colleagues. Senior practitioners especially are predisposed to share knowledge with their juniors. Few are prone to be secretive with information that is of little or no value other than to younger professionals.

Where these conditions do not exist, a bit more effort may be necessary. Noncompeting peers—those in other cities, states, or regions—often can be most helpful. So can professional associations that may track developmental trends on regional and national bases.

Every professional should take the time necessary to get "plugged into the network" in his or her discipline. Membership and participation in the meetings, seminars, and other activities of the profession usually are all that is required. Information exchanged formally and informally at those meetings can be a major source of guidance in professional development.

Other data. One other set of often overlooked sources of information also is important. It consists of associated professionals and vendors, both of whom are necessarily familiar with the profession and sensitive to prevailing developmental trends. Engineers, for example, often can tell a young architect more about local and regional trends in the practice of architecture than can the principals in any individual architectural firm. Engineering firms usually serve many other architects in their geographic areas.

The same patterns exist in other disciplines. Dental surgeons, orthodontists, and endodontists usually are more familiar with trends in general dentistry than are general practitioners. Internists and surgeons often are far more knowledgeable than are general practitioners. Graphics specialists and commercial artists are highly sensitive to trends in advertising.

The pattern also prevails among vendors serving professional practices, from whom even more detailed information sometimes can be obtained. Equipment and supply vendors usually know a great deal about the "state of the union" in disciplines they serve. The nature of services and products they supply keeps them informed as to what practices are growing and which are not. Vendors' casual conversations with professionals and paraprofessionals make them privy to a great deal of sensitive or confidential information, some of which ultimately slips out.

Market Analysis

With all available information in hand—statistics and suppositions, facts and surmise—professionals must make their own analyses of market potential. Analyses must deal with disciplines and with specialties and subspecialties within those disciplines. They must deal with firms and personalities, with cities and regions, with every available insight that may prove beneficial in establishing a course of action.

Results of this process are expressed in a series of practice development strategy decisions:

1. These are the groups the practice will serve.
2. This is the geographic area in which they are to be found.
3. These are the services that the practice will offer, now and in the future.

Each of the decisions must be undertaken with care. Each should be based on careful analysis of primary and secondary variables. Without all possible care in decision making, potential for economically damaging error is compounded intolerably.

Problem potential is as much a function of events that logically follow decision making as of the decisions themselves. Practitioners who have decided upon the nature of the services they will offer, the areas in which they will be offered, and the groups to which they will be offered inevitably proceed in keeping with those decisions. Offices are located or relocated accordingly. Interiors may be modified to meet the needs of existing and prospective clienteles. Personnel often are trained or retrained with specific clienteles in mind. Substantial investments thus may be put at risk as the practice development process begins. Total investment increases as communication strategies are established, vehicles are selected, and programs are implemented.

COMMUNICATION STRATEGIES

No successful communication strategy is created in a vacuum. Each must be designed to meet the requirements of a specific practice development strategy and the foundations or assumptions on which that strategy has been based. The communication strategy must be specific to practice clienteles, existing and prospective; to geographic limits established for the practice; and to services offered or intended to be offered.

Audience size, nature, and geography, in other words, are communicators' primary concerns. With these factors known,

1. audience characteristics can be identified
2. productive messages can be designed, and
3. appropriate media can be selected.

Pragmatically, these steps usually are taken concurrently rather than sequentially. Each is considerably more complex than it appears.

Audience Characteristics

Multiple audience characteristics influence development of communication strategies. Audience size and identity are major factors in identifying media to be used. Audience interests and motivations influence the nature of messages to be transmitted.

In each case, the nature of professional services offered and, most important, the extent and frequency with which they are apt to be needed influence the process. Frequency of professional-prospect communication, as earlier discussed, should be governed by these factors.

Audience size. Size arguably is the most critical of audience characteristics in creating communication strategies. Audience size dictates the viability of alternative communication techniques. The extent to which interpersonal communication can be employed and to which mediated communication is necessary is governed by audience size.

The factors involved are not absolutes. Interpersonal communication is possible in all circumstances. The process becomes increasingly impractical, however, as audience size increases. Engineers logically can make personal calls on architects. Surgeons can regularly contact internists directly or through professional associations. Most accountants and attorneys face much different problems. Their prospective clients are so many that any effort to apply interpersonal techniques in communication would be prohibitive in terms of time demand.

Professionals dealing with a few hundred prospective clients or patients logically should concentrate their efforts in the interpersonal sector. Those who number prospects in the thousands may not abandon interpersonal contact but must emphasize mediated communication in one form or another.

Audience identification. The audience identification question in practice development communication is more complex than in comparable activities elsewhere. Decision makers involved in most merchandise-related transactions are relatively obvious. Spousal influences may arise in terms of major purchases, but most decision makers otherwise are the buyers of the products involved.

These circumstances may or may not obtain where professional services are involved. Pediatricians always deal with parents or guardians rather than with patients. Interior designers and engineers often are employed by architects. Many professionals in law, accounting, engineering, architecture, and a host of other disciplines are employed by organizations rather than individuals.

The identification problem in organizations is especially troublesome. Decision-making authority with regard to products usually is centralized in larger organizations' purchasing departments. Locus of power, as it sometimes is called, is not as evident where professional services are involved. Several individuals or groups often are involved. Decision-making power in national and transnational corporations may be spread over several committees.

The extent to which decision makers can be identified is a major determinant in selecting channels of communication. Interpersonal approaches initially are practical only when decision makers or contact points can be identified. Personal letters followed by telephone calls and possibly appointments require precise prospect identification. Name, title, address, and telephone number must be known. Where these conditions cannot be met, communicators may be forced to resort to alternative communication channels, despite the apparent applicability of the interpersonal channel.

Audience interests. Where members of prospective clienteles cannot be individually identified, individual interpersonal and mail approaches initially are impossible. Other interpersonal techniques, however, continue to be viable. Business, trade, and professional associations, through their meetings, seminars, and conventions, become logical channels for alternative approaches. Attendance or, preferably, participation will lead to contacts with individuals who often can provide information on organizational decision-making processes.

The same principle applies in other situations. Consider, for example, the problem of the plastic surgeon specializing in cosmetic rather than reconstructive procedures. Logic suggests that prospective clients will be relatively wealthy, aging, and, for the most part, female. Since the procedures involved are elective, only a small percentage of the prospect group is apt to be interested in the surgeon's services at any given moment. Successful communicators in these circumstances must deliver messages with some frequency to all members of the primary target group. Those involved can be identified to some extent from a communication perspective. First, every community has a number of groups that attract members of the group involved. Some are charitable or philanthropic in nature. Others are social. Most maintain formal organizations, which means they have membership lists and may meet regularly. These circumstances imply potential for use of newsletters or other mail materials if membership lists can be obtained. They also suggest a possible need for program speakers.

Another alternative applicable in this context and similar situations involves spending and reading habits. Credit card user lists are offered for sale for promotional purposes. So are the circulation lists of magazines. Some credit card organizations and many publications cater to the relatively affluent. Acquisition of their lists permits access to groups whose members may have the economic status to be prospects for cosmetic surgeons' services.

Appropriateness of Media

The audience interest principle identified above must be applied in dealing with large audiences as well as small. Smaller audiences, class audiences as opposed to mass audiences, require special consideration only in that numbers involved permit efficient and productive use of a broader range of communication techniques. Extensive application of interpersonal approaches in dealing with mass audiences is impractical even where those involved can be identified.

Consider, for example, the plight of the residential real estate agent who recognizes that most apartment residents ultimately will buy dwellings. Those involved are so many as to preclude successful application of any interpersonal communication channel. The agent instead must look to such vehicles as magazines that appeal to young, upwardly mobile members of the community.

Knowledge of media that serve prospective clients or patients thus is vital to those who would successfully communicate. Most community media today fall into logical categories. They include print, electronic, and what might be called alternative media. Each category is worthy of examination in light of its applicability to professional development programs.

Print media. The print media include newspapers and magazines. Most larger communities have daily, weekly, legal, and business newspapers. Many have a so-called city magazine. A few have specialized magazines directed to specific types of businesses or professions.

The magazines, because of their relatively narrow audience groups, are most applicable in professional development programs. Legal and business newspapers may be used as well. Traditional daily and weekly newspapers, other than where the latter serve affluent suburbs, seldom are appropriate vehicles for those seeking to market professional services.

Print and electronic media both can deliver professional advertising. News and feature releases published and broadcast without charge are far more productive but require greater skill and effort in preparation. News coverage also is usually perceived to be well within any traditional ethical limitations. Some professionals consider advertising as less than wholly ethical.

News releases usually are based on changes in professional practices. Appropriate subject matter includes new services, personnel, and facilities, as well as professional activities ranging from research to publication of books or articles in professional journals.

Print media exposure, especially in daily and weekly newspapers, seldom is optimally productive in and of itself. Users of these media should remember, however, that material they contain readily can be reproduced for use in other applications.

Electronic media. The electronic media include radio and television, including cable systems. These are primarily entertainment rather than news media. Most can be effectively used, however, to distribute information delivered to them in the form of news or feature releases.

Electronic media are more demanding of professionals than are the print variety in that the electronic require more than appropriately written material. Radio news directors often want professionals to provide taped statements for broadcast. Television criteria call for visuals as well. Visuals in most cases must involve activity that will capture viewer attention when broadcast. "Talking heads," as they are called, are anathema to stations competing for audience share.

Most cable systems offer public access and other channels to which professionals readily can gain access. Audiences are so small, however, as to make these media of marginal value other than in one context: copies of videotapes made for cable can be successfully applied elsewhere—in waiting rooms, in speaking engagements, and in a host of other situations. Cable systems' production facilities often are also made available to the public at little or no cost.

Alternative media. Other situations include a broad range of communication settings and applications that are becoming increasingly important in practice development. Most important among them are those that can be characterized as synergistic in nature. These are communication channels and devices that are amenable to what might be called multiplier effects.

Consider, for example, a research or other paper prepared for presentation at a professional meeting or publication in a professional journal. Announcements of the presentation or publication are often acceptable to local print and broadcast media. Reprints of the article then can be used in professional offices, in calling on prospective clients, or in direct mail applications.

Potential is even greater if the paper presentation was recorded on audio or videotape. Local radio and television stations will be more interested than otherwise would be the case, and copies of the tapes subsequently can be used in local speaking engagements as well.

Local speaking engagements can be as beneficial for those whose services are of interest to small groups as are state and national presentations for others. The best audiences necessarily consist entirely of prospective users of professionals' services. This standard seldom can be met, but audiences can be selected by economic status or interest group to include significant percentages of prospective clients or patients.

Benefits will accrue even from presentation to "weaker" audiences, however, in that information involved also can be conveyed through print and broadcast media. Daily and weekly newspapers often print articles about presentations that have been given or are going to be given. Occasionally, both advance and follow-up stories will be published.

MESSAGE STRATEGIES

Beneficial mass media exposure can be achieved by virtually every professional. Gaining exposure, however, requires that several conditions be met. The most important among them is that information conveyed to the media must meet contemporary definitions of news.

Several other criteria also are important. Information must be conveyed on a timely basis and in keeping with media standards. When these conditions have been met, information qualifies to be printed or broadcast.

Qualifying does not insure broadcast or publication. Every news and feature release—print and broadcast—is at the mercy of events beyond the ability of professionals and media to control. Natural disasters and other events can prevent publication of the best of releases, leaving communicators with nothing to show for their efforts. Such incidents are to be expected. Those who want to insure publication or broadcast can do so, at considerably greater cost, only by purchasing advertising in the same media.

Nature of News

Information becomes news in a manner that meets practitioners' professional development needs only by meeting several standards. Two are paramount. First, content must be of significant interest to a large portion of the group that the target medium considers to be prospective audience members. Second, content must meet the needs of the professional.

Looking at the mass media from another viewpoint, those who would successfully communicate through them must create a tripartite community of interest. When this construct is understood, as explained below, media economics and simple logic lead to communication success.

Media economics. The economics of the mass media determine the extent to which any news release will be published or broadcast. Mass media economics, in turn, is a numbers game, nothing more, nothing less.

The mechanics of the game are simple. With rare exceptions, as in public broadcasting, the media are for-profit organizations. Their primary loyalty is to the bottom line rather than to the public interest. The bulk of their revenues is produced by advertising sales. Advertising rates are based on print media circulation and broadcast audience size.

The primary responsibility of editors and news directors to their employers, for these reasons, is to build circulation and audience. They accomplish this objective by creating products that will attract the largest audiences possible.

Message content. Given these circumstances, professionals should readily understand the manner in which news and feature releases are evaluated. Each is examined in light of a single question: will it attract the audience? Message content must be of sufficient interest to readers, viewers, and listeners to encourage them to buy the magazines or newspaper or to tune in the radio or television outlet.

Professionals must fashion messages that meet these guidelines and that will also serve their development needs. In other words, as indicated earlier, messages must be of interest to readers or viewers in order to meet the standards of media gatekeepers. They concurrently must be of developmental value to professionals.

Creating News

News can be generated for the media in one of two ways. First, events can be caused to occur which by nature will be newsworthy. Second, and at least equally important in practice development, relationships between professionals and the media can be established through which media come to call upon professionals to comment on newsworthy events in their areas of expertise.

The latter approach to creating news is more time-consuming and requires personal effort on the part of professionals as well as communicators. It is a more durable generator of media exposure, however, than almost any conceivable number of newsworthy events that professionals might engender.

Expert source. Professionals can become expert sources for the media by concurrently applying a number of strategies, some not unlike those used in efforts to communicate with media audiences. Professionals' objectives in this case, however, are to build relationships rather than to generate media exposure.

Relationships necessarily are personal. To be productive, they must involve media gatekeepers—editors and news directors—as well as professionals. Editors and news directors rather than reporters are primarily responsible for deciding what local architect will be called for comment on a construction code problem or what physician will be called for comment on a medical breakthrough.

Professionals can come to know editors and program directors in several ways. First, practitioners can gratuitously provide information to editors and news directors, with business cards attached, on a for-your-information basis. Copies concurrently may be provided to reporters *for* publication, but the objective here is to create a relationship, to establish the professional as a news source and an expert in his or her field. Reprints of articles, copies of speeches, samples of brochures and any other material that might conceivably be of interest should be provided regularly to gatekeepers for all media that might be of value in professional development.

After several months of supplying information in this manner, the professional should make personal calls on those involved. Calls should be timed to avoid news deadlines. Visits should be brief and to the point: "I hope the information has been of help. Please feel free to call at any time. Here are my direct telephone numbers, at home and at the office." The professional's objective here is to strengthen the relationship through personal contact. Gatekeepers are more apt to telephone those they've met in person.

Finally, no sooner than a few weeks after the personal call, professionals should seek opportunities to create their "first big breaks." Big breaks are the first occasions on which professionals are quoted extensively by the media. They usually are more readily obtained in print than electronically. Breaks are obtained by watching or listening to the electronic media for breaking news stories concerning the professional's area of expertise, and then calling the print media to offer "any information that may be helpful to you." Copies of resulting articles then can be mailed to other media—print and electronic—with a brief note saying, "I'd be happy to help you, as well, whenever a need arises." The desired pattern at this point has been established.

Making news. Generating news for the media on a consistent basis is necessarily time-consuming but rewards usually are sufficient to justify the effort involved. Some necessary information already exists in most professional practices, and the remainder usually can be generated without excessive effort. The information comes from three sources: the practice and both professional and personal activities beyond the scope of the practice.

Practice-related information worthy of dissemination includes changes in scope of services, relocation or expansion of facilities, and changes in professional and paraprofessional personnel. All of the information involved will not be published or broadcast, but news releases nevertheless should be distributed to all of them. Extra copies are inexpensively prepared and circulated and help fulfill the professional's expert role in any event.

Feature releases are another matter. They can be developed on a broad range of subjects but are not necessarily intended for the mass media. Most professionals, for example, have developed techniques or tricks of the trade that would be of interest to peers. Others engage in research. Some have devised "better mousetraps" in managing their practices. Such information is highly valued by professional journals.

Information of interest to professional and business journals and to magazines read by prospective clients and patients is especially valuable in practice development. Techniques used by an architect to solve a problem for a manufacturer, for example, may be of interest to others in the manufacturing industry involved or to all industrial managers. Exposure in their professional journals inevitably produces inquiries from prospective clients.

Activities beyond the scope of the practice can be equally productive. Professionals who want to encourage the development of their practices should become involved in their professional organizations. They should volunteer for committee assignments that inevitably lead to officer status. They should offer to serve as faculty in professional development seminars. All these activities can generate information for news releases and much more.

In conducting professional development seminars, practitioners gain opportunities to describe their own accomplishments. Seminars usually require preparing speeches or other accompanying materials that bring with them considerable potential for further exploitation. Speeches readily can be converted for use as journal articles. They later can be circulated, as can journal articles, to gatekeepers and reporters. Finally, presentations can serve as a basis for news releases.

Communication techniques in this manner can be made to feed upon themselves. A news release can lead to an invitation to speak, which can lead to a news release. A journal article can trigger further news releases and additional speaking invitations. The overall results can be a cyclical progression that becomes self-sustaining in much the same manner as can occur when professionals take time to cast themselves in expert roles.

Finally under the heading of making news is the matter of professional activities that are not strictly professional related. The word *strictly* is applicable because the "distance" between professionals' community activities and their practices can be a major variable. Most activities can be sorted into one or both of two categories: governmental and nongovernmental.

Many professionals accept, and should accept, appointment to governmental and quasi-governmental bodies that relate to their areas of professional competence. The presence of an engineer on a construction codes panel, an architect on a zoning panel, or an attorney as an interim judge can be highly beneficial to professional practices. Such appointments are especially valuable where they enable those involved to speak out in public on issues that involve public interest and professional expertise. A great deal of salutary media exposure is almost certain to result.

Service of this sort may or may not be of benefit where professionals are attempting to develop expert status with the media. In general, public service in appointive, relatively nonpolitical positions produces favorable results. Difficulties can arise, however, when professionals seek elective office. Their efforts toward practice development then may be misunderstood by media gatekeepers as politically rather than professionally oriented. Where this is the case, media exposure can decline rather than increase.

Nongovernmental service is another matter. Potential for misunderstanding is absent and results in the form of media exposure can be almost equally beneficial, provided that professionals elect to join and serve in appropriate organizations. Appropriate groups, in this case, are those that, while nongovernmental, nevertheless are related to professionals' interests and expertise.

An architect, for example, would find service with preservationist or beautification-oriented groups to be appropriate. An oncologist logically might volunteer to assist the American Cancer Society. An attorney might associate with the Freedom Foundation. As in the situations described above, these affiliations, to the extent that professionals are active, also can generate speaking engagements, media exposure, and the like.

Capitalizing on News

Professionals who employ the techniques described above to generate media coverage find themselves and their work better known and their practices growing as a result. Too often, however, they permit significant portions of the potential benefits of their efforts to go unrealized.

The problem involved, fortunately, is readily solved. It arises out of an increasing questionable assumption: that information published or broadcast by the mass media is quickly disseminated through the populations professionals serve or seek to serve. The solution requires that practitioners act on a contrary assumption and insure that the content of media reports is conveyed to those most important to their practices: clients and patients, existing and prospective.

Audience problems. Failure of information published and broadcast in the United States to circulate adequately is a product of media proliferation, which in turn creates audience fragmentation. The problem exists in broadcast and print sectors alike and has progressed to a point at which many media experts contend that the term *mass media* is a misnomer, much akin to *airline food*.

One may agree or disagree with the terminology but the problem is real. Media have been proliferating and audiences have been declining in size. Daily newspapers are fewer in number, but there are more weeklies as well as business and legal newspapers. Magazines—special rather than general interest magazines—are proliferating at an unprecedented rate. Network television outlets now face competition from independent stations and cable systems. Each medium that survives necessarily captures a part of the audience and revenue of its predecessors, with inevitable results.

Defeating the trend. Professionals bent on having their messages conveyed must turn to other channels of communication to supplement that which they accomplish through the mass media. They can and should take advantage of the alternatives, especially where communication programs make these channels amenable to use at relatively low cost.

Printed materials of all kinds are most useful in offsetting media audience problems. They can be distributed in any of several ways, only some of which add significantly to professionals' communication costs. Economies tend to be greatest if reprints are extensively used and if distribution is accomplished in conjunction with speaking engagements and other activities.

The most obvious and most expensive of the options is mail distribution, which may or may not be appropriate. The nature of the profession and the practice are the primary variables involved. Those who see patients or clients regularly, as in the case of dentists or accountants, may find waiting room distribution sufficient. Where patients or clients are seen irregularly, as in the case of architects or surgeons, mail distribution is indicated.

ALTERNATIVE STRATEGIES

The foregoing pages deal largely with uncontrolled channels of communication. The few controlled channels that have been mentioned—mail distribution of reprints, for example—generally have been well within traditional ethical constraints. This should not be taken as suggesting that professionals should neglect the potential of controlled communication channels to the extent that it exists.

The audience problem addressed above is very real. It is progressively eroding the ability of most forms of advertising to deliver real market penetration. In general, the strongest media are metropolitan daily newspapers. In most cities, they penetrate 50 to 60 percent of all households. Some weeklies may perform somewhat better, but they are rare.

Few professionals can afford to tolerate message distribution systems that deliver such low percentages of prospective clienteles. They must instead make extensive use of uncontrolled systems and handle the controlled, with the possible exception of direct mail, with caution.

Other than as discussed above, there are but two strategies worthy of consideration. One is controlled; the other, uncontrolled. The first, involving extensive use of interpersonal communication, is a strategy that promises success only where prospective clienteles are quite small, as in the case of architecture, engineering, advertising, and the like. It will be discussed at length in the ensuing chapter. The second, a controlled approach, involves use of media advertising. Some of the advertising media are acceptable across all professions. Others are not.

Mass Advertising

Members of some professions draw distinctions between mass media and other forms of advertising. At a minimum, they consider some acceptable and the remainder unacceptable from an ethical standpoint. Boundaries of the two classes are inconsistent across professions. Two other categories, mass advertising and class advertising, thus will be considered here.

Mass advertising involves the mass media, those discussed briefly above in which professionals today legally can advertise if they wish. Whether professionals can ethically use newspapers, magazines, radio, and television to promote their practices is another issue in many professions. These media generally are considered acceptable in podiatry, chiropractic, optometry, and some other professions. They are viewed far less favorably in law, medicine, and other areas.

Competitive circumstances in many communities are encouraging more and more members of the older professions to experiment with mass media advertising. Few, however, appear to find this vehicle sufficiently productive to warrant protracted use. Whether this continues to be the case remains to be seen. Competitive pressures in some professions conceivably may force newcomers to use extreme measures.

Class Advertising

Precise boundaries between class and mass advertising may be difficult to draw. There nevertheless appear to be some more or less traditional media that are more ethically acceptable than others. Yellow Pages advertising, for example, has long been used by most professionals. In some professions, display advertising in these directories has taken hold as well.

Medical and dental practitioners who specialize in cosmetic procedures appear at this writing to be using advertising more extensively but on a selective basis. City magazines and other media that appeal to those with high disposable income levels seem to be most used.

As in the case of mass advertising, these trends may or may not continue. The continuing effectiveness of the media involved doubtless will be the primary determinant of their use. Whether any will be able to retain a degree of effectiveness in a progressively more competitive marketplace remains to be seen.

IN SUMMARY

Clearly defined practice development strategies are necessary to guide professionals' choices from a broad range of communication techniques. Development strategies and communication strategies are mutually dependent. Defining a practice development strategy thus is a prerequisite to developing communication programs.

Using information drawn from a host of sources, professionals first must examine the several variables that can govern practice strategy development. Then they must select the groups that their practices will be designed to serve, the geographic area from which those groups will be drawn, and the services that will be offered by the practice.

These decisions permit practice developers to successfully characterize the audiences with which they must communicate and, thereafter, to design productive messages for delivery through carefully selected channels of communication.

Audience size and precise identification of decision makers are critical in selecting communication channels. The latter element governs the manner in which interpersonal communication and mail techniques can be employed. Size of audience influences economic factors that enter into the media selection process. When decision makers cannot be precisely identified and when practices involved are narrowly based, alternative approaches must first be used to identify prospective clients. The interests of audience groups often can be used as a point of departure to make initial contact with prospects through business or professional organizations or, in the alternative, through media serving them.

Audiences and their interests are equally significant in dealing with larger groups. The print media especially offer communicators opportunities to direct their messages to groups with specific interests or demographic profiles. Electronic media cater to broader audiences.

Two basic media strategies are used in delivering messages through the mass media. One uses activities in which professionals are involved or can become involved as bases from which news releases attractive to the media can be generated. The other involves a set of procedures designed to bring professionals to the attention of editors and news directors in a manner that encourages these media gatekeepers to come to professionals as information sources. While more time-consuming in its development, the latter strategy also is more productive to the professional in that it ultimately leads to continuing media exposure without further effort.

The latter benefit should not discourage professionals from extending the use of media exposure through reprints or otherwise. Media proliferation has fragmented audiences to a point at which so-called mass media are relatively inefficient. Professionals must behave accordingly, using reprints and similar materials to magnify the results of initial exposure.

ADDITIONAL READING

Gray, James G., Jr. *Managing the Corporate Image: The Key to Public Trust*. Westport, Conn.: Quorum, 1986.

Nash, Edward L. *Direct Marketing: Strategy, Planning, Execution*. 2nd. ed. New York: McGraw-Hill, 1986.

14

Targeted Communication

Most professional development programs deal with broadly based existing and prospective clienteles. Communication efforts supporting these programs must be designed accordingly. Communication strategies are oriented primarily toward mediated rather than interpersonal communication. All professions, however, are not alike. Existing and prospective clienteles are relatively small among many professions, and among some practices in other professions. Mediated communication in these circumstances is impractical for tactical and economic reasons. Programming instead must be reoriented toward the interpersonal end of the communication spectrum.

Any profession in which the average practice numbers clients in the dozens or hundreds logically is better served by targeted or focused communication efforts than by the broad-spectrum variety. The professions involved, including architecture, engineering, public relations, advertising, and the like, differ significantly from medicine and dentistry. These professions deal with few clients at any given time. They usually provide their clients with more intensive and extensive services over longer periods of time. Average annual revenues per client in these practices usually are in the thousands or tens of thousands of dollars rather than in hundreds of dollars.

STRATEGIC DIFFERENCES

Where clienteles are small and revenue per client is high, practice development involves systems very different from those used where clienteles are larger. Techniques that can be highly effective in what might be described as high-volume, low-ticket practices often are valueless in low-volume, high-ticket situations.

The two groups of professions early follow the same practice developmental path. Practitioners in both sectors fashion attractive surroundings for existing and prospective clienteles. Physical environments and the performance of practice personnel must be managed to create client or patient satisfaction. Scope of services must be defined to meet the needs of clienteles involved.

When developmental prerequisites have been met, communication becomes the order of the day. Practice realities must be communicated to existing and prospective clienteles. The different types of practices at this point have reached a fork in the road. One group must deal with relatively large numbers of prospects, while the other focuses on smaller audiences. In the first instance, individual prospects seldom can be identified by name or address. Communication efforts at best might focus on specific census tracts or socioeconomic groups. In the second instance, prospective clients can be identified with considerable precision. Organizations that hire architects, engineers, Big Eight accounting firms, and corporate attorneys are well known among the members of those professions. Names of companies, their locations, names of their officers and directors, their products, their sales volumes, and much more data are available for the asking or for a fee.

Mass Communication

Where practitioners deal with large numbers of "faceless" individuals, no matter how precisely they can be described, techniques of the sort described in chapter 13 become essential. A mass approach would be necessary, in fact, even if prospective clients for the family practitioner or the general practice dentist could be individually identified. Costs associated with individual contact by letter, telephone, and in person would be far too great in relation to potential revenue involved.

These conditions lead professionals logically to a blend of communication strategies that places greater emphasis on mediated information transfer. Early interpersonal contact usually is unnecessary and economically impractical in bringing patients or clients to the door.

Selective Communication

The circumstances are reversed when prospective clients are relatively few. Competition is almost always more intense. Services often are developed to meet the specific needs of prospects by industry if not on an individual basis. A great deal of time and effort often is expended early in the marketing process in three preliminaries:

1. monitoring environments within which prospect groups operate,
2. identifying emerging needs among those groups, and
3. designing services to meet those needs.

During the heyday of organized labor, and as late as the early 1980s, for example, attorneys and labor relations consultants offered a broad range of services designed to assist clients in resisting union organizing efforts. Those efforts largely had subsided by the end of the decade as demographic trends created a seller's market for labor. As a result, many consultants who earlier worked as union busters reoriented their efforts to assist employers in creating more attractive environments for workers.

Where professionals attempt to stay ahead of the demand curve, to develop and market services in advance of pressing need, communication techniques change radically. Techniques change because communication objectives have changed. Professionals must make prospective clients or patients aware of previously unrecognized needs rather than of services to meet previously acknowledged needs. In the case described above, for example, employers who had used policy and procedure manuals to keep employees in line suddenly found it necessary to redesign systems to attract personnel rather than to discipline them. Policies had to be redesigned to produce compliance rather than punishment.

Success on the part of professionals working in this area thus depended on their ability to *(a)* identify need, *(b)* design responsive services, and *(c)* let prospective users know whom to call when services are required. The latter element is critical. Services of this sort usually are purchased only where prospective users come to know professionals early. Trust and confidence must be established before need develops to a point at which purchase decisions are necessary. These conditions require that professionals

1. make initial social or business contacts long before need develops,
2. make prospective clients aware of the availability of services and build confidence levels, and
3. maintain contact until purchase decisions are made.

Other than where initial contacts can be made socially or in group settings, and perhaps even then, a three-step process usually is most productive. The process involves an initial contact by letter, a follow-up by telephone, and, ultimately, the first of several appointments.

THE CENTRAL PROCESS

Practice development among professions that deal with relatively few largely identifiable clients focuses on face-to-face discussions. The process and several ancillary activities all are oriented toward bringing the parties together in the prospect's office.

Ancillary activities in most cases are supplemental to the primary effort. They may occur before or after the letter-call-appointment sequence begins. Those undertaken early often are education oriented, as in the case of seminars for trade or professional groups. Those undertaken after appointments may vary in content. All are designed, however, to maintain contact and to cement relationships.

Mail Contacts

Initial contacts between professionals and those they hope to serve most often occur through the mail. Personal letters are most frequently used, but other devices can be employed as well. The latter range from announcements and greeting cards to promotional mailings.

Professionals' concerns over the propriety of mailings other than letters tend to restrict promotional mailings in many professions. Levels of reserve usually are lower, however, in some of the younger health care disciplines. Optometry, podiatry, and chiropractic are noteworthy among them.

Formal letters are viable points of departure in any event where prospects can be identified by name, title, and address. They have become increasingly popular in recent years with the advent of microcomputers and their mail management capabilities.

More sophisticated word processing systems, such as WordPerfect, WordStar, and Word, include utilities that enable users to maintain lists of clients or prospects that can be merged with what otherwise would be form letters. The programs involved allow for almost unlimited personalization as well. The result, given letter quality printers, consists of inexpensive, individually typed letters ready for professionals' signatures.

Letters prove most productive when they are short, address a specific need, promise assistance, and provide for follow-up. The letter shown in figure 14.1 continued in use essentially unchanged in the author's consulting practice for more than twenty years.

The letter says, in essence, "You have a problem; we have a solution; I'd like to talk about it; expect my call." It is ambiguous by design. It is intended to pique recipient curiosity. The objective is to induce the prospect to accept the follow-up telephone call and make an appointment.

The Telephone Call

One of two situations results from any telephone call of this sort. Appointments are obtained or they are not obtained. Initial telephone follow-ups more often than not fail to result in appointments. Those to whom letters have been addressed most frequently are too busy to come to the telephone or are out of their offices. At this point, a subtle game begins.

The game might be called "never leave a message." In order to maintain control of the situation, the professional must retain the initiative. It is lost if messages are left. The best course of action in dealing with those who are busy is a request: "Tell him I called and that I'll call again." A viable alternative is

Figure 14.1
Solicitation Letter

```
' ---------------------------------------------------------------

    Dear                      :

    Rising advertising and marketing costs today are
    compounding budgetary problems in organizations
    of all kinds.

    We at The Resource Group have developed a number
    of innovative techniques to economically meet
    contemporary needs.  Consisting primarily of
    selective communication devices, they are designed
    to produce maximum return on user investment.

    We believe that these techniques can be of value
    to your organization and would appreciate a few
    moments of your time to discuss them with you in
    person.

    I'll call next week for an appointment to discuss
    the matter in more detail.

    Sincerely,

    THE RESOURCE GROUP, Inc.



    E.W. Brody
    President
---------------------------------------------------------------
```

to say, "Tell him that I'll be at 234–5678 for the rest of the day and that I'll call again if I don't hear from him."

The game can be played ad infinitum. Secretaries ultimately come to know professionals by voice, at which time, a friendly inquiry is in order: "Can you tell me how best to get through to him?" Or, "What's the best time to catch him in the office?"

Friendliness and persistence are critical in the professional's approach. Given these two elements, appointments ultimately will be granted. It is not unusual for a year or more to elapse between the initial letter and an appointment, but extensive or repetitive delays become psychological assets rather than liabilities. When appointments finally are granted, prospects already feel a sense of obligation toward callers.

The Appointment

Few professionals handle what are essentially sales calls with real proficiency. Most have little or no sales experience and have been "dragged kicking and screaming" into selling. Hunger is an exceptionally powerful motivator, however, especially for those just starting out in practices of their own.

Weaknesses professionals feel in selling situations are more perception than reality. A simple formula always will serve to move the practitioner quickly from the prospect's ground to his own:

1. Briefly define a problem that you have reason to believe the prospect may be experiencing or will soon experience.
2. Describe how your service will solve the problem.
3. Point out that you offer a broad range of services applicable to other problems and that you would like to know of any other with which he or she is concerned.

The latter step is critical. The professional's primary objective in the course of a first call is *not* to sell a service. The call is intended primarily to start building a relationship. Secondarily, it is intended to elicit information about existing or potential needs. Professionals ideally reach a point during initial calls at which they can tell their prospects: "Let me give some thought to what you've told me and get back to you in a week or ten days. It's just possible that we may be able to help."

The latter sentence is critical even when the practitioner already knows precisely how to solve the problem at hand, what the solution will cost, and how long it will take to get the job done. The only exception occurs when the prospect is feeling substantial pressure to act immediately. This might be the case if the caller is a labor attorney and the prospect is concerned about a union organizing situation. Where no such pressures exist, professionals always are best advised to be certain of their ground; to return to their offices and do some research into the prospect company and its recent history. When research is complete, and in any event before the specified week to ten days has elapsed, a second call is in order: "I have the information we discussed last week, and I'd like to stop by at your convenience."

The second call always is easier than the first, covering four points: "Here's the information; here's how long it will take; here's how much it will cost; here's how we can get started." Diverse opinions exist as to the latter point. Some suggest having a formal agreement ready and asking for the business. Others prefer to deliver a formal proposal and agreement at a later date.

No precise formula exists as to which course to follow. Much has to do with the extent to which the professional has established a personal relationship with the prospect over the prior weeks. Some suggest that a second information-gathering appointment is appropriate, preferably over lunch, to strengthen the relationship before a solution to the prospect's problem is proposed. More important, however, is the nature of the organization and the decision-making process with which the professional is dealing. Some chief executive officers can and will make decisions first and tell subordinates later. Others prefer a collegial style of management. Still others must involve boards of directors or executive committees before entering into agreements with professional organizations. The latter circumstances can complicate and lengthen what has now become essentially a selling process.

PROPOSALS AND AGREEMENTS

Most of the complications arise over the circumstances and the manner in which information is to be conveyed to others in the prospect organization. *Circumstances* refers primarily to the matter of competition. Is the professional's proposal going to be viewed alone or are other practitioners to be invited or permitted to make proposals? *Manner* refers to how decision making is going to be handled. Will the professional have an opportunity to personally address all those involved in making the decision or will some confine themselves to reading proposals?

A word of caution is appropriate at this juncture. Professionals willing to engage in speculative presentations always should attempt to attach one condition to their participation: a candid, after-the-fact discussion with the prospect about factors that contributed to the decision, favorable or unfavorable. Competitive presentations may or may not lead to agreements. Where agreements do not result, professionals often can learn much that will help them in the future by attaching this condition in advance.

Competitive Situations

A number of pitfalls can exist in competitive situations. Prospective clients may or may not be serious in requesting proposals. These conditions most often occur in advertising and related disciplines where clients are merely "keeping vendors honest." Significant numbers of professional organizations for these reasons will not participate in competitive situations.

Others exclude governmental contracts from their offices, especially where political matters may be involved. This more often is the case at local, county, and state rather than federal levels, but outcomes may be no less troublesome. Governmental and quasi-governmental agencies in these jurisdictions not infrequently will follow a request for proposals by negotiating contracts with favored vendors. The practice is patently unfair, especially where a favored vendor is asked to execute a concept advanced by a competitor, but nevertheless persists. The only practical recourse open to offended parties is to decline participation in the future.

It is not unusual in some professions to confine practices to noncompetitive situations. The number of firms following this policy suggests that they suffer no adverse economic results. Whether a similar policy should be adopted in any given circumstances can only be answered in light of prevailing conditions.

Preparing Proposals

Almost any organization considering a professional proposal requires that the details be reduced to writing. Information presented verbally must be available for continuing reference even where the chief executive officer alone ultimately will make the decision.

No generally accepted content or mechanical format exists for proposals. The relative importance of these factors varies with the nature of organizations involved. Both usually become more a matter of concern in larger organizations where decision-making processes may be more complex.

A number of questions then must be considered by those responsible for preparing proposals. How much detail should be included? What level of knowledge or sophistication can be assumed on the part of those who will read the proposal? What will be their perspectives of the problem? Professional responses to each of these questions alone must determine the outcome.

Level of detail. Consider, for example, the matter of detail. Is it safe for professionals to assume that all who will be reviewing the proposal are familiar with the evolution and current status of the problem or should background be provided? Those who have worked in an industry for years presumably are familiar with basic issues and problems involved, while newcomers are not. Significant numbers of highly placed executives in many organizations are relative newcomers to their companies, if not to the industries in which those companies operate. Proposal writers should make every effort to determine the nature of their audiences before starting to write.

Two primary schools of thought predominate in professional circles as to the handling of proposals. One contends that they should be short and to the point; that busy executives have neither the time nor the inclination to become involved in functional details. The other takes an opposite perspective, declaring that the proposal must cover all the bases in order to insure that it include an answer to every question that may occur to any reader.

There may be no way to satisfactorily resolve this issue. One technique used by a relatively successful firm of communication consultants appears worthy of merit. That organization depends on the instinct and judgment of those who developed the prospect and handled the bulk of the early contact work. Their recommendations are almost invariably taken in developing long or short proposals. The firm's track record appears neither significantly better nor significantly worse than those of competitive organizations.

Knowledge levels. The question of reader knowledge levels is more readily addressed if practice developers have adequately handled activities preliminary to submitting a proposal. There is no reason why a prospect should not be asked to describe the normal decision-making process within his or her organization. Subsequent questions should be directed toward obtaining information concerning those involved.

Several points are of special interest to professionals preparing proposals in this context. First among them is that mentioned earlier: how well do those involved know the industry and its problems? Others can be equally important. How far down the organization will the primary decision maker reach for advice and counsel? What are the backgrounds of individuals involved?

The questions are directed toward obtaining two different types of information. Organizational level usually is a strong indicator of knowledge level and sophistication. Knowledge of the extent to which the proposal will be circulated downward can be an equally strong indicator of the manner in which content should be prepared. Information concerning individuals also can be significant. Educational and experiential backgrounds are of special importance to proposal writers. These factors are valid indicators of preferred format as well as style.

Reader perspectives. The perspectives of those expected to read the proposal are most important. Perspectives usually can be deduced by the nature of individuals' positions in the organization and can be addressed through calculated response to one question: what positive and negative impacts might the proposed service have on the individual and on his or her department?

The issue, in other words, is more complex than the usual "what's in it for me?" Virtually any change is likely to be resisted to some extent by those who perceive no benefit to them. As a very wise educator once said, "There always are two reasons not to change: 'we've never done it that way' and 'we've always done it the other way.' " At a minimum, change is apt to include inconvenience, which most individuals tend to avoid.

Beyond inconvenience are such matters as potential impact on the size and responsibilities of the operating unit. Most managers measure the relative stature of their positions in terms of these factors. They tend to resist diminution in status even where it is not accompanied by other penalties.

Failure to address all of these issues and any collateral questions that may arise ultimately can prove troublesome if not fatal to a proposal. Issues unresolved in proposals tend to produce questions, requests for further information, and other barriers to quick acceptance.

Technical factors. Finally, those preparing proposals must address a relatively happy question: to what extent should the document be illustrated? Barring contrary indicators, the answer can be expressed in one word: extensively. This especially is the case where statistical information is involved. Graphs and diagrams convey information far more rapidly than mere words. Today's senior managers may be at home with words. Their successors, reared in the age of television, will be more visually oriented.

Visual orientation of presentation recipients should not be a problem today in any professional practice. All should be equipped with microcomputers capable of converting data to graphs at the touch of a few keys. Drawings and other devices are available on floppy disks. Since the mid–1980s, IBM and similar hardware have been fully as capable as Apple computers of producing first quality graphics at little investment in time or cost.

BEFORE AND AFTER

Practice development efforts for professionals who deal with relatively small clienteles do not stop with the submittal of a proposal. Neither, in many cases, do they begin with a letter. Alternative points of beginning exist. Follow-up also is necessary after proposals have been delivered and even where they have been preliminarily deferred or rejected.

Many professionals use several devices to make them and their organizations more visible to prospects. The processes involved are designed to produce "over the transom" or unsolicited inquiries from prospective clients. Most are oriented to produce salutary exposure in business and professional media or, in the alternative, to bring professionals into direct contact with prospective users of their services.

When media exposure is involved, practitioners can also prepare article reprints that can be readily incorporated into follow-up efforts. One of the cardinal rules of counselor selling, as the process sometimes has been called, is "never let go of a prospect." Construction of interorganizational relationships should be an ongoing task. The only real certainty beyond death and taxes is change. Organizational change creates demand for consultant services.

Creating Visibility

Many professionals who deal with small clienteles find alternative paths to first interviews highly productive. Among their preferred techniques are writing for professional media, conducting seminars and other educational programs for members of the industries they serve, and serving actively in those industries' trade or professional associations.

These activities are highly synergistic. Reprints of published material can be used during sales calls, incorporated into proposals, and distributed during or after seminars. Seminar content, in turn, can be readily converted into manuscripts for publication.

All of the efforts involved are designed in part to serve as alternatives to sales letters. They are intended to make practitioners and their organizations known to prospective users of professional services to a degree at which a telephone call readily produces a sales interview.

Journal articles. Public recognition for professional expertise is most readily accomplished in many professions by publishing. The process is mandatory for those who would progress in the academic world. It is almost equally productive, however, in any profession.

Professionals should expect, however, that some publications will be more productive than others. Some, as in the case of veterinarians, accountants, and attorneys, often volunteer their services to community newspapers with moderate but salutary results. Community newspaper audiences involve relatively small numbers of prospective clients.

Professional publications, especially those regularly read by prospective clients, tend to be more productive. Two factors are involved: the nature and the relative prestige of the publications. Editors of these journals are perceived as experts by readers. Their implied endorsements of professionals' qualifications and writings therefore are more credible with audiences.

Journals read by prospective clients usually are expected to be more productive than those serving the professions, but this is not always the case. Practitioners in professions in which referrals are common often find their own journals at least as productive.

All professionals should remember that their articles are welcomed by most editors of business and professional journals. These publications operate with minimal editorial budgets. They lack resources to aggressively cover the news in their fields. Any information of interest to their readers therefore is readily accepted for publication. The same conditions prevail with educational activities.

Educational activities. Well-designed seminars and other educational activities are potentially at least equally productive. They cast professionals in authoritative instructional roles and position them in front of audiences that can consist largely of prospective clients.

The latter conditions are most readily met where professionals work with business or trade associations representing prospective client groups. A civil engineering firm, for example, might arrange to present seminars concerning new road and bridge design techniques to a state or regional association of municipal and county officials.

Presentations of this sort are successful because they meet the needs of all of the parties: association, members, and professionals. Few professional associations are adequately funded. Much of their non-dues revenues are derived from convention and meeting services. They often charge members nominal fees to attend such events. Association members find it necessary to stay abreast of developments in their fields and can readily do so through association-sponsored events. In increasing numbers of cases, members may be required to participate in continuing education activities as a condition of membership.

These circumstances play into the hands of aggressive professionals, especially where they have been writing on prospective seminar topics. Attractive subject matter and potential profit create an irresistible lure for association executives. Professionals often donate their services to obtain access to association platforms. In most other cases, they work for expenses only in order to meet and work with the most active members of client organizations.

Many professionals value the typical half-day to one-day seminar for an organization of prospective clients at one hundred thousand dollars or more. New client relationships almost inevitably result from these presentations, they find, and participants almost invariably will welcome subsequent sales calls. Seminars thus can replace a large volume of letter writing and telephone activity. Appointments with prospective clients are more readily made, and the developmental process leads more quickly to the proposal stage.

Proposal Follow-Up

Many professionals tend to assume that they can relax after proposals are delivered. These circumstances rarely prevail. Most proposals require extensive follow-up. Proposals too easily can be shunted aside in favor of more pressing organizational matters and never returned to center stage even in noncompetitive situations. Proposing organizations must assume responsibility for keeping approval processes moving.

Depth and extent of necessary follow-up varies with the nature of the prospect organization and its decision-making processes. The extent to which professionals successfully manage follow-up requirements usually is governed by their prior efforts in information gathering and relationship building.

Follow-up procedures. Frequency and level of formality are major variables in proposal follow-up. Practitioners must serve as visible reminders that the decision process requires organizational attention. Their activities must keep the process moving, however, without their appearing to be pushy. A sometimes precarious balancing act thus is necessary, varying in its delicacy with the strength of professional-prospect relationships.

Any number of techniques can be used in maintaining contact with prospect organizations where professionals have proposals pending. The most obvious is monitoring of due dates. Every proposal should be followed with a telephone call to "make certain you received the information we provided." That contact and every subsequennt contact must conclude with what might be termed an "I'll call you back" remark.

Professionals must *always* retain the initiative in dealing with prospective clients. The circumstances here are the same as those that apply while in the telephone phase of the process leading to an appointment. Contacts must always conclude with a question or statement designed to retain the initiative for the professional, such as, "When can I check back with you?" Or, "I'll call back in a week to ten days to answer any questions that may arise."

Personal follow-up. Even more can be done where professionals have developed strong relationships with organizations entertaining their proposals. Personal relationships between professionals and members of prospect organizations are not unusual, especially where the professional may have worked with organization members in seminars or otherwise. Informal monitoring of proposal status is readily accomplished when this is the case.

Semipersonal relationships, at a minimum, should be established early in the process. In larger organizations, professionals' primary contacts should have been induced to buy in to proposed projects before formal proposals are submitted. Thereafter, they can serve as professionals' "friends in court," providing information as to potential problems that practitioners might help overcome by providing information or otherwise.

Other follow-up. The follow-up process can and should be further supplemented with mail and/or in-person contacts designed to reinforce prospective clients' sense of need for action. Personal relationships may or may not have developed to the point at which casual luncheons are appropriate. Mail contact is indicated in any event.

Mail contact can be maintained in one of several ways. Where professionals are writing or speaking, copies of their articles or talks always should be forwarded to prospective clients. Accompanying letters are unnecessary. Business cards should be attached with a brief note: "Thought you might be interested in this."

Project-related mail contact can be even more effective. Articles that appear in trade or professional literature and bear on prospective clients' problems should be copied and forwarded with similar notes. In the case of a municipality contemplating building a waste disposal facility, for example, an engineering firm might forward published materials relating to municipal waste disposal problems anywhere in the world.

MAINTAINING CONTACT

When does maintaining contact stop? With few exceptions, never. If the organization is a prospective client, the practice development process never ends. It continues for as long as the professional is in practice or for as long as the prospect remains a prospect.

Professionals conceivably may retire from practice and prospects may go out of business. Each of these events, however, is less likely to occur than is change in the prospect organization. Change in ownership, in the business environment, or in the client's endeavors all can open the door to beneficial professional relationships.

The professional development process is designed to insure that practitioners will have an opportunity to establish relationships when opportunities arise. As most professionals one day learn to their sorrow, nothing is quite so frustrating as hearing the words, "We just signed a contract for that sort of service with _____." These or similar words are emblematic of a lost opportunity that may not soon occur again.

Maintaining contact involves two procedures to guard against such occurrences. One of them literally is a contact process. The other is based on environmental assessment. Both are intended to position professionals to benefit from their practice development efforts.

Maintenance Procedures

Too many practitioners consider rejection of a proposal final and permanent, an "until-death-do-us-part" decision. Nothing can be further from the truth.

While individuals and organizations enter into professional relationships with the intention that they be durable in nature, few realize that objective. Organizations change. Senior managers change. Needs change. Individually or in combination, any of these factors can lead to dissolution of an old or creation of a new professional relationship. Some in advertising contend that client-agency relationships begin to deteriorate with the handshakes that cement them.

Professionals who have made proposals only to have them rejected can and should be prepared to take advantage of changing circumstances. Preparation involves more than sitting back and waiting for the telephone to ring. At least two specific strategies are necessary to insure that the practitioner will be home when opportunity again knocks.

First, he or she must remain known to the prospective client. Out of sight literally becomes out of mind over an extended period of time. Organizational executives see dozens of hopeful professionals over the course of a year. They cannot be expected to remember the names, addresses, or telephone numbers of individuals they have not seen in months.

Second, the prospective client should continue to be seen periodically by the professional in one way or another. The sightings can be social, professional, or in other contexts. They are necessary to reinforce earlier memories and to permit professionals to express continuing interest.

Staying known. Remaining known is the easier of the two tasks for those who maintain active practice development programs. Copies of every article, reprint, and clipping that becomes available can and should be forwarded to every active prospect in the professional's files. An alert secretary should be trained to clip items relative to the businesses of prospective clients as well. These also can be forwarded with a business card and the message, "Thought you might be interested in this."

Efforts to remain an identifiable component of prospective clients' environments also justifies preparing and distributing news releases concerning professional practices and their personnel. The overall objective can be achieved in no other way. Simply stated, it is a matter of having professionals' identities known to prospects at the time need for services again prompts them to pick up their telephones.

Being seen. The phrase "being seen in the right places" is as applicable in professional practice development as in any other endeavor. To the extent that differences arise, they relate to the places involved. Environments related to practitioners' profession or to business matters are far preferable to others. In other words, professionals are better off rubbing elbows with prospective clients at business or professional meetings than at a charity fund raiser or the opera.

Being seen requires only that professionals join and become involved in the activities of community organizations. The organizations preferably should be those that relate directly or indirectly to professional practices. Those in the health care disciplines, for example, might be most at home in organizations dedicated to the conquest of diseases. They also would be most memorable by others when seen in these circumstances.

Two reasons contribute to the latter condition. First, the professional is apt to be looked upon by others involved as an expert. Second, relationships between professional activities and organizational objectives reinforce identification. These conditions suggest that professionals become active in trade or business organizations of which their clients are members. Many of these organizations accept associate members. Memberships involved seldom include voting rights but do permit associates to attend conventions and seminars.

The relaxed atmosphere surrounding convention and seminar events facilitates a great deal of friendly conversation. Participants spend much of their time discussing mutual problems, which presumably will include many that fall within professionals' ability to resolve. Many a professional has used prospects' conventions and seminars to generate sufficient sales leads to keep him or her busy through the remainder of the year.

Environmental Assessment

Where convention-generated leads are inadequate, further springboards for contact with prospects are necessary. These can be generated in surprising volume merely by monitoring the news media, especially those that serve the practitioner's profession and the fields of endeavor in which prospective clients are engaged.

The media involved usually constitute a highly reliable early warning system. They are quick to point out emerging trends and problems as well as innovative solutions. Both can be used by professionals to renew contact with prospects.

A two-step process is advisable. The first step is a copy of the news item in question forwarded to the prospect with a letter suggesting that the professional can help solve the problem or capitalize on the opportunity involved. The second is a follow-up telephone call for an appointment. The process essentially reinstates the mail-telephone-in person sequence described earlier.

Consistent application of the techniques described above will produce continuing practice development. Extended periods of time occasionally may be required in establishing relationships with new clients. Experience suggests, however, that durability of relationships may be a function of time and effort involved in their development.

IN SUMMARY

Narrow-based, as opposed to broad-based, professional practices require different communication strategies in association with their professional development programs. While broad-based programs use mediated communication techniques extensively, narrowly based practices require selective communication approaches leading to personal interviews.

Practitioners in narrow-based professions generally offer more individual customized services or both. Their developmental programs are oriented toward their problem-solving abilities rather than toward the professional techniques necessary in producing solutions to clients' problems. They seek to identify problems originating in client environments that are amenable to solution through professional services, and then sell solutions rather than services.

Practice development in these circumstances requires several steps on the part of professionals involved. Three are most important. Practitioners first must make initial social or business contacts with prospective clients. Then they must make individuals involved aware of the availability of services. Finally, they must maintain contact until need prompts development of client relationships.

Face-to-face discussions of prospective clients' needs and professional services are essential to the development process. A great deal goes before or after, but every aspect of the process is oriented toward obtaining or capitalizing on the first business encounter.

Most professionals use letters to prequalified prospects, followed by telephone calls to solicit needed appointments. These processes require complex systems that enable staff members to identify prospects, generate letters for professional signature, provide necessary call lists, and subsequently record results for follow-up. Follow-up processes continue until appointments are obtained.

Appointments are organized to enable professionals to accomplish two objectives. First, they seek to identify existing or anticipated needs for their services. Second, where those needs are imminent, they attempt to induce prospective clients to consider formal proposals. Proposals are submitted with cover letters through which professionals retain the initiative in dealing with prospects. Most specify follow-up telephone calls in a week to ten days.

Thereafter, and until the initial proposal is accepted or other services subsequently are purchased, regular contact is maintained by telephone, letter, or otherwise. Environmental assessment that originated early in the developmental process is continued, and information generated is used to perpetuate contacts until need develops to a point at which professional relationships can be consummated.

ADDITIONAL READING

Bachner, John P., and Naresh K. Khosla. *Marketing and Promotion for Design Professionals.* New York: Van Nostrand and Reinhold, 1977.

Cleveland, Harland. *The Knowledge Executive: Leadership in an Information Society.* New York: Dutton, 1985.

Cross, Mary. *Persuasive Business Writing: Creating Better Letters, Memos, Reports, and More.* New York: amacom, 1987.

Holtz, Herman. *How to Succeed as an Independent Consultant.* New York: Wiley, 1983.

McCarthy, E. Jerome, and William D. Perreault, Jr. *Basic Marketing.* Homewood, Ill.: Irwin, 1987.

Mueller, Robert K. *Behind the Boardroom Door: The Ultimate Arena of Corporate Power.* New York: Crown, 1974.

Wilson, Aubrey. *The Marketing of Professional Services.* New York: McGraw-Hill, 1972.

15

Managing the Process

The nature and results of development programs add to management work loads in professional practices. One or several individuals must perform the tasks involved. The tasks consist primarily of monitoring results, making periodic adjustments, and generally keeping the process on course.

Several management alternatives are available to professionals who plan to begin or expand practice development efforts. The most popular option, spreading the load among existing personnel, seldom is most practical. Spreading the load is especially risky where no one is primarily responsible for the program. Everyone's responsibility quickly can become no one's responsibility, placing the development effort at considerable risk.

Any of three other alternatives is preferable. One involves assigning resources and responsibility for process management to one or several existing personnel. A corresponding volume of other duties currently assigned to them concurrently must be reassigned elsewhere if personnel involved are to successfully cope with the added work load. The second alternative involves assigning development program management to practice development consultants. Their work requires limited supervision, but costs may be higher than where the process is managed internally. The third alternative usually applies only where practices involved deal with smaller existing and prospective clienteles, as discussed in chapter 14. This approach involves using a combination of internal and external resources and requires considerable effort in its application.

No one of these options is readily applicable in all cases. Often, in fact, more than one will be used over an extended time span as the professional development process progresses. Senior practitioner time available for investment in practice development declines in proportion to programmatic success. Success requires that more and more time be dedicated to meeting client and patient needs, but developmental efforts must be maintained as well.

These conditions suggest applying alternative approaches as circumstances require rather than attempting to select a best option for continuing use. At the outset, for economic if no other reasons, professionals logically should implement development programs internally to as great an extent as possible. As time demands mount, more responsibilities can be allocated to consultants. When practice and program have grown to an appropriate size, an internal development office can be established.

LAUNCHING THE PROCESS

Readers here must be reminded, although perhaps unnecessarily, that formal communication in professional development never should begin before behavioral and environmental factors have been reviewed and modified where necessary. Communication techniques logically and rationally should be limited in their application. Any effort to mislead or deceive ultimately will be counterproductive. Communicators instead must use their skills to enhance understanding. Understanding improves only where gaps between perception and reality and between expectation and experience are spanned.

The first steps in successful development programs involve professional review of practice environment and behavior. Potential sources of negative or conflicting messages in these areas must be eliminated before formal communication efforts begin. Conflict between realities and formal message content renders communication efforts futile at best, counterproductive at worst.

Pragmatically, communication begins with adjustments in behavior and environment. Practice clienteles quickly become aware of significant changes and immediately start communicating them informally to communities that practices serve. Formal communication processes require something more. The steps include the following:

1. Identifying clienteles and prospective clienteles and their attitudes and opinions

2. Determining what behavioral changes are to be sought among these groups

3. Deciding what factors will motivate them to behave as desired

4. Making any tangible changes necessary to create favorable realities

5. Selecting messages to be delivered to existing and prospective clienteles

6. Selecting communication channels most appropriate to clienteles and messages

7. Monitoring results and making appropriate programmatic adjustments

The foregoing chapters have dealt with these matters in detail. They are significant here in that processes involved must be controlled by professionals. Neither practice personnel nor the best qualified consultants can be given free rein. Professionals first must decide who is going to do what. Afterward, they must maintain oversight to insure that programs are properly executed and made optimally productive.

Points of Beginning

Management decisions in practice development will always be governed to a significant extent by available time on the part of professionals involved. Professionals' time invariably can be sold to clients or patients at rates higher than those paid to practice development personnel. These circumstances suggest that professionals delegate operational development responsibilities in keeping with practice demands.

Given a decision to delegate, practitioners face multiple options in implementing development programs. To a great extent, the "neatest" options and the least troublesome among them also are the most costly. Consulting firms in practice development are available to do the whole job—to evaluate practices, recommend environmental and behavioral strategies, and implement subsequent communication efforts. Their services are relatively expensive.

At the other end of the spectrum are practice personnel, whose efforts must be managed and directed by professionals. Unless they are more experienced in practice development than usually is the case, their low wage rates will be more than offset by the problem potential they represent.

Between the extremes are several alternatives that deserve careful consideration. Some are practical only in limited circumstances. Others are generally applicable. The former include use of qualified moonlighters from academic or other institutions. The latter include specialized personnel or consultants employed to perform specific developmental tasks rather than to undertake total programs.

Using moonlighters. The state of the national economy suggests that increasing numbers of highly skilled and knowledgeable individuals will be available for part time or moonlighting activities in their disciplines or professions. Some have always been readily available, as in the case of academics. Others apparently are joining them in increasing numbers.

The academic community is a major source of part-time assistance in professional development. Help can be obtained from students and faculty on formal as well as informal bases. Many marketing and public relations classes, for example, undertake research projects that can be devoted to professionals' needs. Practitioners need be cautious in only one respect: faculty members involved should be experienced in their subject areas. Practical as well as academic credentials should be required.

Hiring consultants. Boundaries between the academic and consulting worlds have become hazy in recent years. Many academics are involved in consulting and increasing numbers of consultants have joined college and university faculties. Two separate and distinct trends are responsible. First, academic salaries have not kept pace with the private sector. Second, educational institutions and especially their students are becoming more practice oriented. Competition among institutions for students therefore has encouraged many to add practitioners to their teaching staffs.

Regardless of their origins, consultants most helpful to professionals in practice development are more readily identified through colleagues, professional journals, or professional associations than otherwise. Telephone directory advertising can be misleading. Experience in practice development and communication should be primary selection criteria. More than consultant experience is necessary, however, to insure productive working relationships.

Allocating Responsibility

Responsibilities of professionals, consultants, and their staffs in practice development situations must be clearly defined and mutually understood if success is to be achieved. The understandings involved must extend beyond the principals involved. All personnel within the practice and the consultancy must be conversant with their individual and collective responsibilities. Only in this way can both parties be certain that nothing will fall through the cracks.

The foregoing should not be taken to mean that every individual is responsible for every aspect of practice development. There must be clear lines of authority and responsibility as well. The practice development effort must be a major responsibility, if not the major responsibility, of one individual within the practice. That individual involved should work with a counterpart in the consultant organization who is primarily responsible for the professional's account. These two must control and integrate the efforts of the two organizations.

Neither control nor integration is readily accomplished. The processes are most productive where clearly understood and logically assigned in one of several organizational patterns. Most consultant organizations are prepared to assume responsibility for all or any part of the practice development effort. Professionals bent on controlling costs are prone to handle as much as possible of the work involved internally. The two approaches are not mutually contradictory but can create counterproductive circumstances.

Potential for conflict increases in proportion to the extent to which responsibilities are shared. Logic suggests that specifics generally be assigned in their totality to one party or another. Professionals and/or their staffs, for example, should be responsible for maintaining practice environments. Consultants usually are best suited by education and training to prepare news releases, brochures, and the like. When consultants are asked to produce office signs or professional staff are responsible for brochure photos, difficulties readily can develop. If signs or brochures are delayed because professional staff members failed to specify content on a timely basis, conflict can result.

At one time or another, conflict will tempt practitioners to handle practice development wholly within their practices or entirely through consultants. These options can be as practical as joint, integrated efforts. Before proceeding, however, the requirements of each arrangement should be thoroughly understood.

INTERNAL DEVELOPMENT

Installing a practice development function within a professional organization appears on the surface to be easily accomplished. If installation is taken only to mean placing warm bodies at desks, appearances are not deceiving. Considerably more must be achieved, however, if the development function is to be cost-efficient and productive over an extended period of time.

Difficulties encountered in producing long-term efficiency were implied in the alternative approaches defined above. The problems occur because well-managed practice development functions can produce rapid short-term growth in professional practices. While welcome, growth can create problems across the practice. Professionals become preoccupied with clients or patients, with recruiting more personnel, and with planning for new facilities and equipment. The practice development function may prosper or collapse during periods of practice growth. Collapse is more likely than prosperity. Prosperity is apt to occur only where professionals are superior managers and development officers are highly skilled in their disciplines.

Prosperity Potential

Continued success in professional development amidst the growth that developmental efforts can create is a function of personnel involved. More specifically, continued functional success requires highly skilled personnel in the development function and unusually well qualified managers in professional roles.

Both elements are necessary because those responsible for managing the professional aspects of the practice quickly find themselves with little time to devote to the development process—directly or indirectly. Demands on their time make direct involvement in practice development more and more difficult. What little time can be made available must be dedicated to those functions in which professionals are irreplaceable—speaking engagements, calls on prospective clients, and the like.

Successful continuation of development efforts under these conditions requires that practice managers take one of two courses of action. Either staffing of the development office must be made adequate to handle increased work loads or substantial portions of the work must be assigned elsewhere, most logically to consulting firms.

The first of the options, while more attractive to many professionals, comes equipped with negative as well as positive implications. The positive, although it may be an illusion, is that perceived higher costs associated with expanded consultant services can be avoided. The negatives involve two major resources: people and facilities.

People Problems

The personnel problem is more difficult than it appears. Professional practice development is a relatively new discipline. There are few highly experienced personnel in the field, and the bulk of those are to be found in consultant firms. These conditions prevail because few professional firms have established development units that can serve as training facilities for others. Most practitioners have elected to use consultants. Most of the knowledge and skill in the relatively young practice development discipline are thus housed in consulting firms.

Developmental personnel can be lured away from these firms, but only at substantial cost. Those involved usually are already well compensated. Most also are reluctant, in light of recent experience, to move from the consulting to the practice side of their discipline. Many professionals have established practice development efforts only to abandon them as numbers of clients grew or as costs mounted.

Facility Needs

Overhead is a more troublesome element in dealing with practice development than many professionals recognize. This especially is the case where practices enjoy moderate to strong responses to early developmental efforts. Growth quickly can cramp the most spacious of practice offices. Multiple demands for more space can develop almost overnight.

More patients or clients inevitably require more practice personnel and space to house them. More equipment—and space in which to house it—may be needed as well. These conditions too often develop precisely at a time when logic suggests that more space be dedicated to the practice development function. Personnel responsible for the development function will be called upon to assume more responsibilities earlier handled by managing professionals. Logic supports such transitions. Short of maintaining adequate oversight, professionals should concentrate on their practices rather than on development functions.

Several options then arise. One that often suffices involves moving the practice development office temporarily or permanently to separate premises. Development functions need be situated on practice premises only to the extent that professionals feel it necessary to maintain close scrutiny of operations. The problem thus develops into what might be viewed as an either/or situation. Professionals must either provide adequate on-premises space for practice development or recruit development personnel of a caliber requiring no direct supervision.

The only other alternative, which may or may not be practical, would involve transferring the practice development function in its entirety to a consultant organization. Managing professionals still would have to maintain adequate oversight, but personnel and space problems immediately would subside. Out-of-pocket costs probably would increase, but net costs—including management time factors—might or might not be significantly different.

EXTERNAL DEVELOPMENT

Assigning practice development responsibilities to consultant organizations may or may not be an advisable alternative for the practitioner. Decisions on this point should be based on the nature and size of the professional practice and on the status of its development effort. At one time or another during the growth of a practice, substantial consultant assistance can be highly productive. Costs may outweigh benefits during other periods.

Differentiating between one period and another requires an understanding of consultant organizations. Most practice development professionals claim an ability to do everything professionals may require. The ability in question usually exists, but often at unduly high cost. Logic suggests professionals use consultant expertise, but only during those periods when it is most cost-effective.

Development Cycles

Effective use of consultant and internal resources requires knowledge of professional development cycles. While practices vary within and across professions, their life cycles and related developmental needs are similarly consistent. The term *life cycle* refers to the fact that organizations, like individuals, go through predictable cycles. The only difference between the two is that organizations can, with adequate preparation and guidance, outlive their founders.

Professional practices, like individuals, progress from birth to maturity before proceeding, too frequently, to decline and dissolution. Steps to prevent the latter developments involve creating succeeding generations of management and necessarily are beyond the scope of this discussion. Considerable effort usually is necessary in the practice development sector, however, well before organizational decline becomes a problem. Much of it logically should come from qualified consultants.

Varying Needs

The problem involved is one of varying needs. Practice development programs require the greatest levels of knowledge and skill at their inception and again as they reach maturity. Younger, less experienced program designers and communicators are ill-suited for the design and start-up phases of practice development. Neither are they usually adequate as the most sophisticated of developmental techniques come into play. Their efforts are needed in varying degrees, however, throughout the process.

The advice and counsel of senior practice development professionals is of inestimable value during the critical periods. Seldom, however, can practitioners afford to develop and maintain this level of expertise internally. Most successful programs therefore pass through several stages. Consultants most often design and implement programs. As internal work loads build, practice personnel assume responsibility for day-to-day functions. When practice and development program approach maturity, personnel complements and external services are adjusted accordingly.

A COMBINED EFFORT

Productive practice development efforts, in other words, are based on a blend of consultant and personnel effort that varies with changing needs. Needs vary during the course of the program and as the practice develops. Determining how various components of the program should be managed requires an overall understanding of the scope of the tasks involved.

Tasks readily can be categorized in keeping with the qualifications of personnel needed to perform them. They usually should be assigned to qualified individuals at the lowest possible organizational echelon. Assigning personnel on this basis is a matter of economic necessity. Patients and clients will not pay the sort of rates necessary to keep highly skilled professionals in clerical tasks, nor should they be expected to do so.

Professionals contemplating installing practice development programs therefore must be prepared to sort out the tasks involved and see that they are appropriately assigned. Some responsibilities, as indicated earlier, necessarily must be assumed by professionals. Others readily can be delegated to consultants or to practice personnel.

Professional Activities

General oversight and management always remain with practice professionals. Theirs is the ultimate responsibility for judging the results of consultant and subordinate efforts. Professionals also must be prepared, however, to assume responsibility for significant parts of the developmental effort.

The latter circumstances arise out of the fact that surrogates are simply unsatisfactory in many developmental settings. Many speeches or other presentations require delivery by professionals. So do interviews with news media representatives. Most importantly, professionals ultimately must assume a role in development itself.

Professionals' roles vary with their disciplines. In general, individual participation is relatively limited where practitioners deal with large numbers of patients or clients and where fees for services are relatively low, as in the case of physicians, dentists, and others in the healing arts. In these disciplines, direct professional participation in the development process usually is limited to speaking engagements and interviews. Almost all other program requirements can be satisfactorily completed by subordinates or consultants.

Where practices involve relatively small clienteles and fees are relatively high, as described in chapter 14, circumstances are very different. Professionals then must become much more involved in day-to-day developmental activities. They must sign letters, make telephone calls to obtain appointments, keep those appointments, and specify necessary follow-up activities. These responsibilities can become burdensome unless appropriate support systems are designed and installed.

Consultant Activities

Design and installation of support systems should be delegated to practice development experts. Professionals only rarely are adequately equipped by education, training, or temperament to deal with the minutiae involved. Minutiae, however, are what make the difference between functional and dysfunctional systems.

The functional are designed to meet standards specified in individual practice development programs. Most standards in this sense are quantitative rather than qualitative. They deal with the magnitude of the effort; the volume of resources to be applied to achieve predetermined goals. Consultant performance always should be judged by the extent to which precisely established goals are achieved. With goals defined, techniques approved by professionals, and budgets established, consultants can proceed to establish systems.

Two separate and distinct types of systems may be involved in any practice development effort. One is common to both of the types of practices mentioned above. The other is used only where prospect groups are small and the letter-telephone call-appointment path is regularly followed.

Common systems. Systems common to both types of practice are established to generate media exposure and to provide communication materials as specified in development plans. These systems are established to insure that all necessary materials meet pertinent quality standards and are produced as efficiently as possible and on a timely basis.

Two types of production schedules usually must be established. One deals with news releases, feature articles, journal articles, and the like. Production in these areas is scheduled to assure a consistent flow of media exposure throughout the year. Other schedules deal with leaflets, brochures, newsletters, and other tools necessary to some practice development plans. These must be produced, delivered, and, in some cases, distributed by mail or otherwise.

Specialized systems. An additional system is necessary to meet the needs of professionals who deal with smaller prospect groups. Materials necessary to maintain the system, ranging from letters and telephone guides to brochures and reprints to be left in prospects' offices, all are created under the system described above. The specialized system is necessary to support professional efforts and to insure that those efforts involve a minimum of professional time.

A well-designed specialized system will include, for example, a set of parameters through which prospective clients are selected as well as mechanisms that will generate lists of prospects on a regular basis. The mechanisms require scanning directories, screening mailing lists, or reviewing other sources of prospects. In addition, the system requires a minimum of several form letters. One of them (see chapter 14) is sent at specified intervals to predetermined numbers of prospects. Another is used later to confirm appointments. A third often is used as an appointment follow-up, although some prefer that follow-up letters be personalized.

The specialized system also must generate (a) lists of names and telephone numbers for professionals to call, (b) an easily used logging system to insure appropriate call follow-up, and (c) any necessary reminders concerning appointments made in advance. The system also must monitor after-the-call activities from thank-you letters to proposals and beyond.

Support Activities

All components of the system specified above should be designed by practice development experts. These elements are too important to the process to be left to novices. Beyond the developmental phase, however, professionals should proceed with caution. A great deal of the mechanical and monitoring activity that is necessary can be successfully accomplished inside or outside professional offices.

Support can be provided, in other words, by consultant or practice personnel. Consultants usually are more efficient and more costly. Practice development is the consultant's only business. His or her successful practice is built on service. Professionals can count on most consultants and their staffs to maintain agreed-upon qualitative and quantitative standards as well as delivery schedule. Price tags attach, unfortunately, to such levels of performance.

Support activity costs generally will be thirty to several hundred percent more when performed in the consultant's office as opposed to the client's. *Cost* in this case refers to more than salary. The term encompasses all overhead factors. Office space, utilities, and fringe benefits are included. Most consultants set the rates they charge as multiples of salaries—their own and those of their personnel. Billing rates of three to four times salary rates are common in most consulting disciplines. Out-of-pocket expenses, such as duplicating, telephone, postage, and the like, are additional and may be marked up as well.

These conditions suggest that professionals use practice development consultant services judiciously. Services that can be most productively handled by consultants should be assigned to them. Others should be handled in professionals' offices. Merging the two into a successful practice development program can only be accomplished, however, with time and patience.

ALLOCATING TASKS

Allocating tasks internally in practice development programs is practical only to the extent that resources permit. Two primary resources are required: personnel and space. Both vary in quality and availability, and their use should be governed accordingly.

Personnel knowledge and skill, in other words, should be the only criteria used in determining what tasks can be assigned to them. Cost, on the other hand, should be the primary determinant where space is involved.

Human Factors

While supplies of professional personnel are relatively large in most disciplines, shortages are occurring with increasing frequency as the so-called baby bust generation enters the work force. Competition for personnel is especially keen where specialized skills are involved, and unusually specialized skills are most needed in professional development.

Those ideally suited for practice development roles are knowledgeable in two areas. They must know practice development, and they must be familiar with the profession involved. Individuals with these qualifications are rare, and with scarcity comes higher price.

These conditions and one other constitute a strong argument for combining internal and external resources in practice development. In using both resources, professionals are able to call upon highly trained and skilled individuals for limited periods of time. Those individuals need not become members of the practice staff and, concurrently, a continuing drain on practice resources.

Spatial Concerns

Office space can become as much a problem as personnel in practice development efforts. Few professional offices are organized or situated in anticipation of rapid practice development. Most offices are leased for relatively long periods and are situated in buildings where little additional space is available, adjacent or otherwise.

These circumstances ultimately can generate space problems of substantial proportions. Growth in practice clientele must be accommodated. Comfort and function in facilities must be maintained at all costs. While colocating practices and practice development offices thus may be practical early in the development process, the circumstances are apt to change in a relatively short time.

Professionals then will be forced to choose how best to physically handle practice growth. Many historically have separated business and professional functions. In the case of physicians, for example, accounting and insurance offices often are located apart from the practices. Some of these situations have resulted from practice growth that could not otherwise have been accommodated within existing offices. Others are the result of deliberate planning to reduce overhead by locating ancillary services in less prestigious and less costly buildings.

If professional development offices ultimately will have to be physically separated from those of professionals, a major argument for in-house as opposed to consultant services is removed. No longer will development staff members have total access to professionals. This being the case, would the practice be better served by consultants or by full-time staff? No uniformly satisfactory answer is available to that question. All the organizational patterns described above have proven to be successful for some professionals and unsatisfactory for others. None has proven universally successful in any discipline or in any given set of circumstances.

Whether dealing with staff or consultants or both, professionals face an unenviable task in making hiring decisions. Practice development experience is a rare commodity among the thousands of firms and individuals who claim expertise in this area. Many have been associated with public relations, organizational development, marketing, or advertising. Experience in any or all of these areas can be helpful in practice development, but backgrounds in neither one nor several can assure success.

MAKING DECISIONS

Potential difficulties in selecting personnel or making decisions as to consultants and offices often drive professionals into the arms of the latter groups. Where consultants are adequately knowledgeable and experienced, outcomes tend to be salutary.

Office space requirements tend to be volatile during the early months and years of practice development efforts, and the best-planned arrangements often must be sacrificed to meet the needs of growing clienteles. Professionals thus are ill-advised to expend substantial time or effort in attempting to colocate practice development and professional offices, although, on a long-term basis, these circumstances are highly desirable. No decision concerning office space can be considered permanent early in the development process.

These conditions also militate against professional tendencies toward economical solutions to practice development needs. Many are tempted to employ younger and less experienced practitioners and compensate for their weaknesses by providing direct personal supervision. Only rarely do such arrangements prove functional. Any significant success in practice development quickly will absorb any professional time not previously committed to patients or clients. Without continuing supervision, the practice development effort then tends to lose early momentum and eventually will require restructuring.

Selecting Professionals

If practice development is to be undertaken within the confines of a professional practice, then relatively knowledgeable and experienced self-starters capable of seeing that programs early become productive are all but essential. They are not easily found, but professionals have no choice but to invest the necessary time and effort.

The knowledge, talent, and skill of individuals selected will exert a strong influence over the future of the professional practice. Extreme care must be used in the selection process, which involves screening applicants against a previously defined set of criteria.

Individual criteria. In practice development, as in any profession, successful experience should be the strongest criterion in the selection process. Successful experience should weigh most heavily in decision making, in fact, almost without regard for the professional discipline with which the practice developer was involved. Preference might be given to those whose experience is with similar practices. Familiarity with the process described in chapter 14, for example, is preferable where the process is applicable. Practical experience in any form, however, should outweigh academic or other credentials.

Few candidates will be able to offer specifically applicable academic preparation in any event. None exists. Many who have held practice development positions historically have come from the profession involved. They were practicing professionals who somehow drifted into practice development or practice management. This role is occupied to some extent today by senior members of large law, accounting, and other firms. Few of them, however, are adequately skilled in applying the developmental and communication processes to produce optimum results. Professionals may make excellent practice managers. They seldom are successful as practice developers because of their narrow academic and experiential backgrounds.

Most successful practice development personnel are trained in one or more of the communication disciplines and gain practical experience in working with members of one or more professions. Accredited undergraduate public relations programs arguably constitute the best academic background. Their requirements span the communication disciplines and require background in advertising, marketing, and business as well. Other than in the nature of their clienteles, professional practices are remarkably similar to one another.

Successful practice developers also tend to be highly knowledgeable in the nature of the industries the professions serve. Those who have worked with larger accounting firms, for example, have become thoroughly acquainted with the workings of the business and financial communities. Those in architecture and engineering are conversant with the workings, problems, and needs of the construction field.

Professionals seeking to establish practice development staffs thus should examine resumés or question candidates closely in at least three areas. The first is practice development experience. The second is academic background. The third is knowledge of the profession and the economic sector in which it operates.

Consultant criteria. A parallel set of criteria generally should be applied in selecting consultant firms. Care should be exercised, however, to avoid those organizations that purport to be everything to everyone. There is a real need for generalists in management consulting. Few individuals or organizations dedicated to management consulting, however, are as well equipped as their specialist colleagues to deal with relatively narrow areas such as professional development. Professionals should be especially wary of the more aggressive consulting and accounting firms, which of late have sought to spill over into a host of associated disciplines in order to facilitate their own growth and development.

When generalists have been eliminated, relatively few consulting organizations remain in contention for practice development assignments. Practice development itself is not a generally recognized consulting speciality. Experience in several associated disciplines can, however, equip practitioners to cope with the needs of professional practices. These disciplines include organizational development, organizational communication, and human resources management.

Consultants in the latter areas who also have had experience in the field in which the professional is practicing often are best qualified for practice development assignments. Development, communication, and human resources professionals who have been involved with any component of the health care industry, for example, probably are well qualified to serve any of the health professions. Those who have served any segment of the development/construction industry are apt to be oriented toward engineering, architecture, and design.

Perhaps the best criterion for professional decision making consists of the track records of the applicants or firms, as demonstrated by comments of their previous employers, their clients, or their colleagues. Most professions, especially those listed above, are tightly knit clubs in which reputations are well known and jealously protected.

Physical Arrangements

Decisions as to physical arrangements are more readily made after consultants or staff personnel have been selected and the capabilities of any prospective staff members are known. A decision to proceed at the outset with consultants to the exclusion of additional staff personnel eliminates any contingent space problems. Unlike accountants, who may operate for long periods in clients' offices, practice development consultants will appear only occasionally on client premises.

Where professionals elect to establish internal practice development staffs, space and pertinent support facilities and personnel immediately become necessary. Consistent personal contact with professionals is essential. Frequency and duration of meetings will vary, however, with the experience and maturity of practice development staff members. Experienced senior practitioners require no supervision and relatively infrequent meetings under normal conditions. More supervision and more frequent contact are usually necessary with junior personnel.

These circumstances suggest that the practice development function need not be colocated with the professional practice if the development staff is highly experienced. Otherwise, especially during the early phases of program development, proximity usually is an asset to both professionals and staff members. Later, professional and development offices readily can be separated, but regular contact between professionals and practice developers will always be necessary.

IN SUMMARY

Practice development should be a continuing component of the professional office. As such, it requires management. Relatively little beyond professionals' usual activities is necessary until the prerequisites of professional development have been met, until environmental and human realities are attractive to existing and prospective clienteles.

Shortly thereafter, and certainly within a few months of the start of the communication phase of practice development, circumstances will start to change. The change can be rapid, especially in younger practices, which can grow with unexpected rapidity. As practices grow, time available for professional development tasks on the part of practitioners declines. The professional development process can suffer, however, unless efforts continue.

Several alternatives are worthy of professional consideration. The most evident involve retaining practice development consultants or establishing practice development functions within the professional organization. Others exist as well. Moonlighters often can be hired from among those performing practice development tasks for other organizations. Faculty of colleges and universities also may undertrake consulting agreements.

Unless the entire process is delegated to a consulting firm, at considerable cost, the professional's most difficult problem involves assigning responsibilities for the different components of professional development. The process must function as an integrated whole. Neglect and conflict can be highly destructive. Professionals therefore are well advised to assign specific responsibility for each task required to insure that the process continues uninterrupted.

Neither internal nor external systems are problem free. The internal require more than warm bodies. Substantial knowledge and skill are necessary, especially where anticipated growth may erode the amount of time professionals can devote to the process. Personnel thus can become a major problem. Potential for difficulties is compounded by the fact that professional development is a relatively young discipline. Few experienced practitioners exist in most communities outside consulting services.

Facilities also can be a problem, especially as the development process takes hold and practices start to grow. Available space early allocated to professional development staff members soon may be needed to provide professional services to new clients. Alternative locations often must be considered. With them, however, come potential internal communication and management problems. These can be minimized in part in the personnel selection process.

Use of consultant firms also can help alleviate the problem, but only in part. The development process continues to require management direction. Consultants are most productive early in the practice development process and again when programs reach maturity. Early, they provide depth of knowledge and skill helpful in establishing the program, and later, they can assist in installing more sophisticated techniques often required as professional practices grow.

A combined effort also usually affords the greatest possible flexibility during periods when professionals need it most. While retaining general oversight and management, they find it necessary to devote more and more time to other aspects of their practices. At the same time, continuing success requires continuing effort in the practice development sector.

ADDITIONAL READING

Cummings, Paul W. *Open Management: Guides to Successful Practice.* New York: amacom, 1980.

Drucker, Peter F. *Managing in Turbulent Times.* New York: Harper & Row, 1980.

Hawken, Paul. *The Next Economy: What To Do with Your Money and Your Life in the Coming Decade.* New York: Ballantine, 1983.

McDonald, James O. *Management Without Tears: A Guide to Coping with Everyday Organizational Problems.* Chicago: Crain, 1981.

Mason, Richard O., and Ian I. Mitroff. *Challenging Strategic Planning Assumptions: Theory, Cases, and Techniques.* New York: Wiley, 1981.

O'Toole, James. *Vanguard Management: Redesigning the Corporate Future.* New York: Doubleday, 1985.

Rosen, Stephen. *Future Facts.* New York: Simon & Schuster, 1976.

Stine, G. Harry. *The Corporate Survivors.* New York: amacom, 1986.

Toffler, Alvin. *The Adaptive Corporation.* New York: McGraw-Hill, 1985.

Selected Bibliography

Alten, Stanley R. *Audio in Media.* 2nd ed. Belmont, Calif.: Wadsworth, 1986.

Ansoff, H. Igor. *The New Corporate Strategy.* 3rd ed. New York: Wiley, 1988.

Beach, Mark, Steve Shepro, and Ken Russon. *Getting It Printed: How to Work with Printers and Graphic Arts Services to Assure Quality, Stay on Schedule, and Control Costs.* Portland, Ore.: Coast to Coast, 1986.

Beck, Arthur C., and Ellis D. Hillmar. *Positive Management Practices.* San Francisco: Jossey-Bass, 1986.

Belkner, Loren B. *The First-Time Manager: A Practical Guide to the Management of People.* New York: amacom, 1978.

Berko, Roy M., Andrew D. Wolvin, and Ray Curtis. *This Business of Communicating.* 3rd ed. Dubuque, Iowa: Brown, 1986.

Blalock, Hubert M., Jr. *Social Statistics.* 2nd ed. New York: McGraw-Hill, 1972.

———. *Conceptualization and Measurement in the Social Sciences.* Beverly Hills, Calif.: Sage, 1982.

Blanchard, Marjorie, and Mark J. Tager. *Working Well: Managing for Health and High Performance.* New York: Simon & Schuster, 1985.

Bove, Tony, and Cheryl Rhodes. *Desktop Publishing with Pagemaker: IBM PC AT, PS/ 2 and Compatibles.* New York: Wiley, 1987.

Burnett, John J. *Promotion Management: A Strategic Approach.* 2nd ed. St. Paul, Minn.: West, 1988.

Burton, Paul. *Corporate Public Relations.* New York: Reinhold, 1966.

Caddy, Douglas. *Exploring America's Future.* College Station: Texas A & M University Press, 1987.

Carpenter, Susan L., and W. J. D. Kennedy. *Managing Public Disputes.* San Francisco: Jossey-Bass, 1988.

Cascio, Wayne F. *Manaaging Human Resources: Productivity, Quality of Work Life, Profits.* New York: McGraw-Hill, 1986.

Castells, Manuel, ed. *High Technology, Space, and Society.* Beverly Hills, Calif.: Sage, 1985.

Center, Allan H., ed. *Public Relations Ideas in Action: 500 Tested Public Relations Programs and Techniques.* New York: McGraw-Hill, 1957.

Cetron, Marvin. *The Future of American Business: The U.S. in World Competition.* New York: McGraw-Hill, 1985.

Clifford, Donald K., Jr., and Richard E. Cavanaugh. *The Winning Performance.* New York: Bantam, 1985.

Congressional Office of Technology Assessment. *Technology and the American Economic Transition: Choices for the Future.* Washington, D.C.: U.S. Government Printing Office, 1988.

Conover, Theodore E. *Graphic Communications Today.* St. Paul, Minn.: West, 1985.

De, Nitish R. *Alternative Design of Human Organizations.* Beverly Hills, Calif.: Sage, 1984.

Deal, Terrence E., and Allen A. Kennedy. *Corporate Cultures: The Rites and Rituals of Corporate Life.* Reading, Mass.: Addison-Wesley, 1982.

Degan, Clara, ed. *Understanding and Using Video.* New York: Longman, 1985.

Derr, C. Brooklyn. *Managing the New Careerists.* San Francisco: Jossey-Bass, 1986.

DeVries, Manfred F. R. K., and Danny Miller. *The Neurotic Organization.* San Francisco: Jossey-Bass, 1984.

Didsbury, Howard F., Jr. *Communications and the Future: Prospects, Promises, and Problems.* Washington, D.C.: World Future Society, 1982.

Dizard, Wilson P., Jr. *The Coming Information Age: An Overview of Technology, Economics, and Politics.* 2nd ed. New York: Longman, 1985.

Doyle, Robert J. *Gainsharing and Productivity: A Guide to Planning, Implementation, and Development.* New York: amacom, 1983.

Fendrock, John J. *Managing in Times of Radical Change.* New York: American Management Association, 1971.

Gellerman, Saul W. *Management by Motivation.* New York: amacom, 1968.

Glatthorn, Allan A. *Writing for Success.* Glenview, Ill.: Scott, Foresman, 1985.

Glueck, William F. *Personnel: A Diagnostic Approach.* 3rd ed. Plano, Tex.: Business Publicataions, 1982.

Goldhaber, Gerald. *Organizational Communications.* 4th ed. Dubuque, Iowa: Brown, 1986.

Goldman, Jordan. *Public Relations in the Marketing Mix: Introducing Vulnerability Relations.* Chicago: Crain, 1984.

Gumpert, Gary, and Robert Cathcart, eds. *Intermedia: Interpersonal Communication in a Media World.* 3rd ed. New York: Oxford, 1986.

Hanan, Mack. *Life-Styled Marketing: How to Position Products for Premium Profits.* 2nd ed. New York: amacom, 1980.

Harris, Philip R. *Management in Transition.* San Francisco: Jossey-Bass, 1985.

Harrison, Michael I. *Diagnosing Organizations: Methods, Models and Processes.* Beverly Hills, Calif.: Sage, 1987.

Holtz, Herman. *The Consultant's Edge: Using the Computer as a Marketing Tool.* New York: Wiley, 1985.

Howard, Carole, and Wilma Matthews. *On Deadline: Managing Media Relations.* Prospect Heights, Ill.: Waveland Press, 1985.

Howard, V. A., and J. H. Barton. *Thinking on Paper.* New York: Morrow, 1986.

Imundo, Louis V. *The Effective Supervisor's Handbook.* New York: amacom, 1980.

Jacoby, Jacob, and Wayne D. Hoyer. *The Comprehension and Miscomprehension of Print Communications: An Investigation of Mass Media Magazines*. New York: Advertising Educational Foundation, 1987.

Johnson, Eugene M., Eberhard E. Scheuing, and Kathleen A. Gaida. *Profitable Service Marketing*. Homewood, Ill.: Dow Jones–Irwin, 1986.

Kaatz, Ronald B. *Cable: An Advertiser's Guide to the New Electronic Media*. Chicago: Crain, 1982.

Kanter, Rosabeth Moss. *The Change Masters: Innovation and Entrepreneurship in the American Corporation*. New York: Simon & Schuster, 1983.

Kastens, Merritt L. *Long-Range Planning for Your Business: An Operating Manual*. New York: amacom, 1976.

Kickson, David, J., et al. *Top Decisions: Strategic Decision-Making in Organizations*. San Francisco: Jossey-Bass, 1986.

Kilman, Ralph L. *Beyond the Quick Fix: Managing Five Tracks to Organizational Success*. San Francisco: Jossey-Bass, 1984.

Kiplinger Washington Staff. *The New American Boom: Exciting Changes in American Life and Business between Now and the Year 2000*. Washington: Kiplinger, 1986.

Kopelman, Richard E. *Managing Productivity in Organizations: A Practical, People-Oriented Persepctive*. New York: McGraw-Hill, 1986.

Lavrakas, Paul J. *Telephone Survey Methods: Sampling, Selection, and Supervision*. Beverly Hills, Calif.: Sage, 1987.

Lele, Milind M. *The Customer Is Key*. New York: Wiley, 1987.

Lerbinger, Otto. *Managing Corporate Crises: Strategies for Executives*. Boston: Barrington Press, 1986.

Louv, Richard. *America II*. Los Angeles: Tarcher, 1983.

Luther, William M. *The Marketing Plan: How to Prepare and Implement It*. New York, amacom: 1982.

Maccoby, Michael. *Why Work: Leading the New Generation*. New York: Simon & Schuster, 1988.

McGregor, Georgette F., and Joseph A. Robinson. *The Communication Matrix: Ways of Winning with Words*. New York: amacom, 1981.

Mackenzie, R. Alec. *The Time Trap: Managing Your Way Out*. New York: amacom, 1972.

MacKuen, Michael B., and Steven L. Coombs. *More Than News: Media Power in Public Affairs*. Beverly Hills, Calif.: Sage, 1981.

Martel, Leon. *Mastering Change: The Key to Business Success*. New York: Simon & Schuster, 1986.

Masuda, Yoneji. *The Information Society as Post-Industrial Society*. Tokyo: Institute for the Information Society, 1981.

Merriam, John E., and Joel Makower. *Trend Watching: How the Media Create Trends and How to Be the First to Uncover Them*. New York: amacom, 1988.

Mitroff, Ian I. *Business Not as Usual: Rethinking Our Individual, Corporate, and Industrial Strategies for Global Competition*. San Francisco: Jossey-Bass, 1987.

Moore, H. Frasier. *Public Relations: Principles, Cases, and Problems*. Homewood, Ill.: Irwin, 1981.

Naisbitt, John. *Megatrends: Ten New Directions Transforming Our Lives*. New York: Warner, 1982.

————, and Patricia Aburdene. *Reinventing the Corporation: Transforming Your Job and Your Company for the New Information Society*. New York: Warner, 1985.

Nayak, P. Ranganath, and John M. Ketteringham. *Breakthrough! How the Vision and Drive of Innovators in Sixteen Companies Created Commercial Breakthroughs That Swept the World*. New York: Rawson, 1986.

Nelson, Roy Paul. *Publication Design*. 4th ed. Dubuque, Iowa: Brown, 1987.

Organ, Dennis W., and W. Clay Hamner. *Organizational Behavior: An Applied Psychological Approach*. 2nd ed. Plano, Tex.: Business Publications, 1982.

Pascarella, Perry. *The New Achievers: Creating a Modern Work Ethic*. New York: Free Press, 1984.

Paxson, William C. *The Business Writing Handbook*. New York: Bantam, 1981.

Perlman, Daniel, and P. Chris Cozby. *Social Psychology*. New York: Holt, Rinehart & Winston, 1983.

Phillips, Jack J. *Recruiting, Training, and Retaining New Employees*. San Francisco: Jossey-Bass, 1987.

Pickens, Judy E. *The Copy-to-Press Handbook: Preparing Words and Art for Print*. New York: Wiley, 1985.

Pinsdorf, Marion K. *Communicating When Your Company Is under Siege: Surviving Public Crisis*. Lexington, Mass.: Heath, 1987.

Ray, Michael L. *Advertising and Communication Management*. New York: Prentice-Hall, 1982.

Reich, Robert B. *Tales of a New America*. New York: Times Books, 1987.

Rice, Ronald E., and William J. Paisley. *Public Communication Campaigns*. Beverly Hills, Calif.: Sage, 1981.

————, and associates. *The New Media: Communication, Research, and Technology*. Beverly Hills, Calif.: Sage, 1984.

Roalman, A. R. *Profitable Public Relations*. Homewood, Ill.: Dow Jones–Irwin, 1968.

Rogers, Everett M. *Communication Technology: The New Media in Society*. New York: Free Press, 1986.

Roxe, Linda A. *Personnel Management for the Smaller Company*. New York: amacom, 1979.

Ruch, Richard S., and Ronald Goodman. *Image at the Top: Crisis and Renaissance in Corporate Leadership*. New York: Free Press, 1983.

Russel, Robert A. *Winning the Future: Succeeding in an Economic Revolution*. New York: Carroll & Graf, 1986.

Russell, Cheryl. *100 Predictions for the Baby Boom: The Next 50 Years*. New York: Plenum, 1987.

Rydz, John S. *Managing Innovation: From the Executive Suite to the Shop Floor*. Cambridge, Mass.: Ballinger, 1986.

Schein, Edgar H. *Organizational Culture and Leadership*. San Francisco: Jossey-Bass, 1986.

Schiller, Herbert I. *Information and the Crisis Economy*. New York: Oxford, 1986.

Sibson, Robert E. *Increasing Employee Productivity*. New York: amacom, 1976.

Stanton, Erwin S. *Successful Personnel Recruiting and Selection*. New York: amacom, 1977.

Steinberg, Charles S. *The Creation of Consent: Public Relations in Practice*. New York: Hastings House, 1975.

Taylor, James W. *Competitive Marketing Strategies*. 2nd ed. Radnor, Pa.: Chilton, 1986.

Torbert, William R. *Managing the Corporate Dream: Restructuring for Long-Term Success*. Homewood, Ill.: Dow Jones–Irwin, 1986.

Tuleja, Tad. *Beyond the Bottom Line: How Business Leaders Are Turning Principles into Profits*. New York: Facts on File, 1985.

Walton, Richard E. *Innovating to Compete: Lessons for Diffusing and Managing Change in the Workplace*. San Francisco: Jossey-Bass, 1987.

Weilbacher, William M. *Auditing Productivity: Advertiser-Agency Relationships Can Be Improved*. New York: Association of National Advertisers, 1981.

Weinstein, Art. *Market Segmentation: Using Demographics, Psychographics, and Other Segmentation Techniques to Uncover and Exploit New Markets*. Chicago: Probus, 1987.

White, Jan V. *Mastering Graphics: Design and Production Made Easy*. New York: Bowker, 1983.

Williams, Frederick. *Technology and Communication Behavior*. Belmont, Calif.: Wadsworth, 1987.

Willis, Jerry. *Desktop Publishing with Your IBM PC and Compatible: The Complete Guide*. Tucson: Knight-Ridder, 1987.

Zollo, Burt. *The Dollars and Sense of Public Relations*. New York: McGraw-Hill, 1967.

Index

ABOUT THE AUTHOR

E. W. BRODY teaches public relations in the Department of Journalism at Memphis State University in Tennessee and maintains a public relations consulting practice in Memphis.

Professional Practice Development is his fifth book. *Public Relations Research*, written with Dr. Gerald C. Stone, was published by Praeger in 1989. Dr. Brody is the sole author of *Public Relations Programming and Production* (Praeger 1988), as well as *Communicating for Survival: Coping with Diminishing Human Resources* and *The Business of Public Relations*, both published by Praeger in 1987.

Dr. Brody's articles on public relations have appeared in *Public Relations Journal, Public Relations Quarterly, Public Relations Review, Journalism Quarterly, Legal Economics, Health Care Management Review, Journal of the Medical Group Management Association, Modern Healthcare, Hospital Public Relations*, and other publications. He serves on the editorial boards of *Public Relations Quarterly* and *PR Strategies USA*.